IN UNDERSTANDING BE MEN

'Be not children in understanding . . . but in understanding be men' – I CORINTHIANS 14:20

IN UNDERSTANDING
BE MEN

A handbook of Christian doctrine

T. C. HAMMOND
edited and revised by DAVID F. WRIGHT

INTER-VARSITY PRESS

Inter-Varsity Press
38 De Montfort Street, Leicester LE1 7GP, England

Sixth edition © Inter-Varsity Press 1968

First edition 1936
Second edition 1936
Reprinted 1937
Third edition 1938
Reprinted 1943, 1944, 1946, 1947, 1950
Fourth edition 1951
Reprinted 1952
Fifth edition 1954
Reprinted 1956, 1958, 1960, 1961, 1963, 1965, 1967
Sixth edition 1968
Reprinted 1970, 1971, 1973, 1974, 1976, 1977, 1979, 1982

ISBN 0-85110-567-x

Printed in Great Britain by
Hazell Watson & Viney Ltd,
Aylesbury, Bucks

Inter-Varsity Press is the publishing division of the
Universities and College Christian Fellowship (formerly
the Inter-Varsity Fellowship), a student movement linking
Christian Unions in universities and colleges throughout the
British Isles, and a member movement of the International
Fellowship of Evangelical Students. For information about
local and national activities in Great Britain write to UCCF,
38 De Montfort Street, Leicester LE1 7GP.

CONTENTS

FROM THE PREFACE TO THE FOURTH EDITION

The aim of this handbook is to make accessible to the ordinary reader, if only in an elementary form, the great treasures of knowledge reposing in the volumes of theological thought. The author has endeavoured to condense into a small compass the main principles of Christian doctrine, so as to afford those whose time is very fully occupied with other intellectual problems an opportunity of appraising the wide reach of theology and its relation to current theories in science and history. The task is by no means easy. There is always the danger that in condensation ambiguous phrases may obtain a footing and mislead the unwary. The necessity of avoiding, as far as possible, technical terms, either of philosophy or theology, has not lessened this danger. Only those who attempt to substitute simple expressions for scientific terms which have become familiar to the user can fully understand the difficulty.

As has been already stated in previous editions, the approach is such as to include, as far as possible, different attitudes on controversial points while preserving the main outline of evangelical thought.

May God bless the efforts of all who seek to extend the knowledge of His will and use this edition to further His gracious purposes.

T. C. HAMMOND

PREFACE TO THE SIXTH EDITION

In Understanding Be Men has nobly served many generations of Christian students since it was first published some thirty years ago. Numerous ministers and missionaries and others involved in preaching and teaching the faith of Christ could speak with warm gratitude of the book which first introduced them to the close study of Christian doctrine. It is a monument to its enduring usefulness that it should be thought worthy of a new lease of life in a revised form.

For time has not stood still in these past three decades. They have seen a new flowering of evangelical biblical scholarship, and even years of declension have witnessed fresh light breaking forth from God's eternal Word. Some of the fruits of this harvest are garnered in this revision, most obviously in the revised bibliographies. For the rest, it set out to be only a minimal revision, paying particular attention to the questions, the arrangement of some of the material, and what our retrograde age likes to call the 'up-dating' of a line here and there. The reviser found his appreciation of the book greatly increased in the course of his work, but he was neither able nor intended to make it all his own, and on some subjects he must beg to differ. His hope is that the revision has enhanced the value of T. C. Hammond's chief literary testament.

D. F. WRIGHT
New College, Edinburgh

METHODS OF STUDY

Each section or group of sections is arranged as follows:

1. An outline of the doctrine and the main problems connected with it, followed in some cases by a historical review of divergent views from various stages of church history.

2. A selection of the Scriptures which bear upon the doctrine which is being examined.

3. Questions concerning the more important aspects of the subject, with the object of forcing the student's attention to a more careful examination of the points of special significance, or of those on which there are widespread erroneous views. These study topics have been provided in the first instance for non-theological students. Technical language has been avoided as much as possible, but current difficulties have been prominently in view.

4. A bibliography, in order to encourage reference to larger theological works in which are made available the findings of the great Christian scholars of all ages. The suggested books have been chosen because they reflect in the main the orthodox Christian position. Their inclusion does not mean that there is entire agreement with all that is in them. Nor does it mean that they are the only valuable books on the subject! A wider and more varied selection of books will be found in *A Guide to Christian Reading*, also published by the Inter-Varsity Press (revised to 1961), which lists approximately 1500 titles classified under about a hundred headings.

It is recommended that the student should work steadily through the book, giving a definite weekly period, or other regular time, to each subsection. After turning up the Scripture references, he should, when possible, write out the answers to the questions without reference to this book. He should check his answers by referring, whenever possible, to one of the larger works mentioned in the bibliography.

For group study, each member of the group should have read through the selected sections and studied the selected Scriptures prior to the meeting. The leader will outline the chief principles of the doctrine to be discussed, showing the doctrine's relevance, and then put two or more of the questions to the meeting. To enrich the combined findings of the

group it is valuable for several of the members to volunteer to consult
different larger works beforehand, if these are available. It is essential that
the leader should sum up clearly, adding to his previously prepared notes
the chief points which may have arisen during the meeting.

The student is recommended to use the Revised Standard Version of
the Bible in conjunction with this book.

GENERAL BIBLIOGRAPHY

L. Berkhof, *Systematic Theology*, Banner of Truth, 1959.

H. Heppe, *Reformed Dogmatics*, Allen and Unwin, 1950.

A. A. Hodge, *Outlines of Theology*, Eerdmans, 1949.

C. H. Hodge, *Systematic Theology*, 3 vols., James Clarke, 1960.

A. Lecerf, *An Introduction to Reformed Dogmatics*, Lutterworth, 1949.

E. A. Litton, *Introduction to Dogmatic Theology*, James Clarke, 1960.

H. C. G. Moule, *Outlines of Christian Doctrine*, Hodder and Stoughton, 1890.

The New Bible Dictionary, IVF, 1962.

A. H. Strong, *Systematic Theology*, Pickering and Inglis, 1956.

W. H. Griffith Thomas, *The Catholic Faith*, Church Book Room Press, 1952.

G. Vos, *Notes on Biblical Theology*, Eerdmans, 1948.

ABBREVIATIONS

Books of the Old Testament: Gn., Ex., Lv., Nu., Dt., Jos., Jdg., Ru., 1, 2 Sa., 1, 2 Ki., 1, 2 Ch., Ezr., Ne., Est., Jb., Ps. (Pss.), Pr., Ec., Ct., Is., Je., La., Ezk., Dn., Ho., Joel, Am., Ob., Jon., Mi., Na., Hab., Zp., Hg., Zc., Mal.

Books of the New Testament: Mt., Mk., Lk., Jn., Acts, Rom., 1, 2 Cor., Gal., Eph., Phil., Col., 1, 2 Thes., 1, 2 Tim., Tit., Phm., Heb., Jas., 1, 2 Pet., 1, 2, 3 Jn., Jude, Rev.

AV   Authorized, or King James, Version (1611)
cf.   Compare
Gk. Greek
Heb. Hebrew
LXX Septuagint Version, that is, translation of the Old Testament into Greek, about 250 BC
NEB New English Bible, New Testament (1961)
RV   Revised Version (1885)
RSV Revised Standard Version (1952)

THE IMPORTANCE OF CHRISTIAN DOCTRINE

A gifted preacher of over a century ago, Dr Thomas Guthrie, drew attention to the difference between dogmatic and biblical theology. He compared biblical theology to the profusion of nature in which the various plants and flowers are scattered with a bountiful hand 'in ordered disorder'. He compared dogmatic theology to the botanical garden where plants and flowers are gathered and arranged according to species. The former is pleasing to the eye. The latter is suited for that closer study which opens to us the secrets of nature.

The botanist cannot disregard the wider scope and greater beauty of nature's arrangement. But he values the botanical garden because it helps him to a fuller understanding of the gifts which nature offers.

The Bible presents us with the work of God in revelation in many forms. At one time we have the voice of the prophet. At another we get the prayer of the saint. God's providence is painted for us on the full canvas of history. God's dealings with men are unfolded in varied records of individual experience. There is a beauty and profusion akin to the lavish hand of nature. But it is our privilege to classify and arrange, and thus to make more intelligible the unifying purpose that governs the whole. Are Christians under any obligation to devote themselves to the study of dogmatic theology? The answer must depend on many circumstances. The simple person who enjoys the beauty of nature is not required to study botany. The gardener must know something about it. The scientist must seek to exhaust the subject, if it happens to be his speciality.

The student certainly ought to know something about the intellectual processes which have governed the interpretation of the message of God through the ages. Those who have been trained to classify and think clearly in their secular branches of learning ought to be applying the principles of their mental training to the understanding and teaching of divine revelation. Unfortunately, we find very often that 'educated' Christians are foremost amongst those who mix things that differ. We often hear it glibly said, 'You see, I know no theology'! And frequently this particular ignorance is regarded as a matter of pride. The study of Christian doctrine is often thought to be dry and uninteresting. By a singular perversion of ideas it is sometimes said to be 'unspiritual'! 'Doctrine', 'theology', 'dogma' are thought to have an unpleasant ring to them, to be solely the art of making hair-splitting distinctions, and altogether remote from the vital issues of salvation.

Every serious study has its dogmas. The medical practitioner speaks a peculiar language of his own and writes prescriptions in an ancient hieroglyphic. The medical man is expected to know the technique of his special study. A student who boasted that he depended on 'common sense' in diagnosis and had never made a serious effort to absorb the principles underlying this art would, we hope, become disillusioned by the absence of patients, who would prefer to suffer than risk his 'common sense'. Yet sometimes even 'professional' ministers of the gospel content themselves with a minimum of theological information. 'Amateur' Christian workers often display commendable eagerness to 'save souls' and yet are themselves satisfied with a very hazy knowledge of the real nature of salvation.

We need to remember that Christian doctrine is important. It has a twofold application. It is of value both in consolidating the spiritual faith and energizing the spiritual life of the individual. In relation to the latter, it would be well if the reader collected and collated all, or many, of the references in the New Testament which enforce 'teaching', 'knowledge', 'understanding' and 'certainty' in matters of faith. He will be surprised at the supreme importance placed on a clear grasp of the Christian tradition. A study of the Epistles to Timothy alone will serve to make this fact abundantly apparent.

Nor must it be urged in reply that such knowledge is 'spiritual' and not 'intellectual'. It is indeed 'spiritual', for it relates to the things of the 'spirit'. But it is attained by those activities of the mind which are called into play in other studies. Our Lord opened the understanding of His disciples. He sought entrance for truth in that way. He does so still. When one of the Pharaohs asked Ptolemy to teach him geometry by a short method, the sage is reported to have replied: 'There is no royal road to learning.' We need to remember there is only one way to enter into the truth of God. 'Through thy precepts I get understanding' (Psalm 119:104). There is no biblical opposition between 'faith' and 'understanding' or 'knowledge'; indeed the possibility of growth in faith and obedience for the Christian student will inevitably depend upon advance in one's intellectual grasp of the content of Christian belief.

In addition to its value to the individual, Christian doctrine is of the greatest importance in Christian service. No clear teaching can be given, either to children or adults, unless the principles of the subject discussed have been clearly grasped.

We need to remember that truth produces its proper result and error always takes its revenge. Even slight deviations from the facts of revelation may lead eventually to graver aberrations. The best way to avoid error is to define as clearly as possible the norm of truth.

CLASSIFICATIONS

1. Accuracy in Terminology

One of the more disturbing weaknesses of modern Christianity, even among Evangelicals, is its inaccurate and even careless employment of words which either in Scripture or in the history of theology possess a precise technical meaning. In other sciences the reason for the employment of Greek and Latin words is found in the necessity for an accurate terminology in which each word will convey one meaning and one meaning only. This is not generally possible in the use of the vernacular. Considerations of this kind are frequently of the highest importance in a subject such as medicine. Why should it be considered less necessary to secure terminological accuracy in the queen of the sciences?

Examples may be given. One sometimes hears a youthful evangelist, who is not always aware of the earlier uses of the term, emphasizing to his congregation that mankind is 'totally depraved'. His manner, and the context, would suggest that man has lost all semblance of good in any form, and that each individual sinner is as corrupt as he possibly could be! Originally 'total depravity' was used to convey the meaning that mankind possesses an evil principle which extends to the whole of his nature. If the theological term is not to be used in its proper connotation, would it not be better to employ a directly scriptural phrase? Similarly, much confusion has resulted because the word 'regeneration' is used in theology in a wide, narrow, and derived or symbolical meaning (cf. Mt. 19:28, AV; Jn. 3:3; Tit. 3:5), whereas it is used by many evangelical Christians solely in the sense of the technical word 'renovation'. Compare also the use of the words 'the faith' and 'faith'.

It is almost too much to hope that a completely accurate phraseology will be recaptured, but, at least, a Christian student should do his utmost to be as accurate as possible in his descriptions of the great cardinal doctrines. It should be his aim to acquire *careful definitions and to use the various terms in only one special meaning in relation to a particular subject*. If this is not possible he should avoid confusion by defining his own terms himself.

2. The Aim of Classification

The aim of classification is to help the student to come to greater definiteness and accuracy, and to enable him easily to handle the mass of material which has accumulated on every subject. Some minds have a strange aversion to classification, but they do not often rise to eminence in their branch of study! It is specially necessary to classify in those subjects where a number of abstract conceptions are presented in an (apparently) disconnected fashion, as in the Scriptures. It is only when some form of collation and grouping of subjects is attempted that a marvellous design and symmetry comes to light in what originally appeared a chaos.

Not merely would many confusing and, at first attempt, difficult principles be mastered; but misleading statements, ineffective attempts to grapple with practical issues and fruitless arguments between Christians would be avoided.

The writer would urge every would-be effective Christian to secure for himself a *clear classification* of the chief theological systems; to grasp clearly the characteristic emphasis in each; and to work out in secondary classifications the outstanding doctrines and practical implications of each. The latter show themselves, for example, in divergent forms of church government, divergent views on such widely differing subjects as the means of grace, the choice of methods, evangelistic preaching, and even in views of the Lord's return! Surely, the reader has wondered at some period in his Christian life at the mutual recriminations of two Christians in an argument on some point, when each has been perfectly convinced that he is right, and doing more justice to God's honour than the other! More often than not the one is arguing from an extreme 'Calvinist' viewpoint, and the other from an extreme 'Arminian' viewpoint. The confused onlooker could have been saved many unnecessary mental contortions by a few simple guiding principles!

As an example may be cited the so-called Antinomies. This term is applied (in theology) to what appear to be conflicting doctrines concerning the same subject. The limitations of the human mind sometimes render it impossible for us to approach nearer to truth than the statement of the two apparently opposing sets of ideas, the truth of each of which is equally capable of demonstration. The student would be well advised to collect and collate examples of this and similar difficulties in sacred subjects. The time spent in collecting and attempting to make one's own classifications of such matters is never wasted if the sole purpose is to arrive at a clearer understanding of the divine revelation. They are chiefly associated with:

1. *God's Approach to Man* (the Infinite in contact with the finite). There is, for example, the question of God's sovereignty (clearly taught in Scripture), and human choice and responsibility (also clearly taught). God alone knows how these apparently conflicting principles can be fully harmonized when applied to certain crises of life—*e.g.*, conversion.

2. *Eternity and Time.*—In all our discussions of God ('the high and lofty One who inhabits eternity', Is. 57:15) and His dealings in time we are able only to approximate to the truth, and we meet apparent contradictions. Compare such statements as 'My thoughts are not your

thoughts' and 'One day is as a thousand years, and a thousand years as one day'.

But, whilst reverent acceptance of the unreconciled scriptural statements is the only course open to us, yet this does not mean that we cannot secure a *practical application* of their principles.

In urging the student to classify, it is necessary to add a warning concerning the danger of carrying this process to extremes. There have been several examples in church history of devoted men who (pursuing their classification too far) attempted to reduce all doctrine to a cast-iron system. The outcome was not only that they themselves were forced into unscriptural statements, but that heresy and division were forced on the church.

It is necessary for the advanced theologian to learn that there will always remain unavoidable gaps in every theological system. Where divine revelation has not pointed the way it is extremely unwise for human speculative philosophy to attempt to do so. When a classification has been extended to a point where (in any particular) it cannot claim the authority of Scripture, it has ceased to be useful and is rapidly becoming a danger. Reverent agnosticism is preferable to unauthorized speculation.

DEFINITIONS

Since a plea has been made for accurate definitions, it may be helpful to introduce several of the most important ones.

1. The Christian Revelation

The main New Testament word for 'revelation' (used only in a semi-technical theological sense) is *apokalypsis*, meaning the 'uncovering, unveiling of what was previously hidden'. Revelation consists of the progressive unfolding by God of His character and purposes and mighty acts, in history and through the words of His specially designated spokesmen. It begins with the history recorded in the Old Testament (largely the history of Israel) and reaches its climax and fulfilment in the coming of Christ, and also in the establishment of His church and the determination of Christian belief by the Holy Spirit through the apostles. Therefore, 'the Christian revelation' comprises the sum and substance of the self-revealing activity of God for man's salvation. This activity, without which a transcendent God could not be known, centres on Christ and is recorded in the Scriptures. In fact, the Scriptures themselves possess for us the character of revelation, because they provide the sole permanent means of access to the raw material of 'the Christian revelation', and were indeed specially inspired by God to mediate the original revelation to succeeding generations. Thus understood, 'the Christian revelation' excludes 'general revelation' (see below), and is sometimes contrasted with it as 'special revelation'. It is the 'gospel and the preaching of Jesus Christ, according to the revelation of the mystery which was kept secret for long ages but is now disclosed and through the prophetic writings is made known to all nations, according to the command of the eternal God, to bring about obedience to the faith' (Rom. 16:25, 26).

2. 'Faith' and 'the Faith'

It has been well remarked that 'faith in man is the complement of grace in God'. God's approach to man is 'in grace' and man's response to God is 'by faith'. God in grace has been pleased to give man a revelation of Himself, and the only adequate response man can offer is confident trust. Our Lord indicated this when He praised the faith of childhood. Faith is *the instrument* by which the divine revelation and all the blessing inherent in *Him* are grasped.

But, used with the article, 'the faith' indicates the sum of Christian teaching, the body of truth. Jude 3 refers to 'the faith which was once for all delivered to the saints'.

3. Religion and Theology

These two words should be kept distinct in thought from one another, and also from revelation. The former is the ordering of one's life, one's conduct and character, in the light of one's beliefs about God, the practical outworking of a man's response to divine revelation. It may be typified as an *art*, whereas theology is more like a *science*. The latter is the study and description of the revelation of God. Therefore, both religion and theology represent responses to the fact of God's revelation; the former seeks to live by it, the latter to analyse and codify it.

4. Biblical and Dogmatic Theology

We have already (see p. 13) given one account of the difference between biblical theology and dogmatic theology. The former studies the distinctive emphases of the different parts of the Bible, dealing, for instance, with 'John's understanding of the Word or *Logos* of God', and 'Faith according to the Epistle to the Hebrews'. It observes the many-splendoured variety of the Scriptures, and concentrates closely on textual study, using all possible aids to understand its original meaning. In expounding the Bible it avoids using non-biblical categories of thought and language, and takes account of the development of teaching within the period of the biblical revelation.

Dogmatic theology, however, unifies and systematizes the diverse and complementary biblical evidence, and endeavours to show the interrelations of individual doctrines within some over-all scheme or in the light of a key theme. It often functions most naturally in contexts demanding defence of the faith against critical attack (apologetic), or involving controversy and refutation of error (polemic), or requiring the exposition of the official standards of belief (confession) of a particular denomination or tradition in the church. It frequently uses concepts and terminology not found explicitly in the Bible (*e.g.*, 'Trinity', 'substance', 'infallibility', 'sacrament') in order to explain and vindicate the full implications of the scattered biblical data. Dogmatic theology takes notice of the historical development of theological understanding in the life of the church.

Normally, the former would appear to be the only form necessary for the Christian, and all else extraneous and unnecessary addition. But in practice the church has found it impossible to do without the secondary use of the findings and writings of her teachers in all ages. Those who object that there is no scriptural warrant for such use will invariably be discovered to be dependent, consciously or unconsciously, upon secondary theological material of some sort, even if only their favourite preacher or commentator.

Similarly, those who say 'the Scriptures alone are sufficient without any constitution, or summary, for our Christian Union' forget that it is impossible to answer certain inquiries as to our belief by quoting Scripture. If asked our belief concerning the immanence of God, we can scarcely quote the whole Bible! Nor are certain subtle heresies met by any clear biblical statements. We then have to choose between our own paraphrase of what we believe Scripture to state, or to call to our aid dogmatic or systematic theology.

Dogmatic theology arose early in the history of the church, owing to the development of heresy—*e.g.*, concerning the Person of our Lord. In dealing with these heresies clear definitions were forced on the early church leaders; and the collection of these statements, together with the writings of early theologians, later additions from every age and in particular the Confessions and works of the Reformation era, have produced systematic theology. Revert again to the illustration used on page 13, *viz.*, that the Bible may be compared to a wild forest where vegetation and foliage are growing in profusion, systematic theology to a botanic garden where plants have been classified. In the latter, a study is made of *the diseases afflicting the plants* as well as of the plant structures.

5. Historical Considerations

a. Principles of Church History

Many Christian students, particularly those who hope to go abroad as missionaries, would do well to acquaint themselves with the main facts and principles of church history. Far from being dull, it can become, if rightly approached, one of the most thrilling and practical hobbies in the world! Many a man has been dragged from his hopeless superficiality in religion, driven to a spiritual life-purpose and made a spiritual hero by a study of the history of the early Christians. To mention only one of its practical values, the various forbidding names which appear (for the sake of rapid allusion) in books of theology—*e.g.*, Gnosticism, Arianism, Pelagianism—have quite unnecessarily frightened off students who in other subjects (even their hobbies) cheerfully tolerate far more 'repulsive' technicalities!

Has it ever occurred to the reader that Gnostics and Semi-Pelagians still abound? Does he realize that the Old and New Testaments have provided the weapons with which he may deal with them? But he certainly will never be an effective warrior unless he can recognize and diagnose the vulnerable points in his spiritual foes.

b. General or Ecumenical Councils

This is the name given to those gatherings of churchmen which were regarded as universal in the sense of representative of all parts of the church. Protestant Christianity in general recognizes only six, and in particular the first four.

1. Nicaea (AD 325): Summoned to deal with the Arian heresy.
2. Constantinople I (AD 381): Summoned to reaffirm the faith of Nicaea as a basis for unity, and to deal with subsequent errors.
3. Ephesus (AD 431): Summoned to examine the Nestorian heresy.[1]
4. Chalcedon (AD 451): Summoned to combat the teaching of Eutyches.[2]
5. Constantinople II (AD 553).
6. Constantinople III (AD 680).

c. Creeds and Confessions of Faith

Of the 'Creeds', or brief statements of belief (Latin, *credo*, 'I believe'), produced in the period of the early church, three in particular came to acquire special importance and continue to be almost universally acknowledged in the church. They are:

1. The Apostles', which really represents an elaboration of the baptismal confession of faith. It is not of apostolic origin.
2. The Nicene, a developed form of the Creed of the Council of Nicaea, containing fuller statements concerning the Person of our Lord and the Holy Spirit.
3. The Athanasian, a detailed definition of the doctrines of the Trinity and the incarnation. (It has nothing to do with Athanasius!)

Between 451 and the period of the Reformation very few additions were made, but at the time of the Reformation, when the foundations of the church were re-examined, there were produced a profusion of such statements, which at this period were generally called 'Confessions of Faith'. Of these, the British Isles produced the Thirty-Nine Articles and the Westminster Confession.

Whereas the Creeds may be said to represent the views of the whole church at the time, the Confessions are truly representative only of the division which gave rise to them. It is largely by their Confessions of Faith that churches may be defined and classified.

6. The European Churches

a. Chief Theological Divisions

1. *Protestant Theology.*—Under this heading is included the doctrine of

[1] See p. 102.   [2] *Ibid.*

those churches which resulted from the break with Rome at the Reformation. They became for the most part either Lutheran or Reformed, with
Anglicanism as a variety of the latter. (See p. 23.)

2. *Roman Catholic Theology.*—This became largely stereotyped by the
rulings of the divines of the Council of Trent, which was called to
investigate the teaching of the Reformers.

3. *Eastern Orthodox Theology.*—The Eastern church repeatedly broke
with Rome over the latter's claim to supremacy, especially in the ninth
century; the breach became virtually final in the eleventh century. The
theology of the Eastern Orthodox churches gives a prominent place to the
stream of ecclesiastical tradition, differing from Roman Catholic theology
mainly in ethos and 'atmosphere', though also on some points of doctrine.
They give special honour to the Patriarch of Constantinople.

The differences between Roman and (representative) Protestant
theologies, which are more widely marked than in any other similar
cleavage, were accentuated by the uncompromising attitude of the Council
of Trent to all distinctly Protestant doctrine. The fundamental differences
(despite some reforming tendencies since the second Vatican Council)
remain:

1. *Ultimate Authority.*—The Protestants make Scripture the ultimate
authority. Roman Catholics make some combination of Scripture,
tradition and the living, speaking voice of the church the final authority.
Protestants cannot accept the claims of the papacy and Roman church
based upon our Lord's commission to Peter and a particular doctrine of
apostolic succession.

2. *Priesthood and Sacrifice.*—Protestants deny that the Roman priest has
need, or authority, to make the sacrifice of Christ present on the altar in
the Mass. The Bible declares that one oblation was offered 'once for all' on
Calvary, and needs neither repetition nor re-presentation. The Catholic
practice undermines the unique mediatorial priesthood of Christ.

3. *Emphasis.*—Because the Roman Catholic church claims to be in
some sense an extension of the incarnation, its emphasis tends to fall on
this point, while Protestantism focuses on the cross and resurrection as the
final message to man and the completion of his deliverance from sin.

b. Chief Divisions within the Protestant Faith

1. *The Lutheran Churches.*—These are represented by the Augsburg
Confession and the writings of Luther. They are found chiefly in Germany and northern Europe.

2. *The Reformed or Calvinistic Churches.*—These are represented by the
Helvetic Confession and the writings of Calvin. They are found chiefly in
Switzerland, central Europe and Holland. The Presbyterian churches are a

branch of the Reformed faith and are represented by the Westminster Confession.

3. *The Anglican Church* and associated Episcopal churches. These are represented by the Thirty-Nine Articles (which have both Lutheran and Reformed elements, but are Reformed regarding the views on the sacraments).

The Methodist church in America incorporates the Revised Articles of Religion of the Anglican church. Wesley himself prescribed his notes on the New Testament and the first four volumes of his sermons as the basis of a common understanding. Assent to these is required of Methodist ministers. Other important divisions exist between churches which baptize infants and those which baptize only after a responsible profession of faith (Baptists and most Pentecostals), and over the doctrine of the church (*e.g.*, the Brethren).

c. Principles Underlying the Divisions

Students may find it helpful to bear in mind that underlying the divisions today in the churches are the great principles connected either with (1) the ultimate seat of authority or (2) the age-long difficulty concerning God's sovereignty and human freedom.

1. *The Ultimate Authority.*—This may be:
   (i) *The church*—the so-called 'Catholic' position.
   (ii) *Human reason*—the 'Liberal' position.
   (iii) *The Bible*—the 'Evangelical' position.

This does not mean that an Evangelical does not recognize the use of the church and reason in a secondary sense, but that he insists on the unviolated supremacy of the Bible in all matters of faith and conduct.[1]

2. *Sovereignty and Freedom.*—The 'Calvinist' (or 'Augustinian', from St. Augustine who more than anticipated Calvin) emphasizes primarily the sovereignty of God, and following Calvin (whose system is the most logical and complete of the confessional theologies), carries this viewpoint into all departments of his life.

The 'Arminian' (so called from Arminius, a Dutch divine who wrote against the doctrine of predestination) places his emphasis primarily on the side of human responsibility and the need for man's co-operation with God. This emphasis, if accentuated, influences other departments of his theology.

Many of the controversies between equally devoted Christians have concerned such questions as extreme teaching on predestination and an extreme doctrine of free will. These two viewpoints (which are divergent

[1] For a further discussion of this question of ultimate authority see pp. 38-40.

when pressed to extremes) are at the root of many confusions in teaching in all departments of Christian work, from the preaching of the gospel and the theology of conversion to subjects such as sanctification, and even the second advent.

Questions

1. Study references in the New Testament to 'teaching', 'knowledge', 'understanding' and 'certainty' in matters of faith, to show the importance of knowing Christian truth.

2. Are the words 'theology', 'religion', 'the faith' synonymous? Define each.

3. What meaning or meanings does the word 'revelation' bear in Scripture? Is every part of the Bible a 'revelation' in the fullest sense of that term? Cf. Hebrews 1:1-3.

4. How far is it true to say that the Bible is sufficient for the needs of the church?

5. Study and compare the three Creeds mentioned on p. 21 (in the Book of Common Prayer, for example), noting their structures and emphases. Do you find any notable omissions? Do the same with the Thirty-Nine Articles (also in the Prayer Book) and the Westminster Confession of Faith (many editions).

BIBLIOGRAPHY

H. Bavinck, *Our Reasonable Faith*, Eerdmans, 1956.

T. D. Bernard, *The Progress of Doctrine in the New Testament*, Pickering and Inglis, 1968.

H. Heppe, *Reformed Dogmatics*, Allen and Unwin, 1950.

A. A. Hodge, *Outlines of Theology*, Eerdmans, 1949.

C. H. Hodge, *Systematic Theology*, James Clarke, 1960.

E. A. Litton, *Introduction to Dogmatic Theology*, James Clarke, 1960.

Handley Moule, *Outlines of Christian Doctrine*, Hodder and Stoughton, 1890.

W. Niesel, *Reformed Symbolics*, Oliver and Boyd, 1962.

James Orr, *The Progress of Dogma*, Eerdmans, 1962.

E. Routley, *Creeds and Confessions*, Duckworth, 1962.

K. Runia, *I Believe in God . . .*, Tyndale Press, 1963.

W. H. Griffith Thomas, *The Principles of Theology*, Church Book Room Press, 1956.

R. A. Torrey, *What the Bible Teaches*, Oliphants, 1957.

G. Vos, *Notes on Biblical Theology*, Eerdmans, 1948.

PART ONE

FINAL AUTHORITY IN MATTERS OF FAITH

1. Sources

Theology speaks of general revelation and the Christian revelation as the two areas or spheres from which knowledge of God may in principle be obtained. All revelation, by definition, is given by the free and gracious initiative of God. To derive knowledge from a supernatural revelation is the reverse of gaining it by scientific research or philosophic speculation. There is no compromise possible for the Christian, in some matters, between (irreverent) philosophical speculation and divine revelation.

a. The Need of Revelation

The hiddenness of a transcendent and sovereign God can be broken only as He chooses to reveal Himself to mankind. God is not accessible to the sight or understanding of even unfallen man, so far is He exalted above man in His essential being. Moreover, man's inability to attain to the knowledge of God by his own unaided powers is reinforced by the effects of sin, which have rendered him unable to recognize and acknowledge God even when He does reveal Himself, unless at the same time God enlightens his mind to a true perception of divine realities.

Furthermore, it is *a priori* likely, if there is a supreme personal God upon whom the world depends for its existence, that He will make Himself known to men rather than leave them to search vainly in the dark.

b. General Revelation

The Bible speaks of a limited self-disclosure on God's part outside the specifically Jewish-Christian revelation, through the created order, the workings of providence in nature and history, and the moral life and capacities of mankind. Such revelation is largely confined to manifestations of His divine power, eternity and glory, and because of the blindness of mental vision in sinful man, is insufficient to lead to a true knowledge of God. In fact, the response of fallen man to this continual self-revelation of God shows up his perversity and provides further evidence of his inexcusable guilt before God. But once a person has been enlightened by the Holy Spirit, he begins to perceive God's general revelation as well as His coming in Christ, and to respond to it in the appropriate way, by worship, repentance, faith, *etc.*

c. 'Natural Theology'

A long-standing tradition in theological thinking has sought to demonstrate a certain minimum of truth about God on the basis of rational
argument from the existence and nature of the world, and the common
moral and religious awareness of mankind. This found classical expression
in the 'natural theology' (to be distinguished from general revelation,
though it will be seen that some of the raw materials of general revelation
are drawn upon in natural theology) of thinkers such as Anselm and
Thomas Aquinas (eleventh and thirteenth centuries), who believed that by
philosophical reasoning along these lines it was possible to establish the
existence of God and some aspects of His being (see pp. 41–43). Others
have argued for the demonstration of other truths, such as the logical
necessity of divine revelation. All such truths of natural theology are
regarded as necessary principles which the biblical revelation assumes and
builds upon.

Evangelicals differ as to the validity of this approach. Many would be
hesitant to use such arguments, except in a very secondary manner, for
instance as a 'neutral' confirmation of the truths of the Christian revelation (in much the same way as such confirmation may be derived from
evidence provided by science, secular history (e.g., the fulfilment of
prophecy), archaeology, etc.—an exercise which some would even
subsume under the heading of 'natural theology'). Most Evangelicals
would abjure any form of 'Christian rationalism' based on natural
theology.

d. The Christian Revelation

The supreme credential of Christianity is the life, ministry, death and
resurrection of Jesus Christ. The New Testament indicates this, for
instance, in statements which describe as saved those who have truly
expressed their belief in the incarnation or the resurrection (Rom. 10:9;
cf. 1 Jn. 4:2). The revelation was given, therefore, in the form of a Person,
and also of course in the preparatory experiences of God's ancient people
of Israel, and the subsequent foundation of God's new people, the church,
through the Holy Spirit. In view of the fact of the limitation of this divine
revelation, both in time and space, we may legitimately assume with some
a priori probability the provision by special divine activity of an authentic
record of the revelation to ensure its permanence and accessibility. The
Bible is this record and authoritative interpretation of the 'revelation-in-
life', and consequently presents this revelation to us not in the form of
systematic theology (though a book like the Epistle to the Romans seems
to come quite near to it), but largely of historical and 'personal' (cf. the
Epistles) writings of various kinds. As the Holy Spirit inspired the full

completion of the revelation of Christ in the experience of the apostolic church, and also the recording of the whole biblical revelation, so too He enlightens the understanding of the Christian reader. To Him we may also ascribe the clarification in the history of the church as it pondered the messages of redemption, of the essential doctrines contained in Holy Scripture, and their emancipation from false judgments of men.

In considering the revelation in Scripture, a primary and all-essential place must be assigned to the life, character and teachings of Christ. He is the Author and Finisher of our faith. It is necessary, however, to avoid the implication that the amplification by evangelists, apostles and other writers in the New Testament can be neglected in what has been called 'the search for the historical Jesus', or that the foreshadowing in the Old Testament, tracing the development of the purpose of God, can be safely ignored. The Christ we know is the Christ of the Scriptures and of the whole Scriptures.

Scriptures

a. *The Need for Revelation and 'Natural Theology'*

Jb. 11:7, 8; 23:3–9; Is. 55:8, 9; Jn. 1:18; 1 Cor. 1:21; 2:6–14; 1 Tim. 6:16; Heb. 11:6.

b. *General Revelation*

Ps. 19:1, 2; Jn. 1:5; Rom. 1:18–25; 2:12–15; Acts 14:15–17; 17:24–29.

c. *The Christian Revelation*

Dt. 29:29; Am. 3:7; Mt. 11:27; 16:17; Jn. 7:17; 14:6; 16:12–14; Rom. 16:25, 26; 2 Cor. 4:3–6; Gal. 1:11, 12; Eph. 1:9, 10; 3:3–11; 2 Tim. 3:15, 16; Heb. 1:1–4.

Questions

1. Wherein does general revelation prove inadequate? What is its value?
2. What are the dangers in an over-confident 'natural theology'?
3. 'The supreme credential of Christianity is the character of Christ.' Comment on this statement.
4. What is the relation between Christ Himself and the biblical revelation that preceded and followed Him?
5. What is the place of the Holy Scriptures in the Christian revelation?

BIBLIOGRAPHY

H. Bavinck, *The Philosophy of Revelation*, Eerdmans, 1954.
G. C. Berkouwer, *General Revelation*, Eerdmans, 1955.
E. Brunner and K. Barth, *Natural Theology*, Century Press, 1946.
C. F. H. Henry (ed.), *Revelation and the Bible*, Tyndale Press, 1959.
J. G. Machen, *What is Faith?*, Eerdmans, 1946.
B. Ramm, *Special Revelation and the Word of God*, Eerdmans, 1961.
P. Carnegie Simpson, *The Fact of Christ*, James Clarke, 1952.
Article on 'Revelation', *The New Bible Dictionary*, IVF, 1962.

2. The Canon of Holy Scripture

a. The Meaning of 'Canon'

The Greek word *kanōn* means a 'rule' or 'measuring rod'. Applied to the Scriptures, it has a double meaning. In the first place it is used to indicate a collection of those books to which a prescribed test has been applied and which have been acknowledged to be authentic or 'canonical'. Then the term is applied to the collection of writings as a whole because it constitutes the Canon, or 'rule of faith', by which all doctrine must be tested. It is the former meaning which concerns us here.

We need to remember that the books were canonical (by reason of their own intrinsic nature or in virtue of the authority of the writers) before they were collected into a Canon as we know it. The production of a list of 'official' writings does not make those writings any more 'official' than they were originally. Similarly, it is necessary to keep distinctly in mind that whereas 'inspiration' relates to the divine control of the writers, the Canon relates to the number of such writers which were admitted to be 'inspired'. One writer has aptly remarked, 'The Bible is not an authorized collection of books, but a collection of authorized books.'

Certain other books which are not in the Canon are termed 'deutero-canonical' (or 'apocryphal'), owing to the fact that they were not, at the first, received as equal to the inspired books, but as valuable for edification. In the early days they were received by only a section of the church and placed by that section in a subordinate position to those books which were included as inspired and authoritative in matters of faith.

b. History of the Old Testament Canon

The details of the final completion of the Old Testament Canon are not known.[1] There is evidence in the Scripture itself of a collection of authorized books and the fact that they were deposited in the sacred buildings. (See, *e.g.*, the account in 2 Kings 22 of the rediscovery of the 'book of the law' by Hilkiah.) At the time of our Lord there were the Hebrew Scriptures, consisting of the Law, the Prophets and the Hagiographa (Holy Writings). He Himself not only accepted these for His own life and ministry, but authorized them for His disciples (Lk. 24:27). In the New Testament, quotations are found from all the Old Testament books except four.

Of great importance is the fact that, among our Lord's charges against the religious leaders of the Jews, He never included that of adding to or taking from the Scriptures themselves. Note also that the present Old

---

[1] There is no reason why a so-called 'Council' of Jamnia (*c*. AD 90) should be credited with forming the Hebrew Canon. On the contrary, there are strong reasons against it. It neither omitted a book nor included any new book.

Testament is, and has been, acknowledged by world-wide Jewry. It is useful, too, to remember that the Samaritan Pentateuch—almost identical with the Hebrew—has had a long independent history.

Josephus (*c.* AD 95) gives an independent confirmation of the Hebrew canonical list.

c. History of the New Testament Canon

The addition of the New Testament books took place gradually by a natural development:

1. Our Lord's words were regarded as absolutely authoritative from the time of His first public ministry.

2. Reports (by those who heard Him) were received as being as authoritative as the living voice.

3. The letters of the apostles were received, and publicly read, with the same attitude as that accorded to their spoken ministry. Our Lord definitely gave the apostles authority of this kind in His church, and gave His confirmation for the (future) additions to the body of revealed truth which took place when the Holy Spirit had come. (See Jn. 16:13, 14.)

4. The exchange of letters between neighbouring churches followed.

5. Then, when the apostles were being removed by martyrdom and imitations of their writings were put into circulation by interested parties, the question of the *authority* of any additions arose.

The actual process of collecting the canonical books occupied some three hundred years. It may be summarized as follows:

1. The New Testament books were written during the period AD 50–100.

2. They were collected and read in the churches AD 100–200.

3. They were carefully examined and compared with spurious writings AD 200–300.

4. Complete agreement was attained AD 300–400.

No single Council was responsible for arbitrarily collecting and proclaiming a list of books as canonical. This is a very important point.

During the fourth century the Scriptures were classified into:

1. *Homologoumena.*—Books which were accepted by all the churches without exception. Revelation, however, appears to have given difficulty to some, and also the Epistle to the Hebrews.

2. *Antilegomena.*—Books which were 'spoken against' by some, but received by the majority. These were James, 2 Peter, 2 and 3 John, Jude.

Other books such as the Didache and the Shepherd of Hermas were included in the deutero-canonical list, which was read for moral instruction but not to establish Christian doctrine. There is no example of the rejection of a book which posterity has judged fit to have been included. It is easy to exaggerate the significance of the length of time and the amount of disagreement. The greater part of our Canon was recognized from the very first.

d. How was Canonicity determined?

This is an important question. There were three chief considerations:

1. *The Authority of the Writers in the Church.*—The books were, for the most part, written by men who were recognized as appointed by God to reveal His will—lawgivers and prophets in the Old Testament and apostles and their immediate associates in the New Testament. Hence in the case of the books which came to form the New Testament, apostolicity (apostolic signature or some apostolic authorization) was a basic criterion.

2. *External Evidence.*—The consensus of opinion among the existing churches as to their historicity was important. There was surprising unanimity (if the factor of the inspiration of the books be neglected) among them as to which books were canonical. Through lack of knowledge as to their origin, a few books were temporarily doubted by a minority in the church. This minority was at all times a very small one, and there is no example of a book which was doubted by any large number of churches having been later accepted. Difficulty was felt concerning some books which contained statements of doctrine which appeared slightly to contradict the teaching contained in other books which had already been accepted, and also with regard to the anonymous books.

3. *Internal Evidence.*—(i) The contents of the books were recognized to be sound doctrine, in accord with the apostolic teaching on which the churches had been reared. Apostolicity in this sense was probably the most important element in determining canonicity. If it had been lacking in any of the books of the Canon no apostolic authority (*per se*) or consensus of opinion would have been able to compensate for it. The reality of this internal evidence will readily be appreciated by those who will compare the Apocrypha—particularly the New Testament Apocrypha—with the sacred writings. (ii) In addition, the books themselves possessed a self-authenticating character, in terms of the spiritual impression made by their teaching as deserving to be received 'not as the word of men but as what it really is, the word of God' (1 Thes. 2:13). That is to say, the spiritual discernment imparted to the Christians almost instinctively recognized and acknowledged the divine inspiration of the scriptural books. It is only the Holy Spirit's witness that produces a true spiritual persuasion of their spiritual authority. The voice of the Spirit in Scripture

answers to the voice of the Spirit in the Christian. (*Cf.* Jn. 7:17; Rom. 8:14, 16; 1 Cor. 2:12-15.)

Scriptures

a. The Old Testament

Ex. 24:4-7; Dt. 31:9-26; Jos. 1:7, 8; 24:26; 2 Ki. 22:8-11; Ezr. 7:6, 14; Ne. 8:1; Pr. 25:1; Is. 8:16; 34:16; Je. 36:1-4, 32; Dn. 9:2; Lk. 24:27, 44; Jn. 2:22; Acts 28:23.

b. The New Testament

Jn. 13:20; 1 Cor. 7:10, 25; 14:37, 38; 2 Cor. 10:8-11; Col. 4:16; 2 Thes. 2:15; 1 Tim. 6:20; 2 Tim. 1:12-14; 2 Pet. 3:16; Rev. 1:1-3, 10; 2:1, 7; 22:18, 19.

Questions

1. What is meant by the phrase 'The Canon of Holy Scripture'? Discuss (a) the stages in the formation of the Canon, and (b) the factors governing the inclusion of books in the Canon.

2. 'The church created the Canon but did not create its authority.' Do you agree with this statement?

3. Consider the *apostolicity* of the Gospels of Mark and Luke, the Acts of the Apostles, and the Epistle to the Hebrews.

4. Since we have no autographed copies, to what extent can we be sure of the substantial accuracy of most texts in the various books? Give your reasons.

BIBLIOGRAPHY

F. F. Bruce, *The New Testament Documents: Are They Reliable?*, IVF, 1960.

O. Cullmann, *The Early Church*, SCM Press, 1956, chapter on 'The Tradition'.

J. Norval Geldenhuys, *Supreme Authority*, Marshall, Morgan and Scott, 1953.

W. H. Green, *General Introduction to the Old Testament: The Canon*, Murray, 1899.

C. F. H. Henry (ed.), *Revelation and the Bible*, Tyndale Press, 1959.

A. Souter, *The Text and Canon of the New Testament*, Duckworth, 1954.

B. B. Warfield, *The Inspiration and Authority of the Bible*, Marshall, Morgan and Scott, 1951.

B. F. Westcott, *A General Survey of the History of the Canon of the New Testament*, Macmillan, 1881.

Article on 'The Canon', *The New Bible Dictionary*, IVF, 1962.

3. The Inspiration of Holy Scripture

a. The Meaning of Inspiration

The Greek word most nearly equivalent to our word inspiration (*theopneustos* or 'God-breathed') occurs only once in the Bible (2 Tim. 3:16). 'The term means *out*-breathed rather than *in*-breathed by God—divinely *ex*-spired rather than *in*-spired' (*The New Bible Dictionary*), and refers to the work of writers specially controlled and directed for the purpose by the Holy Spirit. The following points should be borne in mind when attempting to describe this process:

1. Its exact nature, mode and limitations are not accurately defined in

Scripture itself. But see illustrations such as those in 2 Chronicles 15:1; Matthew 22:43; and 2 Peter 1:21.

2. Exactly the same difficulties will be met as in attempting accurately to express the union of the human and divine in the Person of our Lord. The two problems are almost identical in their form.

3. In studying this problem of inspiration the human mind, believing itself capable of analysing a divine mystery, has again and again demonstrated its presumptive littleness. The student will be well advised, while using all the aids and correctives which scholarship can bring to the subject, to maintain an attitude of reverent caution and not to allow himself to be persuaded into destructive criticism which archaeology has constantly and with unfailing persistence disproved.

4. The implications of inspiration were not questioned until relatively recently. Until the second half of the nineteenth century on no subject had the church been more united.

b. The Mode of Inspiration

An exact definition of the mode is obviously an impossibility.[1] Just how the Holy Spirit operated upon the minds of the writers we do not know. But it *is* important that we should have no illusions on the following matters:

1. The personality of the human writer was not superseded. Many of the books contain passages which reveal that the author's previous training and temperamental characteristics have been used by the Holy Spirit and are even *of importance* to the message.

2. God purposely chose a number of men from all ranks of society, previously training them by varied experiences, so that the Scriptures should be as close to the many-sided circumstances of human life as possible. Compare again our Lord's incarnation. Both forms of the Christian revelation have been made directly in and through human life. *Cf.* Jeremiah 1:5; Galatians 1:15.

3. It appears to be clear that the writing was never 'mechanical' (*cf.* the typewriter) nor were the authors mere amanuenses. The human writers' thought processes were not superseded, and, although they did not always understand what was to them the secondary (to us, the primary) application of the words they wrote, yet they consciously wrote them as the message God had given them for their own and succeeding generations.

4. On the other hand, while the human author was expected to make use of such genealogies, statistics and documents as he possessed (*cf.* Lk. 1:1-4), the Scriptures themselves claim that the Spirit of God so controlled the writer that he could not introduce any human defect such as false history,

[1] Compare the impossibility of a definition of the mode of our Lord's birth.

inaccurate description or misguided doctrine of such a character as to vitiate the revelation contained in the writing or impair its authority.

5. In the nature of the case, biblical inspiration is *verbal*, *i.e.*, the 'God-breathed' message of the writer is presented in *words*, words that were *approved* by the Holy Spirit as they were expressed by the writer. This is not the same as saying that each word was *dictated* mechanically. The author described in human language what he saw of God's message, consciously applying his mind to the description and exhortations. The Holy Spirit, however, being the Revealer and motive Force in the process, saw to it that adequate words were found by the writer.

c. The Extent of Inspiration

While complete definition is again not possible, the extent to which verbal inspiration is present in the Scriptures should be understood in its main features.

1. The position adopted by the older and chief Protestant theologians is that all of the present Canon, as we have it, must be understood to partake in the definition which anyone may give to 'inspiration'. In other words, all of the Old and New Testament books are (save for any copyists' errors and mistranslations in vernacular versions) substantially as the Spirit of God designed them.

2. This does not mean that we are to believe blindly that there are no differences in the purpose of the inspiration. God has caused to be recorded accurately the sayings of misguided men in the Old Testament. For example, God Himself subsequently contradicts the false arguments of Job's comforters. Obviously, we are not expected to deduce Christian doctrine from their speeches! All of those Scriptures were written for our warning, instruction and reproof. But other Scriptures, such as the Pauline Epistles, were written expressly for our acceptance as Christian doctrine. Hence, while all the Scriptures are fully authorized by God, they differ in their application and the *purpose* for which they were inspired. They differ in their ultimate *application*, rather than in the *degree* of inspiration. The student should be on his guard against a remark such as that 'John's Gospel is *more* inspired than Ecclesiastes'. It is rather that in the former the Holy Spirit was imparting to John the supremest and fullest revelation concerning the Son of God, and in the latter He was supplying a record of the ultimate results of the unaided pursuit of mankind for happiness in contrast with the divine revelation.[1]

3. Some have suggested the word 'plenary', instead of 'verbal', to describe the above view of inspiration. The object of so doing is to avoid

[1] See G. Campbell Morgan's book *The Answers of Jesus to Job* (Oliphants, 1964) for a useful study of the New Testament answers to some Old Testament problems.

the criticism of those who mean by 'verbal inspiration' a purely mechanical conception. The word 'plenary' needs almost as much explaining, however, and no amount of defining will satisfy those critics who are unable to see any difference between the Spirit's full control and a dictaphone method, and who would give us the extraordinarily difficult conception of an inspired message in uninspired words. It is straining at gnats and swallowing camels!

d. The Blending of Human and Divine

It is worth pointing out more fully how the difficulty of the mind in grasping the nature and extent of inspiration is due to the fact that we are dealing with a blending of the human and divine. Wherever God is, there is mystery. But it is precisely this element which is the unique glory of the Christian revelation. No mere impersonal supreme object of worship has been deduced from nature, and no mere philosophy of life has dropped from heaven written on tables of stone. But God has appeared and dwelt with us in human flesh, and His written revelation has come in a form which is at once vitally connected with the living Revelation, and is brought as close to the defective apprehension of human nature as God could possibly have made it.

Note the following comparisons. The living Revelation was mysteriously brought into the world without the intervention of a human father. The Holy Spirit was the appointed Agent. The written revelation came into being by a similar process without the aid of human philosophical abstractions. The Holy Spirit was again the appointed Agent. The mother of our Lord remained a human mother and her experiences throughout would appear to have been those of every other mother—except that she was made aware that her child was to be the long-expected Redeemer of Israel. The writers of the biblical books remained human authors, and their experiences appear to have been similarly natural, though they were sometimes aware that God was giving to the world through them a message of no ordinary importance (e.g., 'For I received from the Lord what I also delivered to you . . .' 1 Cor. 11:23). Mary, the mother of our Lord, probably brought into the world other children by the normal process of birth.[1] The writers of the biblical books probably wrote other purely personal letters which were not necessarily of canonical importance. More important still, no student should fail to grasp the fact that the divine-human personal life of our Lord is one and indivisible by any human means of analysis. On no recorded occasions can we say that in the one instance there was a *purely divine* thought, and in the other a *purely human* thought. The two natures were united in one indissoluble Person.

[1] See J. B. Mayor, *The Epistle of St. James* (Oliphants, 1913), for review of the evidence. Here the argument is only one of probability.

From the manger to the cross, the Lord must always be thought of and described from that point of view. Similarly, though the parallel is not quite complete, the student will be saved much unsound thinking, unnecessary confusion and, even, injury to his faith, by observing that in the Scriptures the divine and human elements are blended in such a way that in few cases can we, with any certainty, analyse the record to demonstrate purely human elements.

e. Perspicuity

It is sometimes urged against Bible authority that its meaning is not clear and needs interpretation or correction by an external authority. The following points are relevant in this connection:

1. To assert that God would offer man a revelation incapable of being understood is to take up a scarcely tenable position. It is intended for every age and for men of every social standing and type of education. Any type of book other than one capable of a straightforward meaning would not command universal acceptance.
2. Sufficient knowledge of the Hebrew and Greek languages and of the contemporary history have come down to us to enable almost all topical allusions and other forms of obscurity to be understood and solved.
3. Whatever alternatives to the Scriptures themselves may be brought forward, Creeds, findings of Councils, private interpretations, *etc.*, they must all be given in human language and are open to the same objection.
4. Such obscurities as we find today differ (often radically) from those which troubled the church in previous centuries. The obscurities of today may well be dispelled by the unfoldings of increasing knowledge, and the dawning of new eras in the light of which these particular passages reveal their true meaning.

We hold that Scripture is capable of giving up its proper meaning for every age and circumstance in which a man may find himself provided he is willing to be taught by and to obey the Holy Spirit.

f. Sufficiency

One of the chief grounds for the breach of the Protestant with the Roman church is the question of the sufficiency of Holy Scripture. The latter holds that the church is free to impose teaching concerning faith and morals as binding on her people and necessary for salvation, without requiring direct confirmation from Holy Scripture (*cf.* the definition of the dogmas of Mary's immaculate conception (1854) and bodily assumption into heaven (1950), which obviously lack any biblical foundation). The evangelical Protestant contention, however, while acknowledging that in matters such as forms of worship and church polity the church is free to make its own arrangements provided they are not 'plainly repugnant to Holy Scripture', maintains that without direct scriptural authority nothing must be imposed as an obligation of faith.

Four points must be recognized:

1. 'Holy Scripture containeth all things necessary to salvation; so that whatsoever is not read therein, nor may be proved thereby is not to be required of any man that it should be believed as an article of the faith.'[1]

2. The Scriptures claim sufficiency and finality for themselves. This claim, necessarily, is mostly to be found towards the close of the New Testament. See the Scripture references under this section.

3. The closing of the Canon of Scripture implies the completeness and sufficiency of its contents, just as it expresses a conviction of the fulfilment and completion of revelation.

4. In the everyday practice of Christian communities and in the life of the individual Christian the Scriptures have proved themselves to be sufficient, times without number.

5. The records of church history demonstrate clearly the fact of this sufficiency. Wherever large additions have been made, corruption and weakness have followed.

g. The Bible as its own Interpreter

Under this heading we must remind ourselves that the Holy Spirit who inspired has continued to interpret the sacred Scriptures. He and His mediation are the sources of their perspicuity and sufficiency. Our Lord taught clearly in John 14 and 16 that the Holy Spirit was to be the supreme Interpreter of the meaning of His own words, and the 'teacher' and 'guide' of the disciples' understanding.

The considerations of importance are:

1. Scripture contains within itself the material and ruling principles by which the meaning of any particular verse may be determined. For example, in the New Testament we have many instances of verses in the Old Testament applied to their fulfilment in the Gospels or interpreted by the apostles in the subsequent records. Hence, there is, as it were, an inspired and authorized commentary on the Old Testament. From these instances we may deduce principles for further interpretation.

2. The statement 'The Bible and the Bible *only* is the religion of Protestants' should be interpreted in the light of paragraphs (e) and (f) above. The proper meaning of the Scripture is primarily to be found by a

---

[1] Article VI of the Church of England.

process of induction and *not* by submission to the ruling of any human interpreter.

Scriptures

1. *Instances of Inspiration.*—Nu. 24:2, 3; 1 Sa. 10:6; 1 Ki. 22:5–28; Is. 61:1; Mi. 3:8; Acts 4:8; 1 Cor. 2:9–13; 7:40; Rev. 2:7, 11, 17, 29.
2. *The Inspiration of the Scriptures.*—Mt. 19:4, 5; Mk. 12:36; Acts 1:16; 4:25; 28:25; Rom. 3:2; 2 Tim. 3:14–17 (sufficiency; *cf.* Rev. 22:18, 19); Heb. 3:7; 10:15; 1 Pet. 1:10–12; 2 Pet. 1:21; 3:2.

Questions

1. What do you understand by the word 'inspiration' as commonly applied to (a) the Scriptures and (b) masterpieces in literature?
2. What controversy is properly related to the words 'verbal inspiration'? Can you describe in any *better* language what those who use this expression wish to convey by it? What is the relation between 'verbal inspiration' and the question of inerrancy?
3. What is the connection between the special operation of the Holy Spirit in the production of the Scriptures and His present ministry in the church?
4. Does the doctrine of inspiration require that the writers of the books of the Bible were conscious of being inspired? Were any or all of them so conscious? Cite the passages on which your answer is based.

BIBLIOGRAPHY

R. Abba, *The Nature and Authority of the Bible*, James Clarke, 1958.
C. F. H. Henry (ed.), *Revelation and the Bible*, Tyndale Press, 1959.
James Orr, *Revelation and Inspiration*, Eerdmans, 1953.
J. I. Packer, *'Fundamentalism' and the Word of God*, IVF, 1958.
N. B. Stonehouse and P. Woolley (eds.), *The Infallible Word*, Tyndale Press, 1946.
J. F. Walvoord (ed.), *Inspiration and Interpretation*, Eerdmans, 1957.
B. B. Warfield, *The Inspiration and Authority of the Bible*, Marshall, Morgan and Scott, 1951.

4. The Relation of the Old and New Testaments

The following chief principles guide our attitude to this problem.

1. *The Unity of the Two Separate Collections of Writings.*—There is no hint that the New Testament writers regarded themselves as producing a new and independent Canon. On the contrary, the New Testament appears to enhance the authority of the Old. The basis of unity is found in the progressive prophecies concerning the Messiah in the Old and their fulfilment in the New.

2. *The Extent of Old Testament Authority.*—Of necessity, certain matters are more fully revealed in the New Testament, and also, with the coming of Christ and the Holy Spirit, new statements are made of previously unrevealed truths. In a few cases these amplify the Old Testament teaching. But it should be clearly grasped that *wherever the Old Testament is superseded, clear and distinct guidance is given to us in the matter,*

and the claim is advanced that such supersession is always in the nature not of a contradiction, but a sublimation, of Old Testament truth.

3. *Interpretation of the Old Testament.*—The spiritual meaning of the Old Testament would be largely unintelligible apart from the interpretation and completions to be found in the New. Prophecies are fulfilled and, in many cases, rendered intelligible only when we come to the New Testament. For example, the temporary sacrifices are completed and superseded by the one perfect and complete oblation of Christ. The resurrection of Christ transforms the fears and longings of the Old Testament into a sure and certain hope for the Christian.

4. *The Testimony of Christ.*—The Lord Himself authorized the Old Testament, quoting from several of the main books of the Pentateuch and the prophets. Compare also His use of the Old Testament in Luke 24.

Scriptures

1. *The Old Testament not abrogated by the New.*—Mt. 5:17-19, and 20 with 21-48; 7:12; 22:34-40; Rom. 3:31; 13:8-10.

2. *Christ, the Key.*—Lk. 24:27; Jn. 1:45; 5:39, 46; Acts 8:35; 10:43; 18:28; Rom. 1:2, 3; 3:21; 10:4; 16:25, 26; 2 Cor. 1:20; 1 Pet. 1:10-12.

3. *Fulfilments of Prophecy in Christ.*—*Cf.* Mi. 5:2 with Lk. 2:4, 15; Is. 7:14 with Mt. 1:23; Is. 35:4-6 with Mt. 11:4, 5; Is. 61:1, 2 with Lk. 4:16-19; Je. 31:31 with 1 Cor. 11:25; and many similar passages. *Cf.* also Acts 2:16-21; 13:46, 47, *etc.*

Questions

1. 'The New Testament does not quote extracts from the Old Testament as though the actual words were inspired.' Discuss this statement.

2. In your opinion, in what chief ways are the Old and New Testaments related? Why is it important to understand the connection between them? Give your reasons.

3. Which do you consider to be the most important books in the Old and New Testaments and why? Which of them do you advise a convert to read first?

BIBLIOGRAPHY

G. C. Aalders, *A Short Introduction to the Pentateuch*, Tyndale Press, 1949.

W. F. Albright, *Recent Discoveries in Bible Lands*, Funk and Wagnalls, 1953.

O. T. Allis, *The Five Books of Moses*, PRPC, 1943.

Millar Burrows, *What Mean These Stones?*, Thames and Hudson, 1957.

C. H. Dodd, *According to the Scriptures*, Fontana, 1965.

E. E. Ellis, *Paul's Use of the Old Testament*, Oliver and Boyd, 1957.

A. H. Finn, *The Unity of the Pentateuch*, Marshall, 1917.

James Orr, *The Bible Under Trial*, Marshall, Morgan and Scott, 1907.

James Orr, *The Problem of the Old Testament*, Nisbet, 1900.

E. Robertson, *The Old Testament Problem: a Re-investigation*, Manchester University Press, 1950.

R. V. G. Tasker, *The Old Testament in the New Testament*, SCM Press, 1954.

G. E. Wright, *Biblical Archaeology*, Duckworth, 1957.

5. Scripture as the Ultimate Authority

As we have already seen, the three courts of appeal which may, with some degree of support, be claimed as ultimate in matters of religion are reason, the church and the Bible.[1] It must not be supposed, however, that these are mutually incompatible; in point of fact, they are frequently to be combined. But the student must clearly understand where the emphasis is to be placed. More depends upon proper emphasis than people imagine, and things which appear not to differ may become, in reality, very different because of the unequal values placed upon one word.

a. Reason

This fails as a final source of authority because of its corruption by sin, and consequent inadequacy and inconstancy. The student needs to guard against the popular failure to distinguish between the principle of reason and the exercise of reasoning power upon any particular subject-matter. A man may employ his reason in an erroneous way, and may claim authority on the ground of reason for what is only a mistaken application of the principle. As a consequence what is a fashionable theory today is discarded tomorrow, and in some cases a rationalistic handling of certain aspects of the faith has gravely misled men. Reason is in its proper place not as the maker of doctrine, but as its examiner and assessor.

b. The Church

Both in the sense of a national church or an independent community of Christians, and in the universal sense of the body of all true believers, the church *has a place of authority*, but it is one of subservience to the Word of God. The following fallacious statements need to be guarded against:

1. That by the church is to be understood a hierarchy which may at any time arrogate to itself the right to set aside Scripture.
2. That the church preceded the New Testament and therefore has a prior authority. There is no hint of this in the Bible; in fact, it was the spoken (afterward written) Word of God which brought the church into being.
3. That church tradition may add to Scripture. Compare the traditions of the Jewish leaders so scathingly denounced by our Lord.

It must always be tenaciously held that no doctrinal statement and no ceremony is valid in clear opposition to Scripture.

The appeal to tradition is fundamentally different in the Roman and Protestant churches. The Roman attitude is that in her official Councils the church is the supreme legislature whose decisions are binding. The Protestant attitude is that the individuals in the church may act in the nature of witnesses (and, sometimes, jury) in a court of law, but not as judges.

[1] See p. 23.

c. The Bible

It is at the very root of the evangelical position that the supremacy of Holy Scripture be held in its fullest sense. This does not mean, however, that reason and the church are not to be used as secondary authorities and in confirmation. But it does mean that no words can too strongly express the importance of securing, beyond doubt, the unsuperseded authority of the sacred Scriptures in all religious discussions whether of doctrine or practice.

It follows, as a corollary, that the ecumenical Creeds, decisions of General Councils, the Confessions of Faith, and the rulings of all modern synods must be regarded as authorities only in a secondary sense. Their words can never be finally binding unless they can be proved by warrant of Holy Scripture.

Scriptures

1. *The Authority and Importance of the Scriptures.*—Ne. 8:1, 8; Pss. 19:7–11; 119:1, 9, *etc.*; Is. 8:19, 20; Mt. 4:1–11; 12:1–5; Mk. 7:1–13; 12:35–37; Lk. 18:31; 22:37; Jn. 12:48; Acts 15:14–19; Rom. 4:3; 9:17; 10:11; 11:2; 2 Tim. 3:14–16.

2. *Warning against Neglect or Misuse.*—Mt. 5:19; Mk. 12:24; Heb. 3:15; Jas. 1:22–24; 2 Pet. 3:16, 17; Rev. 22:18, 19.

3. *The Power of the Word of God.*—Is. 55:10, 11; Je. 23:29; Ho. 6:5; Eph. 6:17; I Pet. 1:23–25; Rev. 1:16.

Questions

1. What is the basis of the authority of the Bible?

2. List and criticize the claims made for the church as the final authority in matters of religion.

3. To what extent may the church and human reason act as secondary authorities in conjunction with Scripture? What is the rightful function of the Creeds and Confessions of Faith as 'subordinate standards'?

BIBLIOGRAPHY

O. Cullmann, *The Early Church*, SCM Press, 1956, chapter on 'The Tradition'.

P. T. Forsyth, *The Principle of Authority*, Independent Press, 1952.

J. N. Geldenhuys, *Supreme Authority*, Marshall, Morgan and Scott, 1953.

E. M. B. Green, *The Authority of Scripture*, CP–AS, 1963.

C. H. Hodge, *Systematic Theology*, James Clarke, 1960.

J. G. Machen, *The Christian Faith in the Modern World*, Eerdmans, 1947.

J. G. Machen, *Christianity and Liberalism*, Eerdmans, 1946.

B. Ramm, *The Pattern of Religious Authority*, Eerdmans, 1959.

P. Schaff, *The Creeds of Christendom*, Baker Book House, 1966.

Article on 'Authority', *The New Bible Dictionary*, IVF, 1962.

PART TWO

THE GODHEAD

1. The Being of God

a. The Basis of Theism

1. Theism may be defined as belief in the existence of a God who controls the world. 'God' has always been taken to represent 'the supreme being who is worshipped as the Lord of men and nature'. (See below, pp. 51, 52.)

2. Scripture itself does not attempt to prove God's existence; it merely states that 'In the beginning ... God ...' Although the Scriptures indicate the futility of denying God's existence, men wickedly suppress the truth about God that is before their eyes and turn to idolatry (Rom. 1:18-23). Hence because sinful man is unable to profit from the revelation of God's being in the natural realm, for all practical purposes our knowledge of God is derived entirely from supernatural sources (see p. 25).

3. Though in the nature of the case there can be no fully conclusive intellectual demonstrations of God's existence, there are a number of considerations which, taken together, have been regarded by many as forming a strong cumulative argument for His existence. Some of these are briefly described below. The ontological approach would appear to be the most persuasive. It must be said, however, that apart altogether from the logical validity of these arguments (which many would in fact question), a large body of evangelical opinion considers it improper to try to prove the existence of God to a man whose understanding is darkened by sin.

4. There is a world-wide intuition in the heart of man that there is a supreme being who is to be worshipped. Although this intuition expresses itself in very many different ways, it is at rock-bottom of the same nature in every age and race. This phenomenon may be claimed as presumptive evidence for the existence of a God. It is noteworthy that this intuition appears to demand personality, power and perfection in God. Any description which weakens any of these elements leaves the mind unsatisfied.

b. The Philosophical Arguments

The following are the chief intellectual arguments or 'proofs' traditionally held to justify belief in the existence of God:

1. *Ontological.*—Historically, this 'proof' was the latest to appear. Logically, it is first. It is an argument based on the concept of perfection: 'I have an idea of the most perfect being. This being must be free from all limitations. Also, "the actual" is superior to "the possible". If the most perfect being were merely *possible* logically, there could be no *actual*. Hence, it is concluded, the most perfect being must possess actual existence, as otherwise I could conceive a being more perfect, which is contradictory.' The student must bear in mind that the concept is that of *absolute perfection*, an idea *sui generis*, because it is the governing concept of all existence. In finite things there often lurks a contradiction in the idea of complete perfection because it is a denial of the finite. This is not so in relation to the thought of absolute being. An *Ens Entium*, a being of beings, must exist, otherwise all 'existence' is illusion. Anselm, Descartes, Spinoza, Leibniz, Hegel, support this view; Aquinas and Kant oppose it.[1] It is discussed in H. D. Lewis's *Philosophy of Religion*.[2]

2. *Cosmological.*—This has a logical dependence on the ontological. The universe is not self-existent. Events everywhere are explained by a cause lying outside them—*e.g.*, vapour condensed by cold falls as rain. The cold finds its explanation in something other than the vapour. We are set on an inquiry into causes. If the world is thus dependent, it must have its source in an independent. To avoid a *regressus ad infinitum* we must arrive at a being in which or whom cause is resolved into identity in difference. The universe with its causal law demands this. Even if the universe were eternal it would remain dependent. A self-determined being is a necessity of thought. The progress of modern science does not encourage the idea of a self-sufficing universe which is the postulate of pantheism. Kant saw clearly that the cosmological argument merged finally in the ontological.

3. *Teleological.*—This is the well-known 'argument from design'. Natural forces and the adaptation to them of living things argue that there is an ordered design behind the world. The design had a designer. This tells us something of the nature of the designer, rather than demonstrates His existence. It shows that if there be a 'first cause', He is an *intelligent* cause.

4. *Anthropological.*—This argues that there must be a greater personality, mind and will apart from the existence of man's personality, mind and will.

5. '*Moral Purpose.*'—It is inconceivable to us that there should be any

---

[1] Kant's rejection is based on the view that 'existence' adds nothing to the inner quality of an object. One hundred thalers possible is the same in conceptual content as one hundred thalers actual. But, as Hegel drily remarked, most people observe very considerable difference between the two concepts!

[2] Teach Yourself Books, English Universities Press, 1965.

other purpose for the universe than that it should result in some moral end, which demands a being interested in the pursuit of this end.

It has been pointed out that these arguments relate to different aspects of God's being; the ontological to His completeness, the cosmological to His being the first cause, the teleological to His designing intelligence, and the anthropological to His personal nature.

c. The Argument from the Fact of Christ

This is based on a conviction that the complex of phenomena which form the beginnings of Christianity provides very strong evidence for believing in the existence of God. This complex ranges from Christ's unique personal character and His claims to be the Revelation of God and, indeed, the Son of God, to His resurrection and the birth of the church through the preaching of the resurrection. This is a many-sided argument, seeking to vindicate the consistency of the New Testament account of these phenomena, drawing out their logical implications, and demonstrating that their only coherent explanation lies in the fact of *divine* activity in and through Jesus Christ.

Scriptures

The Being of God is largely assumed in Scripture. The inspired authors hardly seem to think it can be questioned. See, however, Ps. 53:1, 2; Is. 40:12–26; Je. 10:1–16; Jn. 4:24; Acts 17:23–30; Rom. 1:18–20; Heb. 11:6. *Cf.* also Jos. 3: 10; 1 Ch. 28: 9; Dn. 6:26; 1 Thes. 1:9; and the verses listed on p. 49.

Questions

1. What attempts have been made to prove the existence of God by human reasoning, and on what grounds do you accept or reject them?

2. Which argument, or arguments, for the existence of God impress you most? Which of them would be most likely to appeal to (*a*) an arts student, (*b*) a medical student, (*c*) a member of the faculty of science? On what grounds do you form your judgment?

3. On what do you base your own belief in God's existence? How far are your reasons scriptural?

2. The Nature of God: the Divine Attributes

Even if we allow that philosophical reasoning can persuade us of God's existence, it must be admitted that apart from revelation we know next to nothing of God's nature.

The 'attributes' of God are the qualities constitutive of His being and character. Four points must be remembered:

1. Though they are listed individually, each must be taken in the closest association with all the others. It is only by treating each characteristic of the divine nature separately that we can begin to comprehend the full-orbed greatness of God.

2. The attributes speak of God's *essential being*. God would not be God if He were not infinite, righteous, omniscient, *etc*. His attributes are not features which qualify something else which forms the irreducible essence of His being. (Contrast the way we speak of human attributes.)

3. Though we can say that God's nature is the sum total of His attributes (if these could be exhaustively enumerated), we are not to think of them as *parts* of His being. God's *whole* being is righteousness, omnipotence, *etc*.

4. The books of the Bible which contain the most comprehensive portrayal of the attributes of God are those in which personal devotion and the deeper religious experiences are most fully described, for example, the Psalms. This reminds us of the place of worship in a true appreciation of God's being.

Three main classifications, none of them entirely satisfactory, have been suggested by theological writers:

1. One system classifies them into (*a*) those belonging to His *absolute being* (*e.g.*, infinity and self-existence); (*b*) those belonging to His *personal being* (*e.g.*, freedom and personality); and (*c*) the *specific* attributes (*e.g.*, omniscience, omnipresence, *etc*.).

2. A second classification suggests (*a*) *related* attributes (*i.e.*, related to the creation), and (*b*) *unrelated* attributes. These are sometimes described as the *communicable* and *incommunicable* attributes.

3. The division adopted here distinguishes (*a*) the '*natural*' *attributes*, and (*b*) *the moral attributes*. These terms are not fully adequate, especially in view of (2) and (3) above, but the value of this classification, as well as its limitations, should be clear from what follows.

a. The 'Natural' Attributes

1. *Infinity*.—This is in itself incomprehensible to man. But what is often overlooked is the fact that what was desired by those who originally used the term was to describe God as limitless, not as a mere endless continuum. If careful thought be given to the word, it will readily be seen that neither man nor any other being can know an infinity in quantity. But it is possible to conceive of a being who is free from limitation. 'Infinite holiness or love is not a boundless *quantum* of holiness or of love, but a holiness and love which are qualitatively free from all limitation and defect.' Perhaps we may say that ultimately infinity in God is first internal and qualitative absence of all limitation and defect; and secondly, boundless activity. 'Man has potential powers, but God is "Active Power".'

2. *'Personality' and Freedom*.—A more accurate definition of God is 'free personal Spirit'.

(i) Personality in God is difficult for the human mind to grasp. But the Bible is insistent on this point, and the marks of personal being—mind, emotions (in a sense differing from human emotion), will, freedom—are attributed to Him. It is as *Spirit* that He is personal without any of the limiting notions attached to our view of human personality. It is our knowledge of His being personal that saves us from frigid and barren reflection on the infinitude and absolute sovereignty of God.

(ii) Freedom is an element in His 'personality'. But it is well to point out that Scripture generally leaves the reader to assume God's freedom. In some places it states more clearly that He is the absolute free personal Cause who is sovereign over all life (*e.g.*, Eph. 1:11).

3. *Immutability and Eternity.*—Scripture plainly declares, as, for example, in the ascription of 1 Timothy 1:17, that God is eternal and immutable. That is, He is unlimited by time and space; and His attributes are completely constant. For example, His love is a constant force, not a fitful emotion.

4. *Transcendence and Immanence (or Omnipresence).*—(i) Christianity is alone in uniting in its description of God His 'transcendence' (*i.e.*, His detachment, as self-existent, from His creatures) and His immanence (*i.e.*, His nearness to, and pervasion of, everything, organic and inorganic). Both are true. God is far removed from man in His essential being. He is external to the world and His creatures as the sovereign Creator and Judge of the world. But at the same time He is in 'all things, and in him all things hold together' (Col. 1:17).

The apostle Paul in his address on Mars Hill proclaimed both. 'The God who made the world . . . being Lord of heaven and earth . . . nor is he served by human hands, as though he needed anything . . . he is not far from each one of us, for "In him we live and move and have our being" ' (Acts 17:24, 25, 27, 28).

These and similar concepts need to be carefully differentiated, and yet they must be carefully balanced. It is lack of such balance which has produced heresies on this subject. Emphasis on one of them to the practical exclusion of another is seen in agnosticism (stressing God's inscrutable mystery); deism (stressing transcendence); pantheism (stressing immanence); and theism (stressing personality). Christianity has blended all four harmoniously.

(ii) An older term very similar to 'immanence' is 'omnipresence'. There are two principles underlying human thought on this subject. In the first place God is so great that He cannot be separated from His own works, and, secondly, as the primary Cause and Preserver, He is actively engaged in every part of His creation. This is the converse of the deist's contention that God has set in motion the world forces and has left them to their fate.

The student must observe that it is not so much that God is Himself everywhere as that He is the 'everywhere' itself. The spatial concept is, at best, a metaphor. It might be clearer to suggest that there is not and cannot be anything beyond or apart from God. Also, the mind must be freed from all temptation to limit God. He is not *partly* present to any given person or in any place—but He is *wholly* present in every place.

The reader may be asked: 'Is He equally present in the same manner everywhere?' The older theologians distinguished His *'general* presence' in the world and His *'special* presence' in the heart of the believer. But it would seem better to regard the difference as a difference in the meaning attached to the word 'presence'. The meaning changes with the purport of the presence. God is creatorially in all His works. He is morally present in the realm of conduct. He is present in grace, both restraining evil and conferring blessing. Again, in the latter sense, He is present for a particular purpose, for example, with the two or three gathered in His Name. Compare Exodus 33:15, 'If thy presence will not go with me . . .' and Psalm 139:7, 'Whither shall I flee from thy presence?'

5. *Omniscience.*—God's knowledge is part of His own nature. It is not attached or 'built on' to His nature as man's acquirements are. It is complete and absolute.

God knows the future as well as the past and is absolute even in the realm of mind. He possesses foreknowledge, an attribute in which He challenges the idols to prove their claims by competing with Him (see Is. 41). It is this which has occasioned difficulty to many, particularly in relation to His knowledge of what would have happened had not some other act or circumstance intervened and His foreknowledge of the acts of men, which are said to be 'free'. Two extremes have resulted. Some deny foreknowledge of *free acts* and others deny that any acts are free! The solution is probably to be found in acknowledging that our notions of 'freedom' are faulty. 'Freedom' and rational determination are not opposed. If we were perfect moral beings, for example, we would do only one thing in any given circumstance, *i.e.*, the right and best thing. The absence of alternatives would be the highest exhibition of freedom. There are certainly spiritual principles governing our 'freedom' which God alone understands, so that while we are to regard ourselves as 'free' and are held responsible for our acts, God's foreknowledge can infallibly read a man's future, because He knows what ought to be and the defect which impedes its development.[1]

6. *Omnipotence.*—The thought of power in God must be separated

[1] If a man knew what was wrong with the steering-gear of a car, he might be able to calculate the deflection of the car over a given road. There are illegitimate applications of this in necromancy and the reading of the horoscope.

from analogies with the limited applications of power in man. Man's power consists in little more than the existence and use of *will*, which harnesses and employs pre-existing power. In God power is to be regarded as always *creative*.

Three difficulties need to be commented upon.

(i) God's power does not extend to anything which is self-contradictory. For example, God cannot cause seven times six to make nine. Certain acts would be incompatible with His nature and contradictory to another of His attributes, which are all consistent in themselves and with one another. His power is not arbitrary, and such conceptions are really limitations of God, *not* evidences of His free activity.

(ii) Certain limitations are *self*-imposed. He abides by certain laws which He Himself has set in motion. The opposite view, again, is really a limitation of God as it involves a change of purpose.

(iii) He frequently acts through ordinary measures, as, for example, in healing disease, where He could have displayed His power if He had so willed.

b. The Moral Attributes

1. *Goodness.*—God continually seeks the welfare of creation. There is no hint of deliberately planned evil in creation. All evidence of wrong is properly regarded as a violation of purpose and a negation of being.[1] The *general tendency* of created things is towards goodness, a tendency which is frequently thwarted through man's inherent wickedness and stupidity.

Scripture emphasizes aspects of goodness such as love, loving-kindness, mercy, forbearance and grace. The supreme act of love is seen in redemption, and the New Testament word 'grace' gathers up the manifold Old Testament words used to express the perfection of God's goodness.

2. *Holiness.*—The essential holiness of God is reiterated again and again in the Old Testament—'The Holy One of Israel'. The underlying thought is that of separation from all that is impure. It also conveys the idea of 'loftiness' and complete separation from everything which is finite and imperfect.

It is always necessary to remind ourselves of the grandeur of this absolute moral perfection which encircles the divine Being. Without it true worship would degenerate and man would become presumptuous.

3. *Righteousness.*—In man 'righteousness' is 'to do justly'. This is only a shadow of what the word means when applied to God. He is eternal and

[1] In this connection it is interesting to contrast the teaching of non-Christian religions. See, for example, *The World's Religions*, edited by J. N. D. Anderson (IVF, 1954).

essential righteousness. It is His nature to be righteousness and it is impossible for Him to act otherwise than in accordance with His essential nature. Righteousness is the principle in God which gives rise to and upholds the moral order in the world. Connected with His righteousness are justice, truth and anger.

Some feel that it is difficult to reconcile this teaching with the injustice, inequalities and calamities which abound in the world. The Christian answer would claim:

(i) That these elements emerge as a consequence of man's departure from God—a consequence of the measure of freedom given him as a moral and finite being.

(ii) That grace continually restrains the evil and secures such a measure of good as is possible, granting the exercise of man's freedom.

(iii) That redemption effects finally a new heaven and a new earth.

Read David's statement of the problem and its answer in Psalm 73.

When seeking to avoid the modern tendency to fuse righteousness and love in God, we must beware lest we fall into the opposite error of setting up a dualism in our description of God's attributes, whereby one part of His nature antagonizes another. Righteousness and justice are consistent in Him with love and mercy. They are also never incompatible. God's anger is not 'a resentment or passion, but a judicial disapprobation'.

c. Without Body, Parts, or Passions

Very careful consideration must be given to the types of description which are permissible as applied to the Godhead. Particularly is this true in the case of what are known as 'anthropomorphisms'. Man is unable to conceive of, and to discuss, God's actions without the employment of terms which present analogies with human acts. This frequently involves the use of descriptions which, if taken too literally, would imply that God was limited by a bodily shape and possessed anatomical parts. As *the Spirit*, it is impossible to limit God in any such manner. Hence, it should be clearly understood that it is safest not to employ any anthropomorphisms which are unauthorized by scriptural precedent, and that those which are used must be used on the understanding that they are permitted by God only as aids to the human intellect; for example, 'the Lord's hand is not shortened', 'the eyes of the Lord run to and fro throughout the whole earth', *etc.*

On the other hand, it is necessary to avoid denying moral character to God. Scripture represents Him as suffering (by voluntary self-limitation) from the deliberate ingratitude of man. He is described as experiencing pleasure when His people are obedient to His expressed wishes. Our finite minds can, at best, seek to understand and to discuss in the everyday homely terms which the Spirit of God has been pleased to use in the

Scriptures. After making due allowance for the above exceptions and considerations, the words of Article I of the Church of England remain true: 'There is but one living and true God, everlasting, without body, parts, or passions.'[1]

Scriptures

Note that in certain books, for example, in the Gospel and Epistles of John, there is special teaching on the character of God: *God is spirit* (Jn. 4:24); *God is light* (1 Jn. 1:5); *God is love* (1 Jn. 4:8, 16).

a. The 'Natural' Attributes

1. *'Personality' and Freedom.*—Pss. 94:9, 10; 147:11; Je. 10:10 (and repeated references to 'the living God'); Eph. 1:9, 11, and indeed throughout the Scriptures. God's personal nature depicted by means of *anthropomorphisms; cf.* Gn. 6:6, 7; Dt. 29: 20; 2 Ch. 16:9; Je. 15:6, *etc.*

2. *Eternity.*—Ps. 90:2; Is. 40:28; Rom. 1:20; 1 Tim. 1:17; 6:16. Self-existent: Jn. 5:26; 6:57; Acts 7:25; Rom. 11:33–36. Immutable: Ps. 102:24–27; Mal. 3:6; 2 Tim. 2:13; Jas. 1:17.

3. *Transcendence.*—1 Sa. 15:29; 1 Ch. 29:11; 2 Ch. 6:18; Is. 6:1–3; 40:12–15; Rev. 4. *Immanence.*—Ps. 139:7–12; Is. 66:1; Je. 23:23, 24; Acts 17:24–28.

4. *Omniscience.*—Pss. 33:13–15; 139:1–6; 147:4, 5; Ezk. 11:5; Am. 9:1–4; Heb. 4:13; 1 Jn. 3:20.

5. *Omnipotence.*—Jb. 42:2; Pss. 115:3; 135:6; Je. 32:17; Mt. 19:26; Mk. 14:36.

b. The Moral Attributes

1. *Goodness and Love.*—Dt. 33:3; Ps. 107:1, 8, 15, *etc.*; Zp. 3:17; Mk. 10:18; Jn. 3:16; 13:1; Rom. 2:4; 5:8; Eph. 2:4; 1 Jn. 3:1; 4:8–16. *Aspects of Love.*—(i) *General Benevolence*: Ps. 33:5; Mt. 5:45; Acts 14:17; 17:25. (ii) *Mercy*: Pss. 103:2–18; 145:8, 9; Is. 63:9; Lk. 18:13; Jas. 5:11; 1 Pet. 1:3. (iii) *Faithfulness*: Dt. 7:9; Pss. 36: 5;100:5; 119:89, 90; La. 3:22, 23; 1 Cor. 1:9; Phil. 1:6; 2 Thes. 3:3; 2 Tim. 2:13; Tit. 1:2.

2. *Holiness.*—Lv. 19:2; Pss. 5:4; 99:3, 5, 9; Is. 1:4; 6:1–3; 57:15, *etc.*; Ho. 11:9; Hab. 1:13; Heb. 7:26; 1 Pet. 1:15, 16.

3. *Righteousness.*—Gn. 18:25; Ezr. 9:15; Pss. 11:7; 103:6; Jn. 17:25; Rom. 2:2; 3:4–6, 21–26.

Questions

1. Is it possible to believe in more than 'one true God'? Give reasons for your answer.

2. Suggest various possible classifications of God's attributes. Why is this subject important?

3. 'There can never be a realized quantitative infinitude. Omnipotence in God does not mean an absolute *quantum* of power, but an exhaustless *potency* of power.' Discuss this, stating whether you consider the distinction is properly made, and the grounds on which you base your opinions.

4. God's righteousness sometimes demands retribution. Is this consistent with His all-pervading love? Is it possible to hold that some of God's attributes are mutually incompatible? State as clearly as you can the solution of the problem.

---

[1] By 'passions' must be understood emotional experiences, the cause of which lies partly outside the being affected. God cannot be changed by any action of any other being.

BIBLIOGRAPHY
H. Bavinck, *The Doctrine of God*, Eerdmans, 1951.
E. Brunner, *The Christian Doctrine of God*, Lutterworth Press, 1958.
J. S. Candlish, *The Christian Doctrine of God*, T. and T. Clark, 1888.
K. Heim, *God Transcendent*, Nisbet, 1935.
James Orr, *The Christian View of God and the World*, Eerdmans, 1947.

3. The Divine Names

Space prevents a full discussion of the immense amount of theology which is enshrined in the actual names applied to the Deity in Scripture. The subject is best approached by keeping clearly in mind some general classification and noticing that the use of a particular name appears never to be a matter of chance. There is a connection between it and the particular divine relation described, or message given. Similarly, as also in most Scripture names, each divine name offers an indication of the character of God, or principle on which the message is based. One such classification which has been suggested is:

> a. *General Names*—e.g., El and (plural form) Elohim.
> b. *The Covenant Name*—Jehovah (or Yahweh).
> c. *Particular Names*—such as Jehovah-Jireh; Jehovah-Nissi; Jehovah-Tsidkenu.

a. *General Names*

1. *El* (singular) occurs some 250 times. The underlying thought is that of 'strength' or 'might' and it means 'God' or 'god' in the widest sense. Hence when it is used of the true God it is usually connected with one of God's attributes as, for example, 'a merciful God' (Dt. 4:31); 'a jealous God' (Ex. 20:5).

This usage provides combinations such as El Elyon, 'God Most High' (Gn. 14:18–22); El Olam, 'the Everlasting God' (Gn. 21:33); El Shaddai, 'God Almighty' (Gn. 17:1).

There are numerous such usages, which should be carefully studied with the help of a good concordance.[1]

Two connected singular forms may be noticed, Eloah and its Aramaic equivalent Elah; they have the same meaning as El.

2. *Elohim* (plural) occurs over 2,000 times. It implies 'the God of creation and providence, the supreme Deity'. Though a plural form, it is most probably a 'plural of majesty'.

b. *The Covenant Name*

Yahweh.—'Yahweh' is probably quite close to the original pronunciation of the Hebrew YHWH (consonants only; the text did not include vowels).

[1] *E.g.*, *The Analytical Concordance* by Robert Young (Lutterworth Press), or *The Exhaustive Concordance* by J. Strong (Hodder and Stoughton).

Later, to avoid using the sacred Name YHWH, Jewish scribes read instead 'Adonai', '(My) Lord'. Later still, a combination of YHWH with the vowels of Adonai produced 'Jehovah', which has become the general usage. It is God's special covenant Name with Israel (see, *e.g.*, Mal. 3:6) and occurs some seven thousand times in the Old Testament. The meaning is probably 'the existing, ever-living, absolute, unchangeable One'.

c. Particular Names

Many of these are compounds of the name Jehovah, with nouns or verbal forms. We have, for example, the following: *Jehovah-Jireh* (Jehovah will see, or provide), Genesis 22:14; *Jehovah-Nissi* (Jehovah my Banner), Exodus 17:15,16; *Jehovah-Tsidkenu* (Jehovah our Righteousness), Jeremiah 23:6; 33:16.

There are several other forms of the divine name such as *Jah*, used on forty-nine occasions; *Adon* (singular), used thirty times; and *Adonai* (plural), used some 280 times. These two latter forms are best translated into English by 'the Sovereign Lord', or 'the Owner'. See, for example, Exodus 23:17 and Genesis 15:2, 8.

BIBLIOGRAPHY

J. A. Motyer, *The Revelation of the Divine Name*, Tyndale Press, 1960.
Article on 'God, Names of', *The New Bible Dictionary*, IVF, 1962.

4. Some Rivals of Monotheism

The following rivals of this belief in the one true God (monotheism) may be described:

1. *Atheism.*—This is rarely stated in its original form of a denial of the existence of God. It is, however, widely spread amongst non-churchgoers in the form of 'the universe is self-explanatory'. The arguments described above (pp. 41–43) may be effective to counter it.

2. *Agnosticism.*—This declares that God is 'unknowable'. In another form it tends to pantheism in its undermining of the moral government of the world. There is a limited sense in which it is true that God is 'unknowable'. For example, the Scriptures frequently remind us that 'his ways are past finding out'. But it is the glory of the Christian revelation that our Lord has 'declared him', and that He can be known through Christ. There is a limited sense in which general revelation also permits Him to be known. See above.

3. *Deism.*—This admits that there is a powerful Deity, but separates Him from His own universe and removes Him from active control over it. He is merely the first cause and may even be thought of as impersonal.

4. *Pantheism.*—This describes the universe as a phase of a 'God' who is

reduced to a mere impersonal force. Ultimately it identifies God with His own creation! This is common with a certain type of 'scientific' mind. Needless to say, it destroys all absolute values in the moral realm and undermines the whole structure of the Christian faith. Christians must insist on the clear teaching of Scripture, and the witness of the Holy Spirit and conscience to the 'free personal Spirit' who is distinct from, and Lord over, His universe. As far as the immanence of God is concerned, there is an element of truth in pantheism.[1]

5. *Polytheism.*—In contrast with the belief in one true God, which, in spite of widely diffused modern teaching on this subject, would appear to have been the original belief of mankind, many races have developed a belief in a plurality of gods to account for natural phenomena. The progressive findings of science are so repeatedly demonstrating the essential unity of the world phenomena and the similarity and, in some cases, identity of the forces governing them, that scientific observation should alone suffice to dispel polytheism.[2]

Scriptures

1. *Unity of God.*—Dt. 4:35 and 6:4; Is. 42:8; 44:6; Zc. 14:9; Mk. 12:29, 32; Jn. 17:3; 1 Cor. 8:4–6. See also the Scriptures on pp. 49, 56.

2. *God Active in His World.*—1 Ki. 18:24, 27, 38; Jb. 22:13, 14, 17; Pss. 10:11–14; 73:11; 94:7–9; 121:4; Is. 45:7; Ezk. 8:12; Am. 3:6.

Questions

1. How do you understand the relation between Jewish–Christian monotheism and its 'rivals'? Have these arisen from (a) ignorance, or (b) denial, or (c) perversion, of a true belief in the one God? Cf. Ps. 19:1–4; Jn. 1:9; Rom. 1:18–23, 25; 1 Cor. 1:21.

2. What do you mean when you say that God is personal? Can you suggest any better term to express what is meant?

BIBLIOGRAPHY

H. Bavinck, *The Doctrine of God*, Eerdmans, 1951.
J. S. Candlish, *The Christian Doctrine of God*, T. and T. Clark, 1888.
K. Heim, *God Transcendent*, Nisbet, 1935.
James Orr, *The Christian View of God and the World*, Eerdmans, 1947.

5. The Holy Trinity

From the outset it should be grasped that a clear knowledge of the Trinity is derived only from the Christian revelation; indeed, it would have been quite unknown apart from revelation. Attempts have been made to derive the doctrine of God's tri-unity from Greek philosophy and other sources. There are certainly philosophic resemblances and principles which

---

[1] See above, p. 45.

[2] Christianity admits that there are 'ministering spirits', but these are separate from and entirely subject to the one supreme God.

might have led the thinker to assert that there was a differentiation within the Being of the Godhead. But it is clear that the early church obtained this doctrine by pure induction applied after collecting and collating what the Master Himself and Scripture have to say concerning the Godhead and the three Agents of human salvation. Our Lord Himself has given the clearest teaching on the subject in John 14 and 16.

a. The Basis of the Doctrine

In the Old Testament the first hint is given in the story of creation; God (*Elohim*) creates by means of His Word and the Spirit of God (Gn. 1:1-3; Ps. 33:6). In the New Testament the 'Trinitarian formula', used in our Lord's command concerning evangelization and baptism (Mt. 28:19), provides the first express statement of the doctrine.

It should be observed that the Scriptures introduce the subject in opposition to prevalent polytheism. That God is *One* is insisted upon throughout the Old Testament, even when the plural form 'Elohim' is used. This is one of the cardinal points of Jewish teaching. But, simultaneously, 'the Spirit' is spoken of, and various forms of divine operation described, in terms which provide accumulative evidence of differences in person. The 'Wisdom' literature, especially the book of Proverbs, offered here important suggestions which received expansion at the hands of later Jewish writers. The next development came with the doctrine of the *incarnation*. If this be admitted, there is no philosophic difficulty in the addition of a third Person in our description of the Trinity. Our Lord developed the teaching by impressing on His disciples the fact that there was a distinction between Himself and His Father, and taught clearly that there was another Person, 'the Paraclete', whom the Father would send in His name. He describes the three Persons as quite distinct. Yet it is significant how guarded Scripture is in permitting these distinctions to be stated. For example, the disciples are to baptize not in three names, but 'in *the name*' (singular) of the Father and the Son and the Holy Spirit.

b. Some Definitions

In the apostolic writings the differing functions of the three Persons are clearly described, and, yet again, Their essential unity carefully guarded.

1. *Persons.*—Care must be used when attempting to describe personality in God and in the Trinity. Our definition of human personality as the expression of a being possessing mind, emotions and will is inadequate when applied to the Persons of the Trinity if it implies any degree of limitation. We are certainly taught in Scripture that the three Persons of the Trinity are self-conscious and self-directing, but it is never even hinted that one Person could act in opposition to another. The Greek idea of the

unity of virtue is helpful here. If there were opposition between the Persons, it could only mean that one Person of the Trinity, at least, was defective.

The word 'person' is derived from the Latin word *persona* which was originally applied to the mask which an actor used when representing some character in the drama. But we must not press the illustration in the word so as to suggest that the Trinity merely represents different aspects in which a unitary God displays Himself. That particular error is known as Sabellianism.[1] On the other hand, we must not exalt the difference so as to represent three distinct Beings with different natures in the Godhead. There are three centres of expression in one identical nature. In all probability, *true* personal existence belongs only to God, and the three forms of His Being, or the three modes in which the divine essence exists, cannot be adequately described by men; the word 'person' is the nearest we can get. The differences between men reside not in personality, but in its limitation in 'individuality' with its peculiar basis in heredity, environment, *etc.*, which cannot apply to the Godhead.

It is noteworthy that our Lord should have taught us to call these three Persons in the Godhead by such homely titles as Father, Son and Holy Spirit. It is clear that God Himself would have our finite minds to possess as clear a grasp as possible of the relationship which each of these divine 'principals' or 'agents' bears to the others and to our redemption. There seems to be no word which can adequately take the place of 'person' in these various connections.

2. *Substance.*—Heresy compelled the early church to define more clearly the relation of the Persons to the unity of the Godhead. The most satisfactory word was the Latin *substantia*, and the formula most generally adopted to describe the Trinity was 'three Persons in one Substance'. This safeguarded both the essential unity of the Godhead and the distinctness of the three divine Persons. 'Substance' is, of course, immaterial; it must also not be thought of as a common spiritual 'stuff' or 'material' out of which three Beings of the same divine nature are produced (as we talk of silver as the *substance* from which coins may be made). The divine essence is not *divided* into three: it is fully present in each of the Persons. 'Substance' thus relates to the one Being who is God, rather than to the nature or being of that God.

3. *'Procession'.*—In any teaching on the Trinity the relationship of the three Persons to one another needs to be carefully safeguarded.

There are two chief doctrines to be borne in mind: the subordination (in order of relation, but not in nature, as the word directly suggests) of 'Son' and 'Spirit' to the Father, and the fact that the Spirit of God is said to proceed from *the Son* as well as from the Father. In the case of the first the

[1] See below, p. 55.

Father is to be regarded as the Fount of all deity, by whom the Son was *begotten* (note this word), and from whom the Spirit *proceeds* (again note the word). In the case of the second, in the ninth century, after much difficulty, a majority in the Western church came to accept a formula based on Christ's statement in John 15:26. The addition of the word *Filioque* ('and from the Son'), however, was not accepted by the Eastern church. See the historical notes below.

The truth as expressed in the Nicene Creed is that the Son was the *only begotten of God*, 'God of God' (*i.e.*, 'God out of God' as the Greek preposition directly asserts), and that the Spirit *proceeds* from both the Father and the Son.

Many and varied illustrations have been suggested to indicate something of the nature of the sacred Trinity: from shamrock leaves, the (suggested) tripartite nature of man, and the three elements of consciousness, to evidences of a triad in some of the laws of chemistry and of other sciences. It may not be out of place here to enter a word of caution. While human and natural analogies may legitimately be employed to enforce and illustrate divine truth, no single finite illustration can ever adequately express the infinity of God. Above all, the tendency to unguarded extension of the illustrations must be deprecated and, what is still more dangerous, the drawing of inferences from further seeming parallels in the illustrations.[1]

c. Some Early Divergencies

The two principal divergencies were:

1. *Sabellianism*.—Sabellius (in the early part of the third century), as we have previously indicated, in order to avoid what appeared to him to be a suggestion that there were three separate Gods, taught that in reality there were no permanent distinctions within the Godhead. He asserted that the three names of the New Testament—Father, Son and Holy Spirit—were but designations for three manifestations of the one God, temporarily assumed for the purposes of redemption.

2. *Arianism*.—Arius (*c.*AD 325) went to the other extreme. Although holding that God was one, he placed so much emphasis on his teaching concerning the Persons of the Trinity, that in effect he divided the Substance of the Godhead. This resulted chiefly from his definition of the Son and the Holy Spirit as being lesser, subordinate Beings whom the Father willed into existence for the purpose of acting as His Agents in His dealings with the world and man. In effect, Arius reduced our Lord (and the Spirit) below the level of strict deity. He would admit His deity in a secondary

---

[1] This warning applies with equal force to other departments of truth, for example, to teaching on the atonement.

sense, but denied His *eternal* Sonship, allowing that His Being preceded the foundation of the world, but was not co-eternal with the Father. The disciples of Arius, by teaching that the Spirit was brought into existence by the Son, reduced Him to a relative form of deity (in a tertiary sense).

In recent centuries there have been movements such as Unitarianism (sometimes called, erroneously, Socinianism from the somewhat similar teaching of two Italians in the sixteenth century), and certain modern cults which, although varying in other respects, possess one opinion which is common to them all, that the Godhead consists in one single Person, which necessitates assigning to our Lord and the Holy Spirit some nature and position less than that of true deity. This is one of the most important battle-grounds in the history of the church, and no true Christian should for one moment tolerate any description of our Master other than that which assigns to Him the fullest deity, co-equal and co-eternal with the Father. While, at first sight, it may not seem so obvious, the Christian must equally contend for the full deity of the Holy Spirit.

In short, the full Christian doctrine demands all three of the following:

1. The unity of the Godhead.
2. The full deity of the Son (who was 'begotten') and of the Spirit (who 'proceeds' from the Father and the Son).
3. The subordination of the Son and the Spirit to the Father.

Scriptures

a. The Plurality in the Godhead

1. Anticipations of the doctrine in the Old Testament: *cf.* Gn. 16:7–13; 48:15, 16; Ex. 31:3; Pr. 8:22–31; Is. 6:3, 8; 11:2; 42:1, 61:1.
2. The Son in relation to the Father and the Spirit: Jn. 14:16.
3. The Spirit in relation to the Son: Mk. 1:10–12; Lk. 4:14, 18; Mt. 12:28. In studying this subject the key texts are the baptismal formula (Mt. 28:19) and the apostolic benedictions (*e.g.*, 2 Cor. 13:14).

b. The Persons in the Trinity

1. *The Father.*—He is God absolutely (Jn. 1:1; 17:3; Eph. 1:9, 11; 1 Thes. 1:9).
2. *The Son.*—He is 'begotten', and 'the image of God' (Jn. 1:14, 18—see AV; Col. 1:15; Heb. 1:2–6).
3. *The Spirit.*—He 'proceeds' and is 'proceeding', 'the principle of self-knowledge' (Jn. 15:26; 1 Cor. 2:10, 11. *Cf.* also the particle 'of' in Rom. 8:9; Mt. 10:20).

c. Relation of the Persons

1. *Mutual honour* between the Persons of the Trinity is seen from Jn. 15:26; 16:13–15; 17:1, 8, 18, 23.
2. *Co-ordination* between the Persons of the Trinity in the work of redemption is seen from such Scriptures as Heb. 10:7–17; 1 Pet. 1:2; Eph. 4:4–6; 1 Cor. 12:4–6; 15:27, 28.
3. That there is a sense in which the separate Persons of the Trinity each takes

a special part in the working out of the divine purpose is suggested by such Scriptures as:

(i) Acts 2:23; Rom. 11:33, 34; Eph. 1:4, 9, 11; 3:11 (the Father is the 'Counsellor').

(ii) Jn. 17:4; 1 Cor. 1:30; Eph. 1:7; 1 Tim. 2:5 (the Son administrates and is primarily responsible for the actual redemption of man).

(iii) 1 Cor. 12:13; Eph. 2:18, 22; 2 Thes. 2:13 (the Holy Spirit is the Executor who applies in the church and in the individual the results of redemption accomplished by the Son).

There is an eternal unity in purpose and an external 'economic' distinction of function.

Questions

1. Does our Lord teach anything concerning the Trinity? What previous knowledge on this subject, if any, would His hearers be likely to possess and from what sources?

2. Collect references from the New Testament relevant to the doctrine of the Trinity other than those given above. In what sense(s) can it be called a biblical doctrine?

3. What does Scripture teach concerning the interrelation of the three Persons of the sacred Trinity? What are the *special* functions of each?

4. Do you consider it of any importance to observe that our Lord Jesus is called a 'Son' in two senses? Would it be of any consequence if those Scriptures which imply that He is the 'eternal Son' (Col. 1:15) were overlooked?

BIBLIOGRAPHY

H. Bavinck, *The Doctrine of God*, Eerdmans, 1951.
H. M. Gwatkin, *Studies of Arianism*, Deighton Bell, 1900.
L. Hodgson, *The Doctrine of the Trinity*, Nisbet, 1943.
B. B. Warfield, *Calvin and Augustine*, PRPC, 1956, chapter 4.

6. God the Creator

a. The Narrative of Creation

The student is referred to a book on apologetics for a full discussion of the problems connected with the origin of the material universe.[1] In the following notes, only those points will be discussed which have direct bearing on the doctrine of the creation as usually stated.[2]

In interpreting the actual narrative given in the opening chapters of Genesis, it should be observed that it was not intended to form a scientific description of the origin of the universe as we know it. What would Israel and the first Christians have understood of it, had such a description been provided? Nor is it to be regarded as typical of the form of history which God has given on such matters. It had to be in language which would be understood in each of the successive periods of history.

---

[1] See, *e.g.*, A. Rendle Short, *Modern Discovery and the Bible* (IVF, 1954) and R. E. D. Clark, *Creation* (Tyndale Press, 1946).

[2] For the creation of man, see Part III, pp. 68ff.

A literal description of those things which in their very nature are 'invisible', for example, 'his eternal power and Godhead', is obviously impossible. God has caused to be given what is a partially symbolic record of the underlying *principles* of His creative acts. The reason for such a record is similar to that for the 'anthropomorphisms' which are used concerning God's action. They are both given as aids to faith and they represent to our finite minds the nearest approach to truth concerning the Being and works of God that is open to us.

It is possible that the 'days' of Genesis are to be regarded as periods of time concerning which the narrative presents word-pictures of the form of life which predominated during that period. The emphasis is to be placed not so much on the time factor, but on the nature of God's intervention in each case. Each student will be well advised to gain certainty on this latter point; the other factors are of lesser consequence in the present inquiry. The Genesis account (supported by the New Testament, which includes a statement on the subject by our Lord Himself: *cf.* Mk. 10:6; 13:19) clearly implies that each period of time was accompanied by a definite (supernatural) intervention of God. Nothing less than such a definite operation of the divine will, as is indicated by the word 'create', is adequate as a translation of the Hebrew *bara*, where used in the chapter. Attention, however, needs to be directed to the sparing use of this word. It occurs only three times.

Nor are we told the precise form such a divine act of creation would take; *e.g.*, whether it would be immediate and instantaneous, or gradual and in some sense progressive. The symbolical character of the account, at least in part, has to be borne in mind at this point.

b. The Doctrine of Creation

The battleground in Christianity's struggle with unbelief is not centred in the *time during* which God acted, but in the *nature* of His act or acts. The Scriptures are unique in their unmistakable emphasis upon the fact that it was a definite, powerful and complete operation of the divine will in a manner which must be termed 'supernatural', which ultimately originated the 'material' universe and all forms of organic life, including man. 'Thou didst create all things, and by thy will they existed and were created' (Rev. 4:11). In the case of man, Scripture provides an added emphasis upon the supernatural nature of his origin.

The following points should be noted:

1. *Ex nihilo.*—The statement 'God made the world out of nothing' needs careful definition of the word 'nothing'. It is not true to speak of it in such a way as to imply that 'nothing' was a kind of material which God used. By *ex nihilo*, the mediaeval and Reformation theologians meant that

antecedent to God's first creative act in the universe there was no other material existence.

Someone may ask, 'What would it matter to me today if there had been some existing (eternal) matter when God commenced to arrange the universe?' It matters to the Christian a very great deal, and amongst other considerations are:

(i) If there had been in existence any uncreated (co-eternal) 'matter', we have no assurance that God was, and is, able to control it. It may have proved uncontrollable—in fact, this has been brought forward by one philosophy as a possible explanation of the origin of evil.

(ii) If there is one type of matter, or life, over which God has no control, resulting in setting up a dualism—what assurance have we that there are not other types which are also not under the control of the divine will?

(iii) If He used existing material to make our world, how do we know that He succeeded in doing with it what He originally intended to do? He may have been thwarted by the refractoriness of the material in responding to His (now limited) will and power. An opinion very like this is worked out in the celebrated *Theodicee* of Leibniz.

(iv) It matters because the Christian might otherwise lack assurance of God's final triumph. For if there be some other eternal substance, which exists by as good a right as God Himself, how can we be certain that His ultimate purpose for the church will not be frustrated by a catastrophe over which He will have no control?[1]

2. *Other Creation Stories.*—The biblical doctrine of creation is unique. The mythical accounts in the legends of ancient civilizations are on closer examination found to differ in the meaning attached to words which may be translated 'created' or 'creator'—*e.g.*, Merodach of the Babylonian poems is not a 'Creator' in the same sense as God is stated to be in Genesis.

3. *Rival Explanations.*—With the main alternative theories, the Bible statements should be carefully compared. The chief rival 'explanations' are:

(i) The atheist's contention that the material universe is eternal and independent of any act of will.

(ii) The Platonist's view that God moulded and arranged matter which had pre-existed from a past eternity.

(iii) The Parsee's system of dualism (derived from Zoroaster) which

---

[1] The student of Greek philosophy will observe the very important place that the conception of a primitive eternally existent *hylē* occupies in the schemes of Plato and Aristotle, and will note carefully that the Scholastics abandon Aristotle at this point and substitute the concept of created 'matter' for this original *hylē*.

explains the world as being the arena in which two mutual incompatibles (one good and the other evil) strive for the mastery.

(iv) The pantheist's belief that God is one with and indivisible from His own universe, or that the world is the external manifestation of the internal animating Deity, sustaining a relation to the inner soul similar to that of the human body to the living soul.

(v) The modern scientist's efforts to give more detailed explanations of the process, or processes, by which the material universe and organic life came into being, some of which may in part seem impossible to reconcile with biblical emphases.

The biblical reply to these theories and contentions may be summarized as follows:

(i) The material universe is *not* eternal. It should be observed that the Genesis account leads us to conclude that the world did not have a beginning *in* time, but *with* time—*i.e.*, time began simultaneously with the world and on either side of the world's period of existence is the eternal abyss.

(ii) The material earth was given a definite beginning by God: 'By faith we understand that the world was created by the word of God' (Heb. 11:3).

(iii) There was no compelling force which coerced God into any of His acts in creation. 'In the beginning God created the heavens and the earth' (by a free act).

(iv) The world is not the same as God Himself. While He is immanent in the world, yet He is distinct from it. He remains the 'self-existent One', who inhabits eternity (*cf*. Eph. 4:6).

(v) It is impossible to review here in detail the many explanations put forward by modern science. It is also, happily, becoming unnecessary for the Christian to regard true science as hostile to the faith, because as scientists distinguish facts from 'unscientific' hypotheses, and biblical study clarifies the import of the Genesis story, the area of possible conflict virtually disappears. If it be remembered that Genesis is describing in homely language phenomena for which science uses a large, technical vocabulary, we can give the Genesis account its proper status. We still use the terms 'sunrise' and 'sunset', which are sufficiently accurate for everyday purposes. But science will describe the rotation of the earth about its axis and define its pathway or orbit round the sun. Had the Bible employed such terms as axis of rotation, orbit, *etc.*, what would the earliest uneducated readers of the Pentateuch have understood, or have profited by them? To them 'sunrise' and 'sunset' was a practical experience. Similarly, much of the supposed conflict between Genesis and science it is needless to discuss—so long as it is remembered that the Bible claims quite unequivocally that God originally *created* the heaven and the earth. Also, that certain successive appearances of the chief forms of life on the latter were the results of divine intervention which, similarly, calls for the use of the word 'create'. A good deal of help is obtained by distinguishing 'phenomenal' from scientific language. The former is the language of experience, and remains true so long as our organs of observation are unaltered. For example, grass is 'green' to the savant and the peasant.

Finally, the following four principles must be held tenaciously by the Christian.

1. God was the one and only Creator of the world.
2. The world had a beginning, coeval with time.
3. There was a succession of free creative acts of God.
4. Man was the result of a special creative act and was ordained overlord of the other living beings.

c. Other Spiritual Beings

Before the creation of the visible world there already existed a number of spiritual beings, whom God appointed to be intermediary between the Holy Trinity and the world of men (they are called in Scripture 'ministering spirits'). It is clearly stated that they were *created* by God and were not co-existent with Him. We encounter at least three different 'orders'—archangels, cherubim and seraphim, and angels.

There are also described malevolent spiritual beings. The Scriptures speak of them, too, as 'created'. Of them, the chief, Satan, is also to be described as created. There are, admittedly, philosophical difficulties arising from this conception of a created being embodying within himself the principles of evil (in the abstract). Scripture gives us little information beyond warnings that he is now malignantly hostile to the sacred Trinity, though this was not always so, and is continually active in the affairs of men.

Scriptures

1. See Gn. 1; Jb. 38:4–11 and similar passages in the Old Testament. Compare Jn. 1:1–3 and other New Testament Scriptures such as Rom. 11:36. The Bible teaches that creation was a 'free act' of God (Heb. 11:3; and *cf.* Ps. 33:6–9; Rom. 1:20; Rev. 4:11); that the world still 'subsists' in God (Acts 17:28; *cf.* Col. 1:16, 17); and that He continues to uphold creation (Heb. 1:2, 3).

Particular notice should be taken of the emphasis which the New Testament places upon the Son's part in creation. He is described as intimately concerned in it as the Father. See Jn. 1:1–3; 1 Cor. 8:6; Col. 1:16, 17; Heb. 1:2.

2. The material universe is described as being distinct from the Person of the Creator. He is 'over all' as well as 'in all'. See Eph. 4:6; Heb. 1:2, 12; 2 Pet. 3:10.

3. The Bible clearly teaches that all spiritual being apart from the Godhead was created by God. 'All things' were made by Him (Acts 17:24; Col. 1:16; Rev. 4:11; 10:6).

Satan was apparently created one of the cherubim appointed to have control over angels and creation. Compare Ezk. 28:11–15, a passage which is sometimes taken to refer, under the symbol of the King of Tyre, to Satan or, on another view, to adapt language descriptive of Satan to the correspondent claims of the King of Tyre. A clearer reference to fallen angels is found in Jude 6 and 2 Pet. 2:4 and *cf.* Is. 14:12–15.

Questions

1. Which Person, or Persons, of the sacred Trinity were responsible for acts of creation? Discuss the purpose and value of distinguishing between the 'economic' and 'immanent' relations in the Trinity. ('Economic' comes from the Greek word translated 'dispensation' in Eph. 1:10 (AV—*cf.* RSV and Tyndale Commentary *ad loc.*), and is used of the various divine activities with regard to the world, in creation, revelation, redemption, *etc.* 'Immanent'—*i.e.*, inherent eternally in the Being of the Godhead irrespective of such activity.)

2. 'God created the world *out of nothing.*' Discuss the logic of this statement. (See Heb. 11:3 and Rom. 4:17.)

3. In your opinion is the Mosaic record of creation to be regarded as literal history?—*e.g.*, What meaning do you attach to the six *days* in Genesis?

4. What is the aim or aims of biblical teaching about creation?

BIBLIOGRAPHY

R. E. D. Clark, *Christian Belief and Science*, EUP, 1960.

R. E. D. Clark, *Creation*, Tyndale Press, 1946.

R. E. D. Clark, *The Universe: Plan or Accident?*, Paternoster Press, 1949.

K. Heim, *Christian Faith and Natural Science*, SCM Press, 1953.

K. Heim, *The World: Its Creation and Consummation*, Oliver and Boyd, 1962.

B. Ramm, *The Christian View of Science and Scripture*, Paternoster Press, 1955.

N. H. Ridderbos, *Is There a Conflict between Genesis 1 and Natural Science?*, Eerdmans, 1957.

A. Rendle Short, *Modern Discovery and the Bible*, IVF, 1954.

7. God's Providence and Divine Government

Arising from the doctrine of creation there necessarily follow the subjects of the preservation of the world and control of the creatures upon it. In any examination of these the following must be taken into consideration.

a. Preservation (or Conservation)

This term is used to imply that all existence apart from that of the Godhead derives its continuance, including its powers, from the will of God. Scripture teaches:

1. That the universe cannot continue if left to itself.

2. That all life (both vegetable and animal) does not continue solely by virtue of any inherent principle of its own: it is dependent on the will of God.

3. This dependence upon the divine will applies not only to the being, but to the qualities and powers of all forms of life.

There will be no difficulty in this definition of preservation for those who accept the doctrine of creation. But the following two views deserve notice.

1. The mediaeval schoolmen described creation and preservation as one under the term 'continuous creation'. But this view does not sufficiently emphasize the fact that the world could not exist apart from the maintaining presence of God.

2. Another view represents God's preservation as a mere unwillingness to destroy the world He made. This view is entirely negative, and does not permit us to regard God as an efficient Cause in the process of preservation.

b. The Nature and Extent of God's Providence

It may at once be stated that the Bible teaches that God's providence is complete and all-embracing. See, for example, Psalm 135:6 and Acts 4:28. It includes not only all persons but all events and actions. It is crowned by the certainty that all events have moved and are moving surely to an end purposed by God. But it must be clearly grasped that this possesses no affinity with the belief in the blind fate of the classical religions. It is completely opposed to the doctrine of chance which rejects the conception of a controlling Deity.

God's providence extends to the whole of nature (including animal life), the acts of individual men, and the affairs of the nations. It even has a relation to the acts of evil men.

Indications of the all-embracing nature of God's providence may be gathered from considerations such as the following.

1. The evidence of the operation of a supreme intelligence everywhere in nature.

2. The moral and religious nature of man demands a corresponding and controlling providence.

3. The fulfilment of prophecy and the promises of God, which abound in Scripture, afford strong confirmatory evidence.

4. It is a matter of individual experience that 'there's a divinity that shapes our ends, rough-hew them how we will'.

A number of questions have been raised on this subject.

1. Some find themselves able to admit that there is a general providence, and that the world is controlled by certain invariable laws, but they are unable to allow that there is a *special* providence in the case of individuals. This view presents a very low conception of God. It removes His sphere of action from all connection with detail, whereas the further man's observations go the more it is clear that God is possessed of an infinite capacity for detail. Not only so, but the fixed laws are themselves interwoven and modified in a way which argues the very opposite of

incapacity for, or unwillingness to trouble with, minutiae. Special providence, however, has been degraded in another direction, by suggesting intermittent action by God in the interests of one individual against others. We need to avoid this.

2. Some are troubled to know how God's providence can be reconciled with man's freedom. They contend that if God's hand is continually at work in a man's life he cannot be said to be free in his actions. But man's volition is always only a small part of a general situation. While he is free to act within the limited bounds of his own abilities, his very freedom, as well as the many strong influences around him and beyond his control, are the results of divine providence. The more this is thought through the clearer it will become that the smallest change in the chain of events leading up to a given act would be sufficient to alter drastically the ultimate results.

3. It has often been debated what God's relation can be to acts of sin. Some are content to speak of God's 'permissive' will in relation to these, in order to avoid any suggestion that God could be the cause of an evil act. But it is clear that, in some cases at least, there is more than mere permission. For example, note how the crucifixion is described in Acts 2: 23 (cf. Ps. 76:10). Help may be found by reflecting that God not only 'permits' an evil act, but, by consequence, all the results dependent on that act. The will to permit man to fall carried with it all that sin subsequently meant.

c. The Nature of the Divine Government as Applied to Man

In addition to the providential care over the works of His hands, God governs the intelligent beings He has created (both men and angels) according to fixed moral laws. For example, it is clear from Scripture that He has provided for the cure of sin by redemption, has ordered a process for man's recovery from it and that, while controlling all things for the good of His church, He will ultimately vindicate His own holiness.

Was it an accident, for example, that Oliver Cromwell was arrested on the eve of sailing for America and detained in England, ultimately to devote himself to the cause of religious freedom? Many Scriptures support the view that God is able to, and does, use every known means for the moral government of the world. See, for example, God's challenge to the gods in Isaiah and His prediction that Cyrus should perform His will. 'He is my shepherd, and he shall fulfil all my purpose ... whose right hand I have grasped, to subdue nations before him' (Is. 44:28; 45:1).

d. The Divine Fatherhood

In modern theological teaching the word 'Father' is applied to God far too loosely. In the Scriptures it is rarely used except when referring to the relationship between the divine Father and Son, and with regard to those

who are brought into the relationship of 'sons of God' by the redemptive
act of the *Son* of God.

In relation to man, God's Fatherhood is threefold.

1. He is the Father of all men in *creation*.

2. He is the Father of individuals and of Israel *by covenant* (*e.g.*, 'Sons
have I reared and brought up, but they have rebelled against me').

3. He is the Father of the Christian in a special sense, and this is attained
only in Christ (*e.g.*, 'I am ascending to my Father and your Father').

New Testament usage, while not ignoring the other senses of the word,
lays special emphasis on the use of the term to describe God's relationship
to Christ and the Christian.

Scriptures

a. God's Providence and Divine Government

1. *Conservation of the Creation.*—Gn. 8:22; Ps. 104:29, 30; Is. 40:26; Col. 1:17;
Heb. 1:3.

2. *Providential Care.*—We may note God's care for His creatures (Ps. 145:15, 16;
Mt. 6:26; 10:29); for the human race (Pss. 139:16; 145:9; Acts 14:17; 17:26), and
His special care for the objects of redemption (2 Ch. 16:9; Mt. 6:33; 1 Pet. 5:7). The
book of Psalms provides many passages indicating God's providence, for example,
Psalm 104 (in nature), Psalm 121 (for man), Psalm 103 (for those in covenant relation).

3. *The Divine Government.*—The whole of Scripture, from the time when human
government was first permitted till the consummation of biblical history (in the
supreme exaltation of Christ), is one long record of divine government. See, for
example, Isaiah 45:1–7 (in relation to a world conqueror); Daniel 2:20–22; 4:34, 35,
and the following: Psalms 33:13–17; 75:6–8; Romans 13:1; 1 Timothy 6:15.

Students are strongly recommended to make time for a comprehensive study of
God's governmental dealings with the nations and the gradual unfolding of His
purposes.

b. The Divine Fatherhood

1. *In relation to Christ.*—See Romans 15:6; 2 Corinthians 1:3; Ephesians 1:3, and
the many references in John's Gospel, such as 1:18; 3:35; 5:36; 6:57; 10:38; 16:15,
etc. Compare also Mt. 11:27; 17:5.

2. *In relation to Man.*—We may note God's Fatherhood in *creation* (Acts 17:28,
29; Mal. 2:10; Heb. 12:9); by *covenant* (to individuals and to Israel) (Is. 1:2;
63:16; Ex. 4:22, 23; Dt. 14:1; Ps. 89:26; Je. 31:9), and in *redemption* (realized only
through Christ) (Jn. 14:6; 20:17; Gal. 3:26; 4:6; 1 Jn. 1:3; 3:1, 2.

Questions

1. What do you mean when you talk of providence? How far does God's
providence extend? Do you believe that the world is upheld by a continuous display
of power on the part of God?

2. According to the teaching of the Bible, what is the bearing of the Fatherhood
of God upon (*a*) God's dealings with His people, and (*b*) their response and character?
Cf., *e.g.*, Eph. 5:1; Heb. 12:7.

BIBLIOGRAPHY

G. C. Berkouwer, *The Providence of God*, Eerdmans, 1952.
James Orr, *The Christian View of God and the World*, Eerdmans, 1947.

8. Miracles

a. Definition

The Westminster Confession states that 'God, in ordinary providence
making use of means, yet is free to work without, above, or against them at
pleasure'. In other words, a miracle is any event within the sphere of
human observation which is brought about by the direct volition of God,
normally, but not always, as distinguished from the ordinary manifestations of divine power operating according to intelligible laws, and which
is not only a remarkable exercise of God's power but also of special
significance (*cf.* the 'signs' of John's Gospel, *etc.*) in God's dealings with men.
It must be stressed that the Bible depicts God as sustaining and governing
the *whole* natural order, and does not draw a complete distinction between
His normal providential direction and His miraculous activity. From this
standpoint, 'natural laws' are not fixed eternal forces which God has to
'break' in order to work a miracle, but descriptions of His regular upholding of nature, and even 'natural' occurrences can become miraculous by,
e.g., significant timing or an accompanying word of revelation.

b. Objections Raised

The following are some of the objections which have been raised against
miracles and hence against the authenticity of the Christian revelation:

1. Some object to the possibility of miracles generally and the relia-
bility of the witnesses to them. This is summarized sometimes in the form
supplied by Matthew Arnold: 'Miracles do not happen.' Hume anticipated this argument by the statement, 'It is inconceivable that a man
should rise from the dead, but not that witnesses may be mistaken.'

2. Some miracles are described as too trivial to be considered.

3. The New Testament is said to contain statements (*e.g.*, our Lord's
own words in Jn. 4:48) which disparage those who rely on miracles as
evidence.

4. It is claimed that miracles have been, and often are, brought about
by agencies other than the divine power.

The replies to these objections are not far to seek.

1. It is arbitrary to assume in advance the impossibility of miracles; it
amounts to defining a miracle as 'something that does not happen'. There
is no inconsistency between the biblical account of God's freedom and
sovereignty in relation to the world, and His altering His 'normal procedure', *e.g.*, in the birth of Jesus. The biblical witnesses of miracles have
proved themselves trustworthy in other respects, and often a happening of
miraculous dimensions is alone congruous with the consequences and

other factors present in a given situation (cf. the virgin birth and the resurrection).

2. Scripture uses the various forms of miracle, from the smallest to the greatest, to enforce such lessons as the special providence of God. (See 2 Ki. 6:5–7 and Jos. 10:12–14.)

3. Whilst Scripture discourages the pursuit of miracles as ends in themselves, it appeals to them as evidence on numerous occasions (e.g., Jn. 5:20, 36; Acts 2:22). Miracles are normally associated either with critical stages in the history of redemption (cf. the exodus and the law-giving, the advent and resurrection of Christ and Pentecost), or with periods when the cause of true religion was in jeopardy (cf. the time of the judges, and of Elijah and Elisha). That is to say, miracles are directed to vindicating the true revelation and knowledge of God, and hence we have a criterion for distinguishing the true miracle from the false (cf. Dt. 13:1–3; Mt. 7:22; 24:24; Rev. 16:14). The Bible does not deny the fact of wonder-working by the ungodly, but it does deny that their portents are miracles in the full biblical sense.

c. The Value of Miracles

The Bible appeals to miracles as being important and conclusive evidence, but definitely places them as secondary to the truth itself. The chief value of miracles is not to prove the message, but the divine ordination of the messenger. Help is here afforded by the reflection that miracles are un-common even in divine revelation.

Scriptures and Questions

1. List the biblical words used for 'miracle', and note their respective emphases and frequency. Cf., e.g., Ex. 7:3, 9; 15:11; Ps. 145: 4–6; Acts 2:22; 2 Cor. 12:12.

2. Begin to compile a list of the miracles recorded in the Bible, and observe (a) the purposes behind them, and (b) the contexts in which they occur most often. Cf. Dt. 4:34; Ne. 9:10; Ps. 78:43; Mt. 21:18, 19; Jn. 2:11; 3:2; 9:3; 11:4; Acts 2:22; Rom. 15:19; Heb. 2:4.

3. How far must a miracle be 'super-natural'? Does a 'natural' explanation automatically disprove the presence of a miracle? Cf., e.g., Ex. 14:21; 2 Ki. 2:19–22; 4:32–35, 38–41, 42–44; Jb. 5:9, 10; Jn. 9:6, 7.

4. How does the Bible relate miracles to faith? Cf. Ex. 14:31; Mt. 13:58; 17:19, 20; Lk. 7:2–10; Jn. 2:11, 12; 10:37, 38; 20:29–31; Acts 8:9–13, 18–21.

5. Do you think miracles can still happen today? Give biblical reasons for your answer. Cf. Jn. 14:12; 1 Cor. 12:10; 2 Cor. 12:12.

BIBLIOGRAPHY

R. Hooykaas, *Natural Law and Divine Miracle*, Brill, Leiden, 1959.
C. S. Lewis, *Miracles*, Bles, 1947.
R. C. Trench, *Notes on the Miracles of our Lord*, Pickering and Inglis, 1958.
Article on 'Miracles', *The New Bible Dictionary*, IVF, 1962.

PART THREE

MAN AND SIN

1. The Essential Nature of Man[1]

a. His Origin

Scripture does not provide us with a classified anthropology. But, on the other hand, it does state a number of principles concerning the nature of man which are of great importance because the whole of subsequent scriptural doctrine is based upon them. Again, while the references to man's origin are comparatively scanty, yet the biblical statements must be given priority over all philosophical speculation. Only in this way will the reverent student be prevented from adopting types of fallacious thinking which ultimately give rise to widespread deviations from the plain New Testament teaching on this and allied subjects.

To the New Testament writers, Adam was as much an historical person as our Lord Himself. They are frequently contrasted as, for example, in the Epistles to the Romans and Corinthians. Our Lord's own references to man's origin are of the same direct nature. By no process of literary interpretation can these references to Adam be made to mean other than that he was considered as much a person as the patriarchs subsequently described in the same book.

It is impossible to review here the various alternative theories. The clash between religion and true science has never been so real as many appear to imagine. The tendency of most scientific writers (by which is meant the leaders in research and foremost authorities in its various branches) is to confine themselves to the facts and principles of their own speciality and to admit that the ultimate explanation of origins is still a matter for philosophic speculation. There are, of course, popular authors who speak with far greater precision, and who claim far more for their branch of study than the majority of its leaders. But the average attitude current among prominent exponents of the various sciences would appear to be one of indifferent agnosticism and a greater concentration upon their ever-narrowing and over-specialized fields of research.

In such matters the chief aim of the reverent student of Holy Scripture should be to obtain a clear grasp of basic principles which must be firmly held. What are they?

[1] A full discussion of the many problems connected with this and the following sections is impossible within the limits of this book. Students are advised to read the appropriate chapters in the larger books referred to in the bibliographies.

1. The ultimate origin of the material universe by the free, purposive action of God.

2. The origins of the main divisions of life by similar progressive action.

3. The communality of all mankind. To many it would seem legitimate to add that Scripture teaches the descent of the race from a single human pair, whose being resulted from a similar, but *special*, act.

In the case of 1 and 2, the time factor is of little or no importance; and, in the case of 3, it becomes so only if it can first be proved that the scriptural genealogies are complete (having been designed to contain mention of *each* of the generations), and that the suggested chronologies have been properly deduced.

The doctrine of Scripture as to man's origin is, in its full details, unique in literature.[1] He is said to be the result not merely of God's creation but the subject of deliberation on the part of the Godhead prior to the act. Genesis 1:26, 27 would have us take the view that man's creation had something unique attached to it. It is clear that true science is not competent to pass judgment on this and the above two assertions. The biblical revelation is not accessible to scientific adjudication, and there is neither call for compromise nor room for conflict. Indeed, in some matters such as the following, science may even be said to provide partial confirmation of biblical teaching:

1. Man is to be regarded as the apex of the system of living things. He is the 'head' of creation.

2. The race of mankind is one, and is derived from a single origin (Acts 17:26). The theories of a series of 'cradles' for the human race now appear to have been abandoned.

3. By whatever developments his body may have been produced, explanations of a different nature are required to account for man's mind and his moral nature.

For a review of opposing theories, see books on apologetics. Students should beware of using the term 'evolution' loosely. In its original connotation it may legitimately be employed. The Old Testament Scriptures show an evolution in the sense of an 'unfolding' of successive stages of a divine plan in human history and of a progressive revelation to men. But the term is best avoided altogether when its use is merely a high-sounding substitute for vague expressions such as 'somehow came into being' or 'for the first time appeared'. Used in this way, it means absolutely nothing. If it is to be substituted for the normal biblical, and much more satisfying,

---

[1] With regard to the two accounts of man's creation, in Genesis 1:26 man is considered in his relation to the rest of the universe and as a moral being. In Genesis 2:7 it is the physical details which are described.

term 'create', then it should be confined to its original connection with the mode or the time factor in human origin. Nothing has done more to confuse the issues than the shallow thinking which goes hand in hand with a careless use of this term. The individual Christian may justifiably accept the term as describing the *mode* of divine intervention, but he must utterly reject it as in itself a sufficient *cause*.

b. Body, Soul and Spirit

There have long existed amongst Christian thinkers two views of the components of man's being. Some regard man as tripartite (body, soul and spirit); others as bipartite (body and soul with the spirit as the essence, or another aspect, of the soul). Many accept the view that man is to be regarded as bipartite, for the reasons given below. A third view, increasingly dominant of late, emphasizes the unity of man, and regards words like 'body' and 'soul' as denoting not distinct components of man but different aspects of the *whole* man's life and activity in his various relations to God and the world, *i.e.*, man as spirit, man as flesh, *etc.*

1. Scripture never teaches us to take the view that the body is a useless impediment and clog to the soul, which is to be shed at the earliest possible moment. It is important to observe we are never encouraged to dishonour or maltreat the body. On the contrary, the period of human life in the earthly body is of considerable importance. At the judgment-seat, for example, we are to receive for the deeds *'done in the body'*. The body is obviously regarded as providing the means whereby the moral values inherent in the soul may be given expression.

2. While the human body may possess few anatomical and physiological advantages, and, in comparison with some creatures, even disadvantages, yet Scripture teaches us to regard it with a measure of respect greater than that accorded to the bodies of other living things. For example, God the Son has been pleased to enter into association with a human body, and the Holy Spirit is willing to dwell in redeemed men.

3. 'Soul' and 'spirit' are certainly not to be regarded as synonymous in scriptural language. But, on the other hand, they are not kept invariably distinct. Compare Psalm 74:19 with Ecclesiastes 3:21; Matthew 10:28 with Luke 23:46; Acts 2:27 with 7:59, and see 1 Corinthians 15:45 (AV, RV).

4. In general, Scripture perhaps favours a division into soul and body. The former is used for the whole person, the human individual, as in our usage 'a kindly soul', *etc.*; *cf.* AV and RV with RSV in Leviticus 4:2; 5:2; Romans 2:9; 13:1, *etc.* It is further used for the immaterial part of man which survives death.

5. The references invoked in suggesting the tripartite division are those such as 1 Thessalonians 5:23; Hebrews 4:12; *cf.* Luke 1:46, 47. But those who suggest tripartism admit that soul and spirit in the body are separable only in thought. It would seem best to regard them as differing aspects of the same essence and to remember that, whatever distinctions are made for the spiritual purposes of scriptural teaching, there is a substratum which is common to both soul and spirit.

6. The Bible nowhere depicts man as enjoying fullness of being apart from the body. The body is not merely a temporary abode for the soul regarded as the real man. This is made triumphantly clear by the doctrine of the resurrection of the body, and is not refuted by the difficult passage in 2 Corinthians 5:1–8 (see the Tyndale Commentary, *ad loc.*). Man is *essentially* body, just as he is essentially soul or spirit.

The author would suggest that the more important distinctions to be observed are:

1. The soul (*psychē*) is the manifestation of the immaterial part of man towards the world, and spirit (*pneuma*) is its manifestation towards God (He is a *Spirit* and man can properly approach Him only 'in spirit').

2. In 1 Corinthians 2:14, 15 we have a distinction drawn between 'natural' and 'spiritual' men. The unregenerate man (*psychikos*), or 'soulish', is unable to appreciate God's revelation, but the regenerate man (*pneumatikos*) is alive towards God. Hence we can speak of the 'spirits of just men made perfect' (Heb. 12:23).

The essential difference appears to be in the possession of the divine Spirit. Jude 19 describes those 'devoid of the Spirit' as (lit.) 'soulish'. This throws a light on the position of the unbeliever as 'dead', and the believer as 'alive from the dead' in relationship towards God.

3. Some teachers have pressed this distinction to the point of describing the unregenerate as bipartite and the regenerate as tripartite; and there is a sense in which it is true. So far as man originally was concerned, however, he was possessed of soul as well as body, and the soul was capable of a spiritual relationship with God.

c. 'Image' and 'Likeness'

What is the meaning of these terms, which are used to describe man's original state?

What they certainly do not mean are:

1. That man's body resembles anything in the divine 'form'. As Spirit, God is 'without parts'.

2. That, as the Socinians taught, it merely describes human dominion over the rest of creation.

3. That man was an incarnation of God. Our Lord's incarnate life illustrates man's original relationship to God, but is essentially different in its nature.

4. That since God pronounced man 'very good', he possessed inherent perfection apart from his relation to God.

The image and likeness of God are expressed in man by:

1. His personality. Compared with the animals he is self-conscious, possesses the power of abstract thought, and has a spiritual nature.

2. He normally has a moral resemblance to God. This may be seen in the laws which govern human relationships and human government at their best.

3. He possesses dominion, of a limited type, over creation.

4. He has characteristics which argue in favour of his hope of immortality.

Though he was righteous in his unfallen state, that righteousness was obviously not inherent, for God *told* him His will. He required tuition in righteousness, and having received it, he disobeyed. On the other hand, the Fall was not a necessity. By maintaining his communion with the upholding Creator he need not have sinned. At his Fall the image was retained (although permanently defaced and debased), but the righteousness was lost.

d. Freedom

Scripture makes it abundantly clear that Adam was free to act either in accordance with the divine will or against it. Though he was capable of being tempted (like our Lord when on earth), he was under no compulsion to sin. His act of sin was disobedience by choice. (Compare the action of our Lord, who freely chose not to sin.) He was better placed than we find ourselves in this matter; for, unlike us, Adam had no inward urge to sin. In one sense, we are less free in this respect than he was.

The original righteousness of the first man, however, was not a part of his inalienable right or an inherent characteristic. His remaining righteousness depended upon his relationship with his Maker. All the while that his communion with God was unabrogated by disobedience, the divine power was, as it were, a prophylactic. It cannot be made too clear, or sufficiently emphasized, that Adam's revolt was entirely unnecessary, deliberate and blameworthy. It had no vestige of being a mere accidental slip. In its nature, the first sin was comparable with that hinted at in the suggestion of the fall of Satan.

Man was in a position *not* to sin had he wished (*posse non peccare*); though he was not in a state in which it was impossible for him to sin (*non posse peccare*).

e. Immortality

In an absolute sense, immortality belongs alone to God. Immortality of the creature is derived. That is, it is dependent upon conservation by the Creator. Also, man was not *created* incapable of death (as subsequently became evident). There had even been death in the world before his creation, as is shown by many fossilized forms in the lower geological strata. But it is evident from the sacred text that death is not *natural* to man. The very nature of man as body-and-soul renders death the negation of all that to which man's characteristics point. It is difficult to believe philosophically (and in spite of the objections and alternative theories which have been devised) that man is not destined for immortality. In the Old Testament a disembodied spirit in Sheol is regarded with a sense of foreboding and gloom; and, even in the case of the Christian, the New Testament does not give any encouragement to us to regard the 'unclothed' spirit with satisfaction. 'The spirits of just men' await the consummation of the resurrection morning, when they will be made finally perfect, by the redemption of the body (Rom. 8:23; Phil. 3:21).

'The tree of life' in Genesis 3 is to be regarded as symbolic of God's immortality. The breaking of man's relationship with God removed him from its influence, thereby affecting his derived immortality.

Immortality does not merely mean endless 'survival', but 'eternal life'. It is its *quality* which is important. While the souls of the unregenerate will survive the disintegration of the body, only the regenerate can experience the life, which is of the same quality as the divine life that has been 'brought to light' through the gospel. See 2 Timothy 1:10.

f. The Origin of the Soul

The question how the souls of individual men come into being has long been discussed by theologians, and has received in the main two different answers. The Creationist teaches that God implants the soul in each new human being at, or a short time prior to, birth. The Traducianist avers that soul, as well as body, is transmitted from the parents.

The importance of the subject has generally been held to lie in its bearing on the problem of the propagation of original sin. However, the question presupposes that the soul is a separate entity to be distinguished from the rest of the human being, and is not really meaningful when the soul is seen as an aspect or relation of the whole person regarded as a unity (see above). From this latter standpoint, the debate about the 'origin' of the soul is resolved by the creation of (the whole) man in God's image.

Scriptures

1. *Creation.*—That man was *created* is stated in Gn. 1:26, 27; 2:7, 8, 21–23; 5:1, 2; Mal. 2:10, and is confirmed by our Lord. See Mt. 19:4; Mk. 10:6.

2. *Original State.*—'Little lower than the angels' (AV) or 'than God' (RV, RSV), Ps. 8:5; 'the image of God', Gn. 1:26; 9:6; Jas. 3:9. Compare the New Testament statements that the image of God is being restored (Rom. 8:29; Eph. 4:23, 24; Col. 3:10).

3. *Body, Soul, Spirit.*—1 Thes. 5:23; 1 Cor. 2:14 (where Paul differentiates between 'spiritual' men and 'natural' (sensuous) men).

The following distinction is sometimes made on the basis of scriptural references:

(i) Hebrew *ruach* (breath, wind, spirit) = Greek *pneuma*. *Cf.* Gn. 41:8 and 1 Cor. 5:5. It is suggested that this is the part of man capable of God-consciousness and survival of death.

(ii) Hebrew *nephesh* (soul) = Greek *psychē*. *Cf.* Ps. 86:4; Mt. 26:38. This word is taken by some to denote the ego or self-conscious part of man.

Many scholars reject this interpretation on the ground that the words are not consistently used in Scripture with such a distinction. See above.

4. *(Spiritual) Immortality.*—Immortality in the fullest sense belongs only to God (1 Tim. 6:16; *cf.* Gn. 3:22). True immortality for man is secured only through Christ (1 Cor. 15:53, 54; 2 Tim. 1:10), but see also Mt. 22:31, 32; 25:46; Jn. 3:36; 5:28, 29; Rev. 20:10, 15.

5. *Each man is directly influenced by the headship of the race.*—Rom. 5:12–21 and 1 Cor. 15:20–22, 44–49 (*cf.* Col. 3:9, 10).

Questions

1. To what extent can biblical and scientific views of man's origins be regarded as complementary?

2. Do you regard man's nature as bipartite or tripartite, or neither? Give reasons for your answer.

3. What importance may be attached to the similarity in phrase between the descriptions of our Lord in Col. 1:15 and Heb. 1:3 (RV) and the description of man's nature as created by God in Gn. 1:26? Discuss the phrases used. *Cf.* also Ps. 8:4–6 with Heb. 2:5–9.

BIBLIOGRAPHY

G. C. Berkouwer, *Man the Image of God*, Eerdmans, 1962.

D. S. Cairns, *The Image of God in Man*, SCM Press, 1953.

J. Laidlaw, *The Bible Doctrine of Man*, T. and T. Clark, 1905.

J. G. Machen, *The Christian View of Man*, Banner of Truth, 1965.

James Orr, *God's Image in Man*, Eerdmans, 1948.

H. W. Robinson, *The Christian Doctrine of Man*, Scribner, 1926.

A. Rendle Short, *Modern Discovery and the Bible*, IVF, 1954.

W. D. Stacey, *The Pauline View of Man*, Macmillan, 1956.

2. The Fall of Man and Original Sin

a. The Origin of Evil

The ultimate mystery of the origin of evil is not open to explanation by man, whether he approaches the problem through philosophy or through revelation. The most that the latter supplies is found, for example, in the form of scattered hints relating to the remote past and suggestions as to the motives behind Satan's persistent hostility to the Son of God. Scripture does not encourage philosophical speculation on this subject and, ever keeping itself to the practical needs of mankind, focuses the attention on the acts of human responsibility. The present-day Christian would be well advised to do the same.

But the reader should have settled views on certain underlying principles which are abundantly clear in Scripture. We can give no final answer to such questions as 'Why did not God's foreknowledge lead Him to anticipate and to prevent sin both in the first man and also at its first entry into the universe (in whatever form this may have been)?' But we can state the following on the authority of revelation.

1. God is not the author of sin.

2. God has no need of sin in order to enhance His glory, and He did not permit it solely in order to demonstrate His moral grandeur.

3. The subsequent responsibility of mankind in relation to sin is in no way diminished nor excused on the ground that the men now living were not guilty of its inception.

4. God is not to be regarded as a 'party' to the repeated acts of sin— *e.g.*, those of sex—which man has all too successfully perpetuated, nor is He to be held as partly responsible for the perpetuation of vice simply because He has not withdrawn His sustaining power from the universe. If man freely chooses to misuse certain of his wonderful endowments and to prostitute his remarkable abilities to base ends, it is scarcely just to blame God.

Space forbids a review of the theories and speculations of philosophy. It is worth reflecting upon the possibility, as was suggested by Augustine, that evil, being essentially negative, is not to be regarded as having an origin in the usually accepted sense.

b. The Consequences of the Fall

It is essential to realize that man's constitution—his mind, his emotions and his will—remained intact. Their powers were certainly diminished, but their chief characteristics were perpetuated. Scripture concentrates its emphasis upon man's *spiritual* loss. The most valuable thing he forfeited was his right of free communion with God. Heaven would appear to have been very close to the first man and the veil between earth and the unseen very thin. Man's rebellion has dislocated his power of communication with the Godhead and thrust between his posterity and the divine Being a barrier which only Christ can remove. Fallen man still has a capacity for such communion, but he has no power to exercise it until he receives reconciliation in Christ and is 'renewed' by the Holy Spirit. A consequence of the loss of this upward 'pull' is that man is now a prey to 'the law of sin' in his members, which continually exerts a downward force which we may compare with that of the law of gravity. Man is unable to escape its

continuous operation until he is made free by the operation of another
and stronger law introduced and controlled by the Spirit of God.

The further disabilities imposed by the divine providence are in the
nature of a discipline, and their object is chiefly to restrain man from further evil. Among these disciplinary measures are the continuous toil for
livelihood against the relentless course of nature, the difficulties of child-
birth, the limitation of the duration of physical well-being to an average of
seventy years, and finally physical disintegration. In the thought-life, the
accusations of conscience, a sense of shame and fear of retribution all
combine to restrain from further evil.

Man forfeited also his 'original righteousness' or conformity to the will
and purpose of God, although he is still under the necessity (now become
partly disciplinary) of being subject to the divine law. He can regain a
position of righteousness only through the obedience of Christ. In Christ
he is free from the condemnation of the law and, through the operation
of the Holy Spirit, is gradually freed from the corruption of sin.

c. Original Sin

Revelation provides the explanation of what is a matter of universal
experience—the hereditary tendency to sin which sooner or later makes
itself evident in every child. Scripture declares that the consequences of sin
have descended upon all men, and particularly the inherent and persistent
bias towards sin, already referred to above as 'the law of sin'.

A full discussion of the problems underlying this most important
subject is impossible within the limits of the present study. Students are
strongly advised to refer to some of the books mentioned in the bibliography in order to arrive at an accurate understanding of the nature of
man's spiritual condition. The following brief notes are intended to
indicate several of the most important aspects of the inquiry.

1. *The Teaching of Scripture.*—Passages such as Genesis 8:21 and Psalm
51:5 indicate that from the moment of conception man becomes subject
to a persistent tendency to sin and rebellion against the divine will. The
condition in which man finds himself is the reverse of 'original righteousness', and he has lost the power to become, and habitually to remain,
righteous. This is a matter of universal experience. The word used by the
mediaeval theologians to describe this condition was 'deprivation'. The
state of subjection to the evil principle continuously operating is one of
depravity. The states of deprivation and of depravity are always transmitted
at birth (Jb. 14:1, 4; 15:14; Jn. 3:6). There is no evidence that anyone has
ever escaped these birth-taints, except our Lord. Scripture gives no hint of
the Roman Catholic doctrine of the immaculate conception of the blessed
virgin. By the incarnation of our Lord, and only in the case of that

incarnation, was the process interrupted so that the Lord was free from this law as Him 'who knew no sin'.

The condition is both negative and positive. Negatively, it may be stated that 'man is very far gone from original righteousness' (*i.e.*, in a state of 'deprivation'); positively, he 'is of his own nature inclined to evil, so that the flesh lusteth always contrary to the spirit' (*i.e.*, there is a condition of 'depravity' or the persistence of an evil principle acting as a downward force).

2. *Total Depravity.*—Care must be taken to see that this phrase is used only in the sense originally given to it by theologians. It was never intended to convey the meaning that man is as bad as he possibly can be, and that every trace of moral rectitude has been lost in fallen man. Total depravity is intended to indicate that the evil principle above described has invaded each part of human nature, so that there is no part of it which can now invariably perform righteous acts or invariably think righteous thoughts. That is to say, the totality applies rather to the field of operation of the evil principle and not to the actual degree of evil in the individual. The depravity is also total in the sense that, apart from divine aid, it is irreversible. A good illustration of the theological position is the difference between a straight and a crooked line. A line that is not the shortest distance between two points is crooked or depraved (*i.e.*, turned aside). If it cannot straighten itself, it is totally depraved, whether it is an inch or a mile out of plumb. There is no means known to man by which he can alter the bias of his nature.

3. *Some Objections.*—Various objections have been urged against this doctrine. A few examples may be given:

(i) God would not be righteous to give men a hopeless start in their race of life and then to condemn them to failure.

(ii) This doctrine makes God the Author of sin, since He is the Author of human nature and therefore of sinful nature.

(iii) It conflicts with man's 'freedom'.

(iv) As a consequence man is responsible only for voluntary acts, and if he is subject to an inexorable law, he is not able to be righteous.

In reviewing these, and all such difficulties, the student is strongly advised to be very careful about the use of terms. For example, in (ii) the word 'nature' is used in two senses—God is certainly the Author of human nature in the sense of its essence, but He is not the Author of our present disposition to sin except in so far as He is the Author of man's freedom. Because He has not destroyed man's power to perpetuate human existence, He cannot be accounted to be the active *Author* of mankind's perversions! The student is also advised to note carefully the emphasis of Scripture in all such problems. The problems, as stated above in (iii) and (iv), place the emphasis upon man's limitations, though of course it should be realized that all created beings are necessarily limited. Angels, for example, act 'freely', but under a constant law of righteousness. If they had not been 'free', none could have fallen. Scripture, on the other hand, places the emphasis on man's *freedom to choose Christ*, if he will. 'This is the judgment, that the light has come into the world, and men loved darkness rather than light.' Nothing can excuse a man who deliberately refuses Christ. There are hints of similar moral choices open to men even without 'special' revelation (*cf.* Acts 17:27, 30; Rom. 1:19–25; 2:14, 15). Scripture does not regard man's depravity as conflicting with his responsibility.

The student is advised to consider carefully several problems outside the range of theology proper before committing himself to hasty generalizations on the subject of 'free will'. Freedom is used in many different senses. It means frequently nothing more than the absence of external constraint. A drunkard drinks freely if he is not forcibly compelled to imbibe liquor. It sometimes means ability to control impulses. A man acts freely when he disregards an inner craving. Closely akin to this latter view, freedom is identified with conformity to our reason. We speak of men 'blinded by passion', *etc.* All men are rational, yet no man acts always in a perfectly rational manner. This is a problem of ethics that runs parallel with the theological problem of original sin.

Then, again, psychology takes account of a man's 'history'. Psychoanalysis explains irrational action by subconscious obsession. Race and environment are requisitioned to explain many of our simplest and apparently freest acts. 'Good form' is partly a tradition and partly a discipline imposed on life. So we ask in relation to objection (i) above, 'Where shall we place the start?' It is impossible to regard men as unrelated unoriginated units. There is no more facile, and no more ultimately baffling, mental process than that which separates the person and nature of the individual, giving to the former 'freedom' and to the latter a history. It is the bane of theology as well as of psychology.

The problem of freedom centres in the question, 'Can we secure moral choice in a finite being without granting the possibility of a wrong moral choice? Given the wrong turning, what would be the possible effects?' The problem of objection (iv) is, 'Can we isolate an act from its history and make it voluntary in the sense of being unrelated to a previous moral condition? If we cannot, what meaning attaches to voluntary?' The answer must be that voluntary means the free expression of an individual at any moment, his nature and history entering as real elements into his choice, which is free but not unconditioned. If this be not so, all attempts at a science of psychology are in vain and education is meaningless.

It has often been pointed out (without sufficient attention having been paid to it) that the difficulties felt by some modern minds to the individual's sharing in the fate of the race are unnecessary if the following be observed. It was open to God to organize human life on either an individual or some collective basis. In His wisdom He selected the collective method and bound men together. This, it must be acknowledged, is in many cases for their common good. When sin entered, short of arresting the progress of human generation altogether, God could not prevent the perpetuation of 'racial sin'.

On the other hand, it has also not been fully appreciated that the cross of Christ saved man from utter ruin. In the mediatorial and redemptive work of Christ there is a constant provision for the uplift of the fallen race. God, to whom time stands in a different relation from that which it bears to us, was able to apply the virtue of the cross both before and after the event (Rom. 3:24–26; 5:6, 8, 10 and 12–19). But while the obedience of 'the last Adam' benefits all men indirectly, its eternal redemptive value is experienced only by those who, having committed actual sin, renounce their own disobedience and obey the gospel. It needs to be emphasized that just as racial sin has descended upon all men under the collective system of human organization, *on exactly the same principle* the obedience of the new Head of the race is able to benefit those who receive Him as their Head. If we do not allow the one, we must disallow the other. In addition, it should be added that by virtue of the new covenant the penitent sinner who acknowledges Him as his Head is assured of all that Adam and the race could ever have attained had original righteousness not been lost.

It has been said that had there been no story of the Fall in our Bibles we should have been compelled to invent something of the kind to account for human history.

d. Pelagianism and Other Divergent Theories

Several of the chief divergent views are worth noting:

1. In the early part of the fifth century, Pelagius developed teaching which differed radically from that held generally in the church. He contended that God could not justly demand from man more than man could at any time perform. The essence of his teaching was that obligation is relative to the ability to perform. 'If I ought, I can.' The following is a brief summary of the chief points.

(i) Human freedom is such that man has complete power at any moment to choose between good and evil and to perform the good if he so wills. Sin, therefore, consists only in deliberate and, as it were, momentary choice of evil.

(ii) There is no hereditary principle of sin, and men are born into the same moral condition as Adam possessed before his Fall.

(iii) Adam was created mortal and would have died in any case. His sin affected no-one but himself.

(iv) Men are able to live free from sin if they wish, and some have actually done so apart from the supernatural influence of Christ and of the Holy Spirit. Pelagius did, however, recognize the force of the habit of sin.

The implications of this teaching lead finally to the narrowing of the nature of sin to a series of isolated acts of rebellion (without relation to what precedes or follows) and to a denial of the absolute necessity of divine grace in human redemption.

Briefly, the doctrine of the Pelagians is contradicted by:

(i) The common experience of men that they know they should perfectly love God and their frequent wish to do right; but they habitually fail in both.

(ii) The moral nature of men who know that their thought-life is the chief source of the trouble: they are the victims of jealousy, hatred, malice, pride, over which they can gain no control.

(iii) Man's experience that freedom and ability to perform are not identical.

(iv) The Word of God. This is utterly at variance with these doctrines and states categorically that Adam's sin has affected all men and that the grace of God is a necessity.

Augustine met Pelagianism with a clear definition of the nature of sin and an overwhelming emphasis upon the necessity of the work of Christ for human restoration. Augustine taught that sin, being a lack of conformity to the law of moral good, is in the nature of a negation and therefore is not a necessity. He also stated the traditional doctrine of inherited depravity and the necessity for divine grace.

2. There is a marked divergence between Roman Catholic and Protestant doctrine on this subject. The former is, in practice, semi-Pelagian (although the findings of the Council of Trent are anti-Pelagian). There is no consistency in the scheme of the Tridentine Council, but the following is a valid summary.

(i) The effects of the Fall were loss of original righteousness, physical disabilities which have been transmitted, and spiritual death (not closely defined). Trent is not clear about a condition of depravity.

(ii) The consequences of original sin are transmitted to each child and can be removed only by Christ in the grace of baptism.

(iii) Baptism remits not only the guilt but the whole nature of original sin and, though a desire to sin remains after baptism, it is not itself to be regarded as having the nature of sin, though it may issue in actual sin. The stress is upon the virtue of the church's baptism.

The Protestant divines strongly asserted that there is also an evil principle in man, that there is no power in human nature which can lead to recovery and that the grace of God alone can effect his salvation. They protested that the desire to sin (concupiscence) had the nature of sin and was 'an infection of the nature' whether in the baptized or unbaptized. The Reformers taught that as a consequence of Adam's Fall every man is in a condition both of deprivation (the loss of original righteousness) and depravity (the existence of an evil principle).

3. There are a number of modern theories, most of which are modifications, or advances upon, the philosophic difficulties debated during the Middle Ages. Reference is made to them in order that the student may be on his guard against any teaching which underestimates the serious nature of sin. It has been well said that the point of departure in many heresies is traceable to an inadequate view of sin and its far-reaching consequences. Modern psychology, as taught and practised by some, would tend to deny the fact of sin as such and to explain away the responsibility of man on the grounds of sex abnormalities or endocrine gland disturbance. But those who would thus disprove the reality of sin appear oblivious of the fact that it is human sin which is the root cause of the abnormalities and disturbances. At the most, their contentions affect the question of responsibility in certain cases only.

Scriptures

1. *The ultimate origin of evil* is not described in Scripture and no attempt is made to give us a solution of the mystery as to why God permitted the first sin of man. Note carefully that Isaiah 45:7 means that God ordained the consequences of sin, not the sin itself. Scripture begins by stating Satan's malignant attitude to God and, incidentally, to God's most recent creature—man. See Gn. 3:1-7; Is. 14:12-15; Ezk. 28:12-19; Jn. 8:44; 2 Cor. 11:3; Rev. 12:9.

2. *The Consequences of the Fall.*—Gn. 3:14-19; *cf.* the development of the many vices in Gn. 6 and 9-19; Jb. 14:1-10; Ps. 90:5-12; Rom. 3:10-18; 5:12-21; 7:5-24; 8:10, 19-22; 1 Tim. 2:13-15; Jas. 4:14.

3. *Original Sin.*—Gn. 5:3 (NB 'in *his own* (not God's) image'); 6:5, 12, 13; 8:21; Jb. 15:14-16; Pss. 14:1-3; 51:5; 143:2; Je. 17:9; Mt. 7:12; 12:33-35; Mk. 7:20-23; Rom. 1:18-3:23; 8:7, 8; 1 Cor. 15:22; Gal. 3:10; Eph. 2:1-3; 4:18, 19; 1 Jn. 3:8.

Questions

1. Do you believe that there is a personal devil? If you do not, can you give any other satisfactory explanation of the origin and prevalence of evil in the world? State why you find this explanation satisfying.

2. List the changes which occurred at the Fall in the relationship between (*a*) God and man, (*b*) man and man, and (*c*) man and the rest of creation.

3. 'Separation from God is in itself a sufficient punishment of sin.' Discuss this statement.

4. What are the main views as to the perpetuation of sin? Do you think that the term 'original sin' is satisfactory? Can you suggest a better?

5. Does the view that God permitted the transmission of an 'hereditary taint' rather than 'hereditary sin' relieve the problem connected with the justice of original sin?

6. Explain the meaning of 'total depravity' in non-technical language. Can you think of a less ambiguous phrase to convey its full traditional connotation?

3. The Nature and Extent of Sin

a. *The Nature of Sin*

It should be remembered that the Bible is 'a chronicle of redemption' and not a textbook on sin. Hence the scarcity of precise definitions. But the biblical view of sin is that of wilful disobedience to the divine will, or, in other words, it is ultimately an act or attitude of deliberate rebellion. It may be described in various terms and its manifestations may be variously viewed according to the relations in which it is being examined, but the ugly facts of its true characteristics should never be overlooked.

'Sin' is a generic term describing such ideas as 'failure to attain to a prescribed standard', 'self-will' and 'lawlessness' (in the sense of active opposition to law, as well as of neglect). It takes for granted the possession by man of personality and assumes his understanding of what is required, and his responsibility, contingent upon his freedom. It must be distinguished from the term 'evil'. Evil may exist apart from human responsibility for it, but sin is connected with the volition of an individual or group. In this connection, sin must be regarded as the voluntary separation of man from God.

In considering God's view of sin, two aspects must be distinguished. In relation to God's nature it is unholiness, and in relation to His moral government it is direct disobedience to the divine law. So far as God's requirements are concerned, man has been constituted a moral being and he is universally aware of the fact. For instance, he is fully aware both from his own consciousness and from divine revelation that he is under law to God. He is also aware that he is responsible to obey; and his conscience constantly witnesses to his duty to obey. In the last analysis, man's personal demerit is expressed through his will. Hence, in relation to God's government, sin is ultimately the refusal of man's will to yield obedience to the divine requirements. It must be noticed, however, that in relation to God Himself, sin exists in man's mind and heart. Human nature is sinful, and it is because of this sinful nature that there is expression in overt acts (Mt. 15:18).

b. The Extent of Sin

At this stage we need only summarize the points made in our full-scale discussion above. The state of sin is declared by Scripture to be shared by every individual who has been naturally born. Our Lord alone is excepted because of His supernatural birth. It must also be emphasized that not only is every individual involved, but every part of that individual's nature. Together with human characteristics there is transmitted to each new individual a sinful bias, involving liability to endure the consequences of human sin, and the evil principle ('the law of sin') which will uncompromisingly work in antagonism to the requirements of the divine law. The objection that this view is not that of the Old Testament writers, but was introduced by the apostle to the Gentiles, is surely disproved by Genesis 6:12; Job 25:4; Psalm 51:5. It was also deduced by later Jewish writers before the New Testament came into existence.

c. Sin and the Individual

The personality of fallen man is in a state of disharmony. Emotions, mind and will which should be perfectly and continually balanced in a movement for his highest good are repeatedly found in a state of conflict. Most damaging of all is the ascendancy of the lower and sensuous departments of his nature over the higher and spiritual. He knows and approves the good, yet he continually performs the evil which he hates (see Rom. 6 and 7). That is to say, 'original sin' is the root of the actual sin manifested in the individual's repeated acts.

Scriptures

1. *Sin primarily is 'Rebellion'.*—Je. 44:4; Dn. 9:5, 6, 11; Rom. 8:7; 1 Jn. 3:4. For other aspects of sin see Mt. 15:18; Rom. 14:23; Heb. 3:13; Jas. 4:17; 1 Jn. 2:16. That it is also a relentless evil principle may be inferred from Rom. 6:6; 7:17, 23.

2. *Sin and the Individual.*—Jn. 3:3; 1 Cor. 2:14; Col. 2:13; Gal. 5:17-21; Rom. 7:5-24; 8:6-8; Heb. 3:13.

Questions

1. What factors were present in the first act of human sin? What did the sin consist of? *Cf.* Jn. 8:44; 2 Cor. 11:3; 1 Tim. 2:14; Jas. 1:14, 15; 1 Jn. 2:16.

2. Classify the scriptural definitions and descriptive phrases connected with sin.

3. Trace the development in the teaching about the nature of sin in (i) the Pentateuch, (ii) the Psalms, (iii) our Lord's attitude to sinners, (iv) the teachings of St. Paul and St. John.

4. Is it correct to tell children that they are 'sinners'? If not, give your reasons and state precisely what they are to be taught on the subject of wrong-doing.

BIBLIOGRAPHY

J. S. Candlish, *The Biblical Doctrine of Sin*, T. and T. Clark, 1893.
D. M. Lloyd-Jones, *The Plight of Man and the Power of God*, Pickering and Inglis, 1945.

J. Murrray, *The Imputation of Adam's Sin*, Eerdmans, 1959.
James Orr, *Sin as a Problem Today*, Hodder and Stoughton, 1910.

4. Guilt and Retribution

a. The Nature of Guilt

It is frequently objected that it is not just for God to impute guilt to an individual who was born involuntarily into the world without power to resist and who started life with a bias towards the sin to which guilt is attached. Others (not observing the nature of guilt) will go further and protest that it is grossly unfair for the divine justice to extend Adam's guilt to each individual of today.

A careful distinction must be preserved between the guilt of an individual act and guilt resulting from corporate responsibility. It often happens in our ordinary life that one man becomes involved in responsibility for another's wrongdoing. No man today is condemned by God for the guilt of Adam's individual act, but if Adam is the fountainhead of the race, then it is reasonable to assume a corporate responsibility for the first act of sin. It lies in the very principle of the perpetuation of the race that man, coming into the inheritance tainted by early rebellion, is not only involved in the guilt but adopts for himself an attitude of revolt from the beginning of his conscious existence.

Scripture implies that just as 'original sin' is imparted to the individual, so what may be termed 'original guilt' is reckoned by God. Indeed, it is not possible to conceive of sin without its correlate of guilt. The student ought to compare carefully the application of the efficacy of the atonement of Christ. For example, the impartation of 'original sin' is met by the impartation of the 'new nature'; and 'original guilt' is met by 'remission' of sin on the basis of our Lord's sacrificial death. The two principles are closely parallel. As from Adam men derive sin and guilt, so from Christ, the new federal Head of the race, we derive forgiveness and righteousness.

Finally, man is not eternally condemned for sin other than his own. Actual sin and guilt are joined by God. Men themselves deliberately choose to sin. Those who have heard the gospel message are left wholly without excuse, since they have deliberately rejected the pardon offered.[1]

b. Conscience

A small separate section has been allotted to the subject of conscience, in order to emphasize its nature.

[1] The fate of those who have never heard of Christ is more difficult. Many find in Romans 1:18–25 and 2:12–16 evidence for a judgment based on the measure of light they have enjoyed. We must remember that the judgment related concerns itself with those who have been faced with Christ (*cf.* Jn. 3:19), but on the other hand, Scripture provides no grounds for complacency as to the fate of the unevangelized.

Conscience is to be regarded as nothing more than man's constant assessor, witnessing to the extent or otherwise of his conformity to the divine law (Rom. 2:15). Hence, imprinted on the mind of the personality which has been created in God's image, is a definite principle which seeks to enforce constant obedience to the divine law. While in itself possessing no power as an aid to obedience, it at least leaves man little excuse for not being aware of the nature of his acts, and to that extent increases his responsibility. Conscience, however, assesses on the evidence before it. In this sense conscience is capable of development.

c. The Justice of Retribution

Punishment is an inevitable sequel to sin. Nor has divine retribution anything of the nature of vindictiveness attaching to it. The object of punishment is the vindication of God as the Lawgiver. To some extent this is true of the punishment prescribed by a human magistrate. Man deliberately elected to separate himself from God by sin; God is just, on His side, in separating Himself from sinful man.

The Bible mentions a form of judicial dealing (in the case of a Christian, for example) which is termed 'chastening' or 'discipline'. The object of this is to bring the individual so disciplined to repentance and restoration. But in the case of the sin and guilt of mankind God is declared to be unalterably opposed to 'all ungodliness and wickedness of men'. The punishment threatened against sin in vindication of the divine law is spiritual death.

Scriptures

1. *The Nature of Guilt.*—Ex. 9:27; Is. 6:5; Rom. 1:18–21, 32; 3:4–20; 5:16, 18; Jas. 2:9–12.

2. *Conscience.*—Rom. 2:14, 15; 9:1; 13:5; 1 Cor. 8:7, 12; 1 Tim. 4:2; Heb. 9:9, 14; 1 Pet. 3:16, 21; 1 Jn. 3:19–21.

3. *The Justice of Retribution.*—Gn. 18:25; 2 Ch. 36:15–17; Ne. 9:33–35; Jb. 8:3, 4; Ec. 8:11–13; Mal. 3:18; Mt. 10:15; Lk. 12:47, 48; 22:40, 41; Rom. 2:1–16; 3:8; 12:19; Jas. 4:12.

Questions

1. What 'raw materials' does conscience work with and by? How far is its functioning dependent upon previous instruction and training?

2. How are conscience and guilt interrelated? Compare, for example, the common phrase 'to have on one's conscience'. Can conscience be mistaken?

3. How does Scripture's description of man as a free agent bear upon the subject of his guilt?

BIBLIOGRAPHY

O. Hallesby, *Conscience*, IVF, 1950.
C. A. Pierce, *Conscience in the New Testament*, SCM Press, 1955.

5. God's Eternal Purpose and Human Freedom

a. The Nature of the Purpose

There is nothing which more stabilizes faith than the full discovery that God is working to a plan. While the individual Christian is responsible for doing his utmost to extend the knowledge of the gospel and to work for the interests of Christ both in the church and in the world, he is not finally responsible for the results. After all the busy activity of man has done its utmost, the Godhead unerringly pursues the fulfilment of His eternal purpose.

The words of Ephesians 1:11—'According to the purpose of him who accomplishes all things according to the counsel of his will'—reveal the fact of what may be called 'deliberative counsel' on the part of the Godhead, leading to a 'purpose' which is being continually realized. The ultimate purpose of God is that His Son shall be supreme in the universe, that He may 'unite all things' in Christ, that 'in everything he might be pre-eminent' (Eph. 1:10; Col. 1:18). In the completion of this plan, the cross of Christ is stated to be essential. Coinciding with this purpose, and bringing into it all that His love means, is the collateral purpose that the men who shall have received Christ may be 'conformed to the image of his Son'. It should be noticed that it is never termed a 'plan to redeem the race', nor is it ever referred to as an 'absolute decree' in itself. Nor is the reverse ever stated, that God decreed absolutely the destruction and eternal loss of any man. There is a confusion of thought in the notion of an 'absolute decree'. Indeed, the conception of an isolated 'decree', considered apart from the whole condition of life and being in which men find themselves, is a return in thought to the deist position. The means, as well as the end, must be included in God's purpose. There is, however, a plan for the salvation of God's people and, associated with it as well as with our Lord's part in the accomplishment of the eternal decree, is the revelation that God has foreordained that those who receive Christ shall be made like Him (Rom. 8:29, 30). Scripture does not go much beyond this.

b. The Father's Electing Grace and Covenant

Much that is false has been written and much needless controversy has been pursued by theologians and philosophers on the subject of God's electing grace. It is an outstanding case of the need for adhering to what Scripture actually states and for avoiding the temptation to construct a complete logical system. By a process of induction we may obtain the following from Scripture.

1. Preceding human history, as recorded in the divine revelation, there existed in the mind of the sacred Trinity a counsel of redemption.

2. Its precise nature is not revealed to us beyond the fact that it was the 'Father's will', which was accepted for completion by the Son and the details of which were to be put into operation by the Holy Spirit.

3. It is at least clear that the mysterious relations of the Persons of the Trinity permitted of each of the Persons taking a distinct part in the salvation of men[1]—the Father as the Author of the plan; the Son, begotten from the Father, performing the redemptive will of the Father (or of the triune Godhead); the Spirit, proceeding from Both, putting into execution the will of Both and being united with Them in the purpose of redemption. In relation to men, the Father's purpose selected as its chief end the redemption of fallen man, chose the atoning sacrifice of Calvary as its necessary means, and provided for effectual application of the means in its accomplishment.

Dealing first with the covenant in general and then proceeding to the case of an individual who benefits from it, the precise description of this covenant should be noticed. The covenants with Adam, Noah and Abraham are illuminative of, and lead up to, the one supreme covenant which is described as having been kept secret until 'the time had fully come', when Christ was revealed to become its Mediator and Surety. It is described as being between the Father and the Son, that is to say, made 'on our behalf' who were incapable of keeping our side of any contract between God and man. One of the chief 'clauses' in the covenant is that which promises the elevation of man in Christ to a position far higher than that which Adam had attained when he fell. It is to this that God has *predestined* man in Christ, not to be returned to an earthly paradise, but to be elevated into the 'image' of the divine Son.

But the word 'predestination' also implies a relation to the individuals who believe and a divine control of the steps leading up to their acceptance of Christ and to their renewal in His image, and the word 'election' implies this even more clearly. In other words, 'election' is a particular way of speaking of this 'predestination' as applied to those who are chosen to enjoy its fulfilment. Hence the New Testament uses the term 'elect' to describe those who in point of fact have been enlightened and are clearly separated from those around them by their undoubted allegiance to Christ and their different manner of life. But their election is nevertheless depicted as taking place 'in Christ before the foundation of the world', *i.e.*, on a par with predestination.

The chief point of difficulty concerns the Father's electing grace. All agree that repentance and faith are necessary for the individual's salvation. All are agreed that Christ is the sole channel through whom God bestows redemption. All are agreed that sanctity of life is a necessity in the redeemed

[1] See the note on subordination on pp. 54, 55.

man. All are agreed that man is unable to help himself and needs the awakening and empowering touch of the divine Spirit. All are also agreed that after his conversion the redeemed and sanctified person generally becomes aware that his conversion was no mere accident and that he discovers God has had a plan for his life, and is filled with gratitude that he is permitted to be among the redeemed.

But the point of disagreement comes in relation to the *grounds* of their election. To some, election is the result of God's having foreseen their potential faith and the fact that they would turn to Him when they heard the gospel. In this case, the 'election' confirms and seals their response to God, with its consequent fruit of predestinated conformity with Christ. To others, their response of faith and their turning to God were the result of God's prior electing grace, which sought them in time and predisposed their wills to respond to His call. In the former case it is difficult to see why the word 'election' is used at all; in the latter it appears to some as if God's election would be arbitrary and human free will would be impaired.

While it is true that Scripture teaches that it would be just and lawful for God to do what He wished with His own, the whole of Scripture is against the notion of any rigid arbitrariness in God.

What may be called the moderate Calvinist view appears to be in accord with Scripture and free from most of the causes for objection. In order that Christ might be presented with a redeemed church when He is revealed as supreme in the universe, God has ordained that at least some should be gathered out from the mass of men which had forfeited all claim to mercy by a deliberate revolt against God. This gathering of 'the elect' is effected by a preordained 'effectual calling'.[1] The comparative numerical extent to which God's electing grace applies, the just and righteous ground of His elective choice and many kindred problems, are not revealed to us. We are, however, assured from Scripture that whatever man may find himself outside the sphere of the covenant of redemption has not had his chances of coming to Christ reduced one iota by God's electing grace.

Nor can electing grace which controls and redirects a stubborn will impair the original liability incurred by the act of revolt or the consequent attitude, so that man's responsibility remains exactly as it would always have been.

Grace overcomes the spirit of revolt, reversing the soul's attitude to God. The guilt of revolt remains still to be judged where grace does not operate.

c. Some Cautions

Both revelation and philosophy alike do not supply a complete explanation, and the latter in an endeavour to present a uniform system has often

[1] See below, pp. 137, 138 and *cf.* Jn. 6:37 (both parts) and Rom. 8:30.

presented the most improbable and conflicting views. There are some points in the scheme of Christian doctrine where a 'reverent agnosticism' and an earnest attempt to remain faithful to the biblical presentation are far preferable to the production of a completely 'water-tight' scheme. In our attempts to trace the operations of the divine purposes our minds only wreck themselves again and again. The earnest student who essays to probe the profundities of this subject would do well to keep before him the following cautions which are suggested in the book *Outlines of Christian Doctrine:*[1]

1. This doctrine, as with other similar spiritual teaching, is not presented in Scripture *in vacuo*. It is not presented as an abstract problem, but is related both to the goodness of God and to the sin of the creature.

2. Scripture does not give the least suggestion that God forces His will on the creature. Man is always regarded as free.

3. The question of divine choice is presented in such a way as to result in definite moral impressions—*e.g.*, that God's mercy is completely unmerited by the individual who is contemplating it.

4. The question of God's choice, wonderful as it is, is only a part of the doctrine of salvation. It cannot be used to excuse neglect or a moment of wilful sin.

5. The Christian preacher (who in any case is ignorant of God's actual choices) is responsible for beseeching everyone to be reconciled to God. He and the non-Christian have an equal responsibility, the one to foster the world-wide spread of the gospel, the other to respond to its message.

6. The doctrine of the atonement is undoubtedly presented in Scripture as *not ultimately restricted* in its scope. It has a world-wide aspect, and all may be invited to an actual provision without qualification on the part of the preacher.[2]

7. While implying that the man who has 'confirmed' his election practically by whole-hearted acceptance of Christ is eternally secure, Scripture yet abounds in earnest warnings against presumption and any form of dilly-dallying with sin. The Christian is even regarded as under a greater responsibility not to trifle with sin.

8. Like so many other problems, the more we approach it from a personal communion with God the less do various difficulties connected with certain aspects trouble us. *Solvitur ambulando cum Deo.*

---

[1] Handley C. G. Moule (Hodder and Stoughton, 1890). The entire section will be found to be extremely helpful.

[2] This represents the moderating view of Ussher and Davenant, which ultimately found acceptance at the Synod of Dort. The atonement is for mankind generally, but moral response is secured only in the elect. See pp. 124, 125.

d. Historical Survey of the Doctrine

Space forbids more than a few hints as to the chief schools of thought which have arisen during church history. It must also be remembered that the problem is not confined to Christianity. The teaching of the Stoics, for example, results in an extreme form of 'fatalism', and that of the Pharisees and certain non-Christian religions (*e.g.*, Islam) implies this view.

1. *To about the year* AD 350, the early Fathers repeatedly refer to the subject, mostly in order to combat the fatalism of the pagan or Jewish views mentioned above. There was no systematic presentation of the subject.

2. AD 350–600.—Augustine first approached the subject in a fuller manner, developing his strong advocacy of the necessity of divine grace, when combating the Pelagian heresy, which much overemphasized man's power of self-determination, even to the extent of denying original sin. The essential point in his teaching is that God is absolutely sovereign and that any holiness we may possess is invariably the result of God's prior thought and act on our behalf. As for the unregenerate, he taught that God simply left them to the consequences of their sins. The Latin church became chiefly Augustinian, whereas the Greek church left the problem somewhat indefinite, insisting on man's freedom and God's grace without any serious attempt to relate the two sides of the question.

3. AD 600–1500.—The mediaeval schoolmen were mostly Augustinians. A few, however, had Pelagian tendencies.

4. *The Reformation Era.*—At the Council of Trent the Roman Catholic church revealed a tendency away from Augustinian views, although it paid lip-service to them. This tendency was further accentuated by the success of the Jesuits in suppressing the writings and school of the Jansenists in France. That church, in spite of its official formulae, may now fairly be classed either as 'Semi-Pelagian' or else as the chief of the 'Arminian' systems.

The Reformers were not agreed as to detail, but were in the main convinced Augustinians. The matter was made an issue among the Reformers by Calvin's *Institutes*. This remarkable treatise is probably the most severely logical of all Reformation writings. Calvin, especially in his controversial defence of his system against opponents, placed an emphasis on the divine sovereignty which subsequent and less able followers carried to an extreme of which he himself was not guilty. Calvin himself was a logical Augustinian. It was his followers who developed the extremes from which some divines in the next period of history reacted. The prominence given to the doctrine of the sovereignty of divine grace was part of the Reformation insistence on a spiritual and practical creed, freed from the shackles of sacerdotalism. The English Reformers were what would now be called Calvinists.

5. *To the Present Day.*—At the beginning of the seventeenth century several teachers reacted from the extreme view of some of Calvin's followers. Arminius (a Dutch divine) stated a view which, while acknowledging the necessity for divine grace, appeared to the divines of the Synod of Dort, who condemned it, to place too much emphasis on the freedom of man's will in determining his own relation to the divine plan. This view was adopted by Laud and prevailed in England after the Restoration. It was a strong element in Wesley's teaching, whereas the eighteenth-century Evangelicals of the Church of England were Augustinians.

In greater or lesser degree Augustinianism (Calvinism) competes with Arminianism, and even forms of Semi-Pelagianism, for the supremacy in many sections of the church. Others are predominantly of one viewpoint. The Presbyterian churches, for example, are predominantly Calvinistic in creed though not always in practical fact.

This divergence of viewpoint is very frequently (and often without their realizing it) at the root of arguments between two equally earnest Christians. It invades almost every department of Christian doctrine and materially affects the attitude of each preacher to the methods by which the gospel may be presented to men. It might save much well-meant but wasted discussion if both the arguers could awaken to the fact that the Calvinist is usually commencing with God's relation to the problem and working down to man's, and the Arminian is starting with man's viewpoint and working up to God's. The Calvinist will never be able to understand what he regards as a hopelessly low view of the supreme efficacy of the divine operations. The Arminian equally is appalled at what he feels is a lack of appreciation of the dire results 'if man should fail' in his responsibility to respond to the divine requirements.

e. Theories and Problems

It must suffice here to indicate some of the considerations which must be taken into account by those who wish to have even the smallest grasp of the problems confronting the Christian thinker.

1. In the divine revelation there are as clear references to some form of particularism as there are to the broad, universal application of the gospel. There are also examples of an individual, such as Abraham, or of nations, such as Israel, being specially selected to bestow blessing upon others. It is therefore of importance that something of the nature of God's predestination should be known.

2. There is the further intellectual problem as to how man's will can

be considered really 'free' in the matter of the acceptance or rejection of divine grace, if God has predetermined some form of sovereign election.

The two main schools of thought are as follows (though we must not forget that many people endeavour to adhere to some form of synthesis of their viewpoints):

1. *The Arminian View.*—This teaches that God predestinates those whom His attribute of foreknowledge is able to indicate will accept Christ and continue in His service. This emphasizes the responsibility of each man equally to obey God's call in the gospel, but, in the last analysis, narrows the scope of divine salvation to complete dependence upon this human response. It nevertheless claims to preserve genuine freedom of will on man's part without doing injustice to divine sovereignty. It naturally rejects any limitation of the number of the elect determined by anything other than God's foreknowledge and consequent predestination. The biblical use of 'foreknow', however, often seems to carry with it the idea of 'foreordain' or 'choose' (*cf.* Acts 2:23; Rom. 11:2; 1 Pet. 1:2 (AV; *cf.* RSV), 20 (RV; *cf.* AV, RSV); *cf.* the sense of 'know' in Je. 1:5; Am. 3:2.)

2. *The Augustinian (or Calvinist) View.*—This places the emphasis upon God's predeterminate counsels. It says, in effect, that the Godhead decreed human redemption in eternity past, a redemption which should not in any sense be contingent upon the works of men but solely upon the divine grace, and which should be dispensed accordingly to men without reference to human merit. The individual who is to be saved, however, requires the gift of faith for the appropriation of the divinely wrought salvation, and hence faith is bestowed on the elect, who have been chosen for salvation from before the creation of the world, though of course their number and identity are not known to men.

There is much to be said for this view, but unfortunately it has been carried by some to extremes which have blinded many to the fact that it alone does real justice to the grace of God. Extremists have carried the view to limits which are scarcely distinguishable from fatalism, or which make God arbitrarily to select some men for salvation and others for perdition.

For many it fails to give a satisfactory answer to the question why, if God is able to bring all to eternal salvation, He does not do so in every case. There still remains a mystery connected with the operation of divine grace and human responsibility, which extreme Calvinism does not allow for.

The truth seems undoubtedly to lie in a modified form of the Calvinist view, which will allow fully for the mysterious element of human responsibility which Scripture clearly teaches alongside the plain statement that salvation is from start to finish solely upon the basis of divine grace. In practice, the Christian must keep firmly in mind that there are two parallel truths taught in Scripture. There is the divine sovereignty, by which we are assured that God's purposes will be completed, but also we are nevertheless responsible to work and to appeal to men as though everything depends upon our diligence and upon human response to the message. The oft-quoted lines from St. Bernard will bear repetition: 'Remove free will and there will be nothing to save; remove grace and there will be nothing to save with.' The student should seek to keep all his thinking on this subject in relation to the Godhead, to remember that there is nothing arbitrary in God's electing grace, and to understand that it is taught in Scripture in contexts which imply that it is intended to have practical results in the life of the Christian.

It has often been contended that the doctrine of election and its corollary, the eternal security of the Christian, leads to slackness in daily living and to carelessness with regard to the responsibility to bear the gospel to others. The reverse has been the case! As a matter of fact, the Calvinist has more often than not been the leader in religious and social reform and the most energetic of missionaries. One has only to look at the history of the Reformation and the Puritans, or of nations such as Scotland and Holland, to be convinced of the moral power of Calvinism.

Scriptures

1. *The Divine Purpose.*—Mt. 25:34; Jn. 6:37, 44, 45, 65; 17:2, 6, 9; Acts 2:23; Rom. 8:28–30; 9:11–24; 11:5–7; Eph. 1:4–12; 2:10; 2 Thes. 2:13; 2 Tim. 1:9; 1 Pet. 1:2–5, 20.

2. *Human Responsibility.*—Is. 1:19, 20; 65:1, 2; Je. 9:6; 27:13; Mt. 23:37; Jn. 3:36; 5:24, 40; 7:17, 37; Acts 7:51; 10:43; Rom. 1:28; 2 Thes. 2:10; Heb. 2:3; 3:6, 14; 12:25.

3. *Both Combined.*—Acts 2:23 (cf. 3:23); 4:27, 28; 13:46–48; Rom. 6:17–23; Phil. 2:12, 13; 2 Pet. 1:10, 11; 3:9.

4. *Scriptures to Compare.*—(i) Those which state that redemption was for *all:* Mt. 28:19; Jn. 12:32; Rom. 5:18 (cf. 1 Cor. 15:22); 1 Tim. 2:4, 6; 4:10; Heb. 2:9; 2 Pet. 3:9; 1 Jn. 2:2. (ii) Those which appear to restrict its efficacy to the church: Jn. 10:11, 15, 26–28; Acts 20:28; Eph. 5:25–27. Cf. Rom. 8:32, 33; 2 Cor. 5:14, 15.

Questions

1. Are there any Scriptures which would lead us to believe that God has had a 'fixed purpose' throughout the ages? What do you understand by the expression 'the counsel of his will'? What is the precise content of God's eternal purpose of redemption?

2. Is it possible to reconcile satisfactorily God's foreordination and human responsibility in the matter of man's sin and salvation? Follow the course of Paul's argument in Romans 9–11.

3. Is there any scriptural authority for stating that some men are predestinated to eternal condemnation? How has this subject been treated by various Christian writers?

4. Does Scripture give any support for, or reconciliation of, the (apparently) contradictory beliefs in (a) the infallible 'perseverance of the saints' and (b) the possibility of 'falling from grace'?

BIBLIOGRAPHY

G. C. Berkouwer, *Divine Election*, Eerdmans, 1960.

C. H. Hodge, *Systematic Theology*, James Clarke, 1960.

Abraham Kuyper, *Calvinism*, Sovereign Grace, 1930.

E. A. Litton, *Introduction to Dogmatic Theology*, ed. P. E. Hughes, James Clarke, 1960.

Martin Luther, *On the Bondage of the Will*, ed. J. I. Packer and O. R. Johnston, James Clarke, 1957.

H. C. G. Moule, *Outlines of Christian Doctrine*, Hodder and Stoughton, 1890.

J. I. Packer, *Evangelism and the Sovereignty of God*, IVF, 1961.

W. H. Griffith Thomas, *The Catholic Faith*, Church Book Room Press, 1952.

B. B. Warfield, *The Plan of Salvation*, Eerdmans, 1942.

PART FOUR

THE PERSON AND WORK OF CHRIST

1. Divinity and Sonship

a. His Pre-existence

In view of unitarian and other forms of teaching which deny or undermine the divinity of our Lord, too much importance cannot be attached to the biblical statements concerning His pre-existence. If our Lord had no existence prior to His incarnation at Bethlehem, the Christian claim that He came to be the living revelation of God is at once invalidated and His own claim to have revealed the Father (in an intimate sense) is abrogated. There is much else in the record of the revealed purposes of God which would also be annulled if it could be proved that our Lord was not the second Person of the sacred Trinity. It was therefore of supreme importance that the early church should have safeguarded its teaching on this subject and that Athanasius should have vigorously opposed attacks, such as that of Arianism, upon it (see below).

Full attention should be given to Scriptures which refer to His pre-existence (*e.g.*, 'he is before all things') and to His association with God the Father in the work of creation (*e.g.*, 'without him was not anything made that was made'). There can be no doubt as to their meaning.

b. His Godhead

It is sometimes argued that our Lord Himself never claimed to be divine. No doubt He had reasons for not doing so too openly, but He certainly did so repeatedly by implication. The chief charge at His trial was that He made Himself the Son of God, and He did not deny it (Mt. 26:63, 64, and Jn. 19:7). It is difficult to know what else can be implied by the account of Peter's confession of His Sonship other than that our Lord confirmed the truth of his assertion.

The two titles 'Son of God' and 'the Word' ensure that we understand:

1. That He was a personal manifestation of the Godhead, and not merely an impersonal influence.

2. That He is on an equality with the Father of whose Person and glory He is an accurate expression. It was not long in church history before the Christians were forced to define with increasing accuracy the nature of the divine Persons, especially that of our Lord, in the face of increasing

misconceptions and misrepresentations such as those of the Ebionites and the Arians. Heresy has sometimes exercised a beneficial as well as a baneful influence in the church, in that it has forced the orthodox to a more accurate definition of their beliefs.

At the Council of Nicaea, Christian belief as to the Person of Christ was clarified by the insertion into the credal formula of the word *homoousios* (*i.e.*, identity of being with the Father). This has remained a very essential part of the Christian belief. Our Lord is not merely a likeness of the Father, but is 'one substance with the Father'. While nowhere stated in Scripture in this form, it is implied in a number of verses. (See, *e.g.*, Jn. 1:1 and Col. 2:9 and compare Jn. 14:10 and Heb. 1:3.)

c. His Sonship

In what sense is Jesus Christ the Son of God? Scripture uses of His 'origin' the word 'begotten', implying that He is not created as are the angels. What precisely the word 'begotten', in this sense, means will ever remain a mystery to men. It contains in it the idea of true communication of essential essence. But it is at least revealed that He was 'begotten, not made', and human thought is unable to pass beyond the fact that a differentiation exists in the Godhead best represented by the term 'the eternal generation' of the Son. The expression is due to Origen. The idea of Sonship is necessitated by a revelation of the Fatherhood of God in the sacred Trinity. It is of importance, however, to be quite certain as to the *eternal* nature of the Sonship of Christ. Through not realizing its importance, many Christians have tended to overlook the fact that, although there is a human aspect of the Sonship ('Thou art my Son; today I have begotten thee'), it is to be considered a vital article of faith that our Lord was the Son of God before time began. (See *e.g.*, Jn. 1:18; 17:5, 24, and 1 Jn. 4:9.)

A modern opinion, which has received a certain amount of credence among some Christians, contends that the term 'Son' is applicable only to our Lord's human nature, and therefore that it is incorrect to say that He was eternally the only begotten Son of God. It is contended that the Logos was eternal, but that the Logos became a Son only when He was incarnate of the blessed virgin Mary. There is one passage of Scripture that seems directly to contradict this opinion. Hebrews 1:8 reads: 'But of the Son he says, "Thy throne, O God, is for ever and ever."' And indeed the language in the first chapter of St. John's Gospel points in the same direction. Speaking of the Logos, John says 'the Word became flesh and dwelt among us, full of grace and truth; we have beheld his glory, glory as of the only Son from the Father', where the term 'Logos' and the term 'the only Son' are applied to the same Person without any suggestion that there is a period of time in which one term would not be applicable.

Opinions of this sort need to be strenuously resisted because, however unintentionally, they disparage the authority which attaches to the Person of the Son of God.[1]

Scriptures

1. *His Pre-existence.*—Jn. 1:1–3; 8:56–58; 17:5, 24; Phil. 2:6; Col. 1:17; Heb. 1:2; Rev. 1:8. *Cf.* Pr. 8:22–31.

2. *His Godhead.*—Ps. 110:1 (with Mk. 12:35–37); Is. 7:14 (with Mt. 1:23); 9:6; Mal. 3:1; Jn. 20:28; Rom. 9:5 (RV, RSV mg.); Phil. 2:6; Col. 1:19; 2:9; Tit. 2:13; Heb. 1:3, 6, 8; Jas. 2:1; 2 Pet. 1:1.

3. *His Sonship.*—Mt. 16:16, 17; Mk. 1:11; 9:7; Lk. 22:70; Jn. 1:18; 5:18–23, 26, 27; 14:7–12; 17:1; Rom. 1:4; Col. 1:13–17; 1 Jn. 4:9; 5:5, 9–13, 20.

Questions

1. Why was the divinity of Christ surrounded with so many problems for the first few centuries of the church's existence?

2. Why is it vital to the Christian's faith to believe in the deity of Christ? What Scriptures seem to you decisive in the matter?

3. 'The eternal generation of the Son'—what is the precise meaning of this key phrase? What is it intended to safeguard, and how far is it a scriptural expression?

4. In what respects (state them carefully) was our Lord more than a man? In what other respects was He unique?

5. How does Christ's Sonship differ from ours in relation to God?

BIBLIOGRAPHY

G. C. Berkouwer, *The Person of Christ*, Eerdmans, 1954.

P. T. Forsyth, *The Person and Place of Jesus Christ*, Independent Press, 1946.

H. P. Liddon, *The Divinity of our Lord and Saviour Jesus Christ*, Pickering and Inglis, 1968.

L. Morris, *The Lord from Heaven*, IVF, 1958.

B. B. Warfield, *The Person and Work of Christ*, ed. S. G. Craig, PRPC, 1950.

2. The Incarnation

a. *Its Purpose*

Scripture, in almost every case of reference to the incarnation, suggests redemption as its purpose. In order to become 'the last Adam', the covenant Head of a new race of redeemed men, our Lord must needs take a body similar to ours, and as Man offer the fullest obedience to the divine claims. Subsidiary reasons are given by implication. For example, His present intercessory work as High Priest is enhanced by the fact that He Himself 'in every respect has been tempted as we are', and He has shared in our 'weaknesses'. Similarly, it was necessary that He be born of the Hebrew race and be 'under the law'. Even more to the forefront in John's Gospel is our Lord's title 'the Word'. By no means the least important of the reasons for the incarnation is His manifestation of God's wisdom and love in a readily understandable form.

[1] See also the section on 'The Holy Trinity', pp. 52ff.

It is true that there are approximations to the incarnation in some of the religions of the East. But it must be noticed that in them we meet either a transitory 'incarnation' or else a process that is the reverse of our Lord's incarnation—a man is elevated to deity rather than a divine Person humbled to take human form.

b. The Essential Facts

Some Christians do not appear to be aware of the importance of correct views on matters such as this. It was vital to the subsequent work of Christ that His form of incarnation should not impair His deity (particularly His purity), and that, while being truly Man in every sense, He should not be subject to the sinful inheritance which had corrupted the whole of mankind. Many alternative theories have been proposed, and there is a tendency on the part of some to use the incarnation (incredible as it may seem) to exalt humanity. The essential facts as stated by Scripture are as follows:

1. Our Lord had a truly human body and a rational soul. All that was characteristic of unfallen man was found in Him; in this sense He is the second Adam.[1]

2. He possessed the divine nature in its fullest sense.

3. He was yet not two persons, but one Person.

4. Our Lord did not merely pass through the channel of birth (in a symbolical manner) nor was His birth the result of purging and adding to an already developing embryo. Students need to be on their guard against a too facile assumption that the incarnation could be effected in ways other than actually recorded. We can deal only with the existent fact.

c. The Miraculous Conception and the Virgin Birth

1. Scripture states that our Lord's mother was a virgin, that the conception was miraculous, and that the Agent was the Holy Spirit. Thus our Lord was free from the taint of original sin—i.e., the ordinary processes of transmission of the racial heritage were interrupted in His case by the miraculous conception. It must not, of course, be assumed that the mere fact of a virgin birth would break the entail of sin. The point to be emphasized is that the unique circumstances associated with our Lord's

---

[1] There is no true scriptural evidence for the contention that our Lord and not unfallen Adam is the prototype of the human race, and that had Adam not sinned the incarnation would still have taken place. Calvin discusses this matter at great length in the *Institutes*, Book II, chapter xii. He writes: 'So even if man had remained immaculately innocent, yet his condition would have been too mean for him to approach God without a Mediator.' But he adds later: 'Since the whole Scriptures proclaim that He was clothed in flesh in order to become a Redeemer, it argues excessive temerity to imagine another cause, or another end for it.' The student should beware of anything which tends to exalt human nature unduly.

birth assist us in more readily appreciating the fact that He was born without sin.

Even greater significance attaches to the virgin birth when it is realized that here God begins to 'do a new thing' for our salvation. Seen in this light, the supernatural form of the birth of Jesus takes on a profound symbolical appropriateness. It proclaims that mankind is able to make no contribution to its own redemption; God has to start from scratch, as it were, without human aid (cf. Is. 59:15, 16; 63:4, 5; Ezk. 34:5, 6, 10–16). Even Mary is entirely passive; the initiative is all of God. It is God who 'has visited and redeemed his people'. (This emphasis reveals how grossly at variance with the Scriptures are Roman Catholic ideas of Mary's 'co-operation' in the work of human redemption. The virgin birth declares that God acts on His own.) The 'overshadowing' of the Holy Spirit (Lk. 1:35) recalls Genesis 1:2, and perhaps indicates the beginning of the new creation.

2. There is much evidence in support of the fact of the virgin birth (see a book on apologetics). The biblical writers are unanimous on this: cf. particularly the statements concerning Joseph in the Gospel narratives.

3. Christ possessed *two* natures (divine and human), but was one Person. He differed from us in being derived from no human father and in His freedom from sin (either inherited or acquired).

Scriptures

1. *Royal Lineage.*—Is. 9:6, 7; 11:1–3; Je. 23:5, 6; Mi. 5:2; Acts 13:22, 23; Rom. 1:3.

2. *The Birth of Jesus.*—Mt. 1:18–25; Lk. 1:26–2:20. For *the virgin birth*, see Mt. 1:16, 18–25; Lk. 1:31, 34, 35; 3:23; cf. Jn. 8:41, perhaps an echo of a Jewish belief that Jesus was born out of wedlock.

3. *The Purpose of the Incarnation.*—Jn. 1:14, 18; 3:17; Rom. 8:3; 2 Cor. 8:9; Gal. 4:4, 5; 1 Tim. 1:15; Heb. 2:9–18; 10:4–14. For *the Word*, see Jn. 1:1–3; Heb. 1:1, 2; Rev. 19:13 (cf. 1 Jn. 1:1, 2).

4. *The Importance of the Doctrine.*—Heb. 1:17; 1 Jn. 2:22; 4:2, 3; 2 Jn. 7.

Questions

1. Give your own definition of what took place in the incarnation. How does it compare with (a) the statements of Scripture, (b) the Christian Creeds?

2. In theology it is customary to speak of our Lord's 'state of humiliation' and His 'state of exaltation'. What do you understand by these expressions?

3. How far did our Lord come into fellowship with our human nature?

4. Why is it important to hold that (a) the virgin birth, (b) the death and (c) the resurrection of Christ were literal historical facts?

BIBLIOGRAPHY

J. Gresham Machen, *The Virgin Birth*, James Clarke, 1958.
James Orr, *The Virgin Birth of Christ*, Hodder and Stoughton, 1907.
Article on 'Incarnation', *The New Bible Dictionary*, IVF, 1962.

3. Divinity and Humanity in the one Person of our Lord

Here we can only touch on the many problems that surround this important subject. They centre chiefly in *kenōsis*, the 'self-emptying' of our Lord (*kenōsis* comes from the Greek for 'emptied' in Philippians 2:7); the *hypostatic union*, the union of the two natures (of divinity and humanity) in one Person (*hypostasis* means 'person'); and the 'Communion of the Properties' (Latin, *communicatio idiomatum*), the interchange and intercommunication of the qualities and experiences of the two natures in view of the unity of the Person.

a. Kenōsis

Several alternative theories have been held. The extreme view that He 'emptied himself' of His deity and was limited to the natural knowledge and abilities of an ordinary man is untenable in the light of the narratives. Another states that our Lord, while retaining the possession of all His divine attributes, renounced their use and hid them from the observation of men. There are difficulties in this position, because it demands, for example, an act of will on the part of a baby to refuse to use His omniscience and omnipotence. Other theories are that our Lord suspended His divine consciousness from the time of conception and that He reassumed it in manhood; that the divine fullness was gradually communicated by a series of successive effluxes according as the gradual human development permitted; and that the deity of our Lord underlay His humanity (as a kind of subconsciousness). All of these are open to objection.

The truth is that our Lord's attributes of deity were at no time laid aside. Any theory which violates the integrity of our Lord's deity is obviously unsatisfactory. There seems to be no theory which relieves us entirely from objections. The nearest we can get is that our Lord's perfect divine nature (with the possession of all its attributes) was so united with a perfect human nature that one divine-human Person developed with the divine element (if such a distinction can here be made) controlling the normal development of the human. Beyond this we cannot safely go. (Philippians 2:7, in fact, has nothing to do with questions concerning the divine attributes; it simply indicates the humbling *moral* self-renunciation involved for one who 'was in the form of God' in 'taking the form of a servant.')

b. Hypostatic Union

In thinking of our Lord's ministry and manner of life on earth, no distinction should be made such as, for example, that a certain act or saying was divine and another purely human. The wonder of the combination of His two natures in one Person should be given its full prominence, and its value is greatly enhanced when we realize that our Lord (in His resurrection body) has taken a human form and nature to the very throne of God. The wonder of this is scarcely greater than the related teaching that in a similar manner we are also brought into vital union with Him ('partakers of the divine nature') and are destined to be brought into a fuller conformity with His image and likeness.

There are difficulties in the use of such terms as 'nature' (substance) and 'person', and these distinctions must not be unduly pressed. But it is important to realize:

1. That, while the two natures were united, they were not intermingled and altered in their individual properties, so that there resulted a third type of substance which was neither divine nor human.

2. That there were not transfers of attributes from one to the other, such as a human characteristic transferred to the divine, nor was our Lord's deity reduced to human limitations.

3. That the union was not an indwelling such as the indwelling of the Christian by the Spirit of God, but a personal union such that the resulting being was a unit, who thought and acted as a unit.

c. The 'Communion of the Properties'

While each nature retained its own properties they were not held together merely as though the hypostatic union was a ring thrown around two incompatible elements. There was a real harmony. For instance, it is not enough to say that our Lord walked on the sea because His humanity enabled Him to do the walking and His deity prevented His sinking. Much controversy took place about this, particularly at the time of the Reformation, and two chief views, the Lutheran doctrine of the *Communicatio Idiomatum* and that of the Reformed churches, were brought forward. The first suggested that there was an inter-communication of the human nature and the divine, the one giving to and deriving from the other in the one Person. But the Reformed theologians objected that humanity could never fully have contained the divine and the divine could gain little or nothing from the human. They suggested a connecting link (such as the gifts of the Holy Spirit) between the two natures through the one Person. Neither view is entirely satisfactory. Scripture presents to us *one* Lord Jesus Christ who is both God and Man.

In discussing our Lord's 'unity with God and with the human race' the glorious truth of this statement in its proper meaning should be carefully safeguarded from the half-truths and misconceptions with which it is so frequently entangled.

d. Historical Survey of the Doctrine

The clear statements which appear concerning the Person of our Lord in the Creeds were not made without much controversy. They are the result of the earnest endeavours of early Christian leaders who strove against the misconceptions and definite heresies of the first centuries of church history. The following brief review is given in the hope that the subject will be followed up in a larger work.

1. *The First Three Centuries.*—There is no doubt that the deity of our Lord was firmly established amongst Christians and He was worshipped as God. It was not until certain heresies arose that definitions (other than those contained in the Scriptures) became necessary. The reader must guard against the suggestion that the *definition* of our Lord's deity was the *creation* of faith in Him as God.

On the one hand, the *Ebionites* and others denied our Lord's divinity, while at the other extreme the *Docetists* denied His true humanity, suggesting that our Lord's life on earth was largely an illusion—*i.e.*, it was not the divine Christ who hungered and suffered and died. The Docetic tendency was widespread and constituted a serious threat.

2. *Fourth Century.*—(i) *Arianism* became a menace in the church because it implied that our Lord was not God in the fullest sense, being subordinate to the Father by having been in some way created by the Father and not Himself possessing eternal self-existence. It also implied that our Lord's attributes were divine only in a limited form. At the Council of Nicaea, Athanasius and the orthodox leaders insisted on the insertion of the word *homoousios* ('of one and the same substance' as the Father) in the Creed, which reads 'one Lord Jesus Christ, . . . very God of very God, begotten, not made, being of one substance with the Father'. Had Arianism triumphed it would drastically have altered Christianity, if not destroyed it.

(ii) *Apollinarius*, taking the Platonic distinctions of body, soul and spirit in man, suggested that our Lord had a true body and an animal soul, but that the place of the rational human spirit was taken by His divine being. This would mean that He was not fully human, and therefore 'not tempted in every respect as we are'.

3. *Fifth Century.*—Nestorius, or his followers, so exaggerated the distinctness of the two natures as almost to separate them and divide the one Person into two, and Eutyches went to the opposite extreme and insisted that there was only *one nature* in Christ.

The final pronouncement of the early church Councils on this subject was given at Chalcedon, where the doctrine of the two natures united in one Person (the hypostatic union) was clearly enunciated. This has remained the orthodox Christian teaching and presents the most reliable statement yet attained.

Scriptures

Mt. 1:23; Heb. 1:1–14; 2:9–18; Jn. 1:1–18; Phil. 2:5–11. The following Scriptures indicate the two natures: Jn. 1:14; 8:57, 58; Rom. 1:3, 4; 8:3; 9:5 (mg.); 1 Cor. 2:8; Gal. 4:4; 1 Tim. 3:16; Heb. 2:14; 1 Pet. 1:20; 3:18; 1 Jn. 1:1, 2. Occasionally Scripture uses a word which is strictly accurate for one of the natures only: 1 Cor. 2:8; Acts 20:28 (purchased 'with his own blood').

Questions

1. Why is it impossible completely to understand the Person of Christ? Is it sufficient merely to repeat the actual words of Scripture? (*Cf.* the Nicene Creed.) If not, why not? What is legitimate beyond this?

2. Search the Gospels for illustrations of the union of the divine and human natures in one Person. See, *e.g.*, Mt. 4:2, 3; Mk. 4:38, 39; 9:7, 8. Is there any encouragement given us by Scripture to attempt to separate these two natures on any occasion?

3. Examine the parallels to the union of divine and human in our Lord's single Person seen in the Holy Scriptures (see pp. 32, 34) and in our new life in Christ.

4. What errors have been taught on this important subject? Show how each of them affects Christ's fitness to be the Saviour of men.

BIBLIOGRAPHY

Athanasius, *On the Incarnation*, ET, Mowbray, 1953.
G. C. Berkouwer, *The Person of Christ*, Eerdmans, 1954.
E. H. Gifford, *The Incarnation*, Longmans, 1911.
J. N. D. Kelly, *Early Christian Doctrines*, Black, 1968.
R. L. Ottley, *The Doctrine of the Incarnation*, Methuen, 1908.
See also the books listed on pages 97 and 99.

4. The Life of Christ

Any Christian student who has not read carefully and at leisure completely through one of the Gospel narratives should rectify this omission with the least possible delay. Nothing is of such moment in the world's intellectual pursuits as a study of the work, character and teaching of the divine Master. It is surprising to find how many otherwise well-read Christians have not read a reliable life of Christ, as, for example, that of Edersheim. It is almost incredible what loose thinking is constantly expressed without check and how readily Christians accept statements concerning our Lord's acts and teaching which they do not trouble to verify from the sacred text. It will be a great day for Christianity when its devotees rediscover the actual grandeur of the Person they dimly worship.

a. The Personal Attributes of our Lord

It is interesting to note, on the one hand, His claims to be an object of worship, the One who is able to forgive sin, the Source of life and of access to God, one with the Father and able to send the Holy Spirit to His disciples. On the other hand, we also notice His ability to sympathize with human suffering, His understanding of the hearts of men and His yearning over the Hebrew race.

In discussing His attributes controversy has centred chiefly on the following (which can but briefly be reviewed).

1. *His growth 'in wisdom and stature'* (Lk. 2:52).—This has been discussed in section 3 above. Our Lord's humanity was perfect. Luke's statement describes His normal human growth and does not in the least deny His possession of attributes of deity. That He could on occasion summon more than human learning is shown by His knowing the disciples' thoughts. Mark 13:32 implies our Lord's filial relationship with the Father, who is depicted in Scripture as the Source of wisdom and counsel within the Trinity.

2. *'In every respect he has been tempted as we are, yet without sinning'* (Heb. 4:15).—In what sense was He tempted? This is a question which is often asked. By virtue of His non-possession of birth-sin, was He not necessarily better able to resist than we are? Scripture suggests that He was as capable of receiving temptation through His physical channels as was Adam. To be open to temptation is not in itself sin. Sin consists in the consent of the will to the performing of what is suggested to it by the temptation. We must (in spite of the seeming contradiction) insist that our Lord was subjected to real temptation, and yet it was not in the power of the temptation to seduce His perfect nature. The older theologians describe our Lord's resistance to temptation by *posse non peccare* ('power not to sin'), and not *non posse peccare* ('no power to sin'). Think of the consequences if a divine-human Person really fell, and the problem at once presents itself as one of profound gravity. In the last resort, *posse non peccare* may not fall far short of *non posse peccare*.[1]

3. *Omnipresence.*—To suggest that our Lord's divine-human Person restricted His divine omnipresence is surely disproved by the statement 'the only Son, who is in the bosom of the Father' (Jn. 1:18; *cf.* Jn. 7:34). In any case, we in thought localize the presence of the Godhead to His throne, or to gatherings of worshippers, while still believing in His omnipresence. From the opposite point of view—the violation of His humanity—Scripture is carefully reticent in recording the use of His divine omnipresence.[2]

4. *Miraculous Power.*—As to the reality of His miracles and for a full discussion, see a book on apologetics.[3] The point here is that His humanity, any more than that of Moses, Elijah or the apostles, who also performed

[1] See also p. 72.
[2] A parallel may be found in God's creative activity. He is 'in' His creatures and also 'beyond' them. Calvin develops this thought of the Logos *intra carnem* and the Logos *extra carnem* (*Institutes*, Book II, chapter cxiii).
[3] See also pp. 66, 67.

similar acts in God's name, was not invalidated by the possession of miraculous gifts.

b. The Titles of our Lord

The student would do well to study carefully the names applied to our Lord. See, for example, Warfield's book *The Lord of Glory*. There is a wealth of theology in such names as 'the Son of God', the 'Son of man', 'the Second Adam', 'the Word'.

c. The Purpose of His Life

It should be fully realized by the student that the life of our Lord is far more than the leading up to and preparation for His death. But care must be exercised that in giving due prominence to these further considerations nothing be added which detracts from the centrality and necessity of His death. It is necessary to secure the proper balance between the important points in theology without diminishing the value of any. We may note three reasons why our Lord's perfect life was a necessity, especially in respect of its obedience.

1. It qualified Him to become the sacrificial offering. Old Testament illustrations all insist upon the purity of the victim for sacrifice.

2. It meant that perfect obedience was rendered to God in contradistinction to Adam's disobedience. Scripture emphasizes this repeatedly. See Romans 5:19; Hebrews 10:6, 7.

3. By it He became a properly qualified Mediator and High Priest for His people (Heb. 2:11–18).

Scriptures

The Gospels will well repay careful study. See a good 'Harmony' such as that given in *Helps to the Study of the Bible* (Oxford University Press).

1. *Jesus' Full Humanity* (with its normal limitations).—Mt. 8:20, 24; 21:18; 26:38; Mk. 1:35; 11:13; 13:32; Lk. 2:52; 22:28, 41–45; Jn. 4:6; 11:35; 19:28; Heb. 2:17; 5:5, 8. Study the Lord's practice of prayer.

2. *Manifestations of His Divinity.*—(i) Authority and power: Mt. 8:26; Mk. 2: 7–10; Jn. 1:12; 10:18, 28; 11:43, 44; 14:30; (ii) Knowledge: Mt. 17:27; Lk. 5:4–6; Jn. 1:48; 2:24, 25; 6:64; 16:30; (iii) Communion with His Father: Mt. 11:27; Jn. 5:19, 20; 8:28, 29; 14:10.

3. *The Significance of Christ's Perfect Obedience.*—Is. 49:1–6; 50:4–6; 53:11; 2 Cor. 8:9; Phil. 2:5–8; Heb. 2:10; 5:8, 9; 7:28; 9:14; 10:7–9; 12:2, 3; 1 Pet. 1:19.

4. *Names.*—*Jesus* corresponds to the Hebrew 'Joshua', meaning 'God the Saviour'. *Christ* corresponds to the Hebrew 'Messiah', meaning 'Anointed'. The significance of the dove and the voice from heaven at His baptism is that the anointing of the Holy Spirit was to be the special sign of the Messiah (Lk. 3:21, 22; 4:18; Jn. 3:34).

Son of God (also 'the only Son' and 'His Son'): Lk. 1:35; 22:70; Jn. 3:16; Rom. 1:4.

Son of man occurs eighty times in the New Testament and is used on all except three occasions by the Lord of Himself, as, *e.g.*, in Mt. 8:20; 25:31; Mk. 8:31, 38; 10:45; Lk. 19:10; Jn. 3:13.

We have already emphasized the benefit to be derived from collecting and examining the titles given to our Lord in the New Testament. *E.g.*, note the following: *Lord:* Lk. 1:76; *Emmanuel:* Mt. 1:23; *The first-born:* Col. 1:15, 18; *The Lamb of God:* Jn. 1:29; *etc.* Note particularly the combinations used in Peter's Epistles, such as *Our Lord and Saviour Jesus Christ* (2 Pet. 3:2, 18; *cf.* 1:1).

Questions

1. In applying the adjective 'perfect' to our Lord's humanity, what do you mean? Has it the same meaning as 'sinless' or does it mean more?

2. Give a list of all the names and titles applied to the Lord. Consider the contexts in which each is most used (*e.g.*, 'Christ' and 'Son of God' very little by Jesus Himself, 'Son of man' almost exclusively on the lips of Jesus), and show how they severally relate to His divine-human Person and to the stages of His redemptive 'career'.

BIBLIOGRAPHY

A. Edersheim, *The Life and Times of Jesus the Messiah*, Pickering and Inglis, 1953.
A. M. Hunter, *The Work and Words of Jesus*, SCM Press, 1950.
J. G. S. S. Thomson, *The Praying Christ*, Tyndale Press, 1959.
H. E. W. Turner, *Jesus, Master and Lord*, Mowbray, 1953.
B. B. Warfield, *The Lord of Glory*, Hodder and Stoughton, 1907.

5. The Death of Christ

Again the student is urged to make himself thoroughly familiar with the recorded facts concerning the death of our Lord. He should note the injustice of His trial and the exact wording of the descriptions of the Calvary scenes provided in the Gospels. Inaccurate pictures and sentimental descriptions frequently leave erroneous impressions which hinder appreciation of the true meaning of the events at the cross. For a full discussion of the significance and meaning of our Lord's death see the section below on 'The Doctrine of the Atonement' (pp. 115–127).

6. The Descent into Hell

With reference to the period between the death and the resurrection of our Lord, much has been written which must be treated with extreme caution. On some points, for example, with regard to human destiny and the intermediate state following death, quite unwarranted conclusions have been drawn from the few scriptural references to our Lord's experiences between death and resurrection.

The belief expressed in the phrase of the Creed, 'He descended into hell', finds its basis in a group of scriptural passages nearly all of which are involved in some uncertainty as to their precise significance. The clearest reference is in Acts 2:24–32 (*cf.* Ps. 16:8–11 and Acts 13:34–37), where the Greek *Hades* (Hebrew *Sheol*) means 'the place of the departed'. The most that it is legitimate to draw from this plain statement of fact is that not only did our Lord's identification with mankind lead Him into death, but His soul entered into all that a human spirit passes through at the dissolution of the body. The descent is probably alluded to in Romans 10:6–9, but more problematic are Ephesians 4:9, 10, which may well refer instead to Christ's descent to earth in the act of incarnation, and 1 Peter 3:18–20; 4:6 (see the commentaries on these verses by Selwyn, Cranfield and Stibbs, and also Salmond, *The Christian Doctrine of Immortality*). Some interpreters such as Aquinas regard 3:18–20 as pointing to a pre-incarnation activity of the second Person of the Trinity in the days of Noah. Most theologians have taken this evidence to indicate a 'visit' by Christ not to hell in the sense of the place of punishment (*i.e.*, Gehenna) but to the waiting-place of the dead, where some at least were ready to receive the gospel. By Christ's visitation it became 'paradise' for those who should henceforth 'fall asleep in Jesus' (Lk. 23:43). The Pauline Epistles make clear that for the Christian the intermediate state is no longer to be dreaded. This transformation wrought by Christ in His descent and subsequent resurrection, as He triumphantly vindicated His sovereignty over the realm of death, is probably reflected also in Philippians 2:10 and Revelation 5:13 ('under the earth'; *cf.* also Rev. 1:17, 18 and Mt. 27:52, 53). Anything beyond these few inferences seems to be totally unwarranted.

The unique message of these Scriptures is that it is impossible for us to pass through experiences in which our Lord cannot sympathize, and even in death He has preceded us and transformed its claims over us.

Scriptures

Mt. 26:47–27:66; Mk. 14:43–15:47; Lk. 22:47–23:56; Jn. 18; 19.

Question

Study the order of events on the day of the crucifixion by a comparison of the narratives. Note that the Lord in effect had four trials. Also note exactly what happened from the time of the arrival at Calvary, and the cries from the cross. Refer to Tyndale Commentaries or similar helps to check your reconstruction. This exercise will reveal many amazing facts concerning the condemnation of our Lord. It is clear that several elements in the processes of the trial were irregular and conducive to a miscarriage of justice.

7. The Resurrection and Exaltation of Christ

The subject of the resurrection deserves far fuller treatment than can be accorded to it here. A glance at the recorded teaching of the apostles in the book of Acts and the Epistles (including the Epistle to the Hebrews, which, though not mentioning it directly, is based throughout upon the fact of the resurrection) will reveal it as one of the two cardinal points in Christian doctrine. Its fuller meaning was one of the sublimest rediscoveries of the Reformation divines.

a. The Significance of the Resurrection

The resurrection of Christ formed the core of the first apostolic sermons (to a far greater extent than the cross; see Acts 1:22; 4:33; 17:18), because it represented the *vindication* of all that had gone before in the earthly course of our Lord. His teaching and claims, and His 'obedience unto death', as well as His disciples' faith and hopes, were all vindicated by this act of the Father in which Christ was shown victorious over every hostile power, whether man or demon or death itself (*cf.* Lk. 24:19-21 with Acts 5:31; 13:23; also Acts 2:24; 13:34; Rom. 6:6; 2 Tim. 1:10; Rev. 1:17, 18).

1. First of all, then, the resurrection is the vindication of God's faithful Servant, the crucified One, as 'Lord and Christ', the promised Messiah of God. As such it provided attestation of His deity, and also confirmed His designation as the final Judge of all men (Is. 53:10-12; Acts 2:36; 3:13-15; 5:31; 10:40-42; 17:31; Rom. 1:4).

2. As the mark of divine approval of the suffering Servant, the resurrection also stamped God's *imprimatur* upon the *service* of His obedience and death, as a complete atonement for sin and as the fulfilment of the promises made to the fathers. As a result, salvation and forgiveness of sins are now proclaimed in the name of Jesus. The resurrection was thus the motive centre in the evangelization of the ancient world (Acts 2:32; 4:33; 5:31; 13:32, 33, 38, 39; Rom. 4:24, 25).

3. The resurrection confirmed believers in their faith in God and His power, and gave assurance of their ultimate full salvation. Not only does it certify the saving value of Christ's death, it also persuades us that 'if while we were enemies we were reconciled to God by the death of his Son, much more, now that we are reconciled, shall we be saved by his life'. Christ's risen life continues to save us, as the life of the eternal High Priest who has entered into heaven *for us*, ever to intercede for us and to perfect the work of redemption in us (Rom. 5:10; Heb. 6:20; 7:16, 23-25; 1 Pet. 1:21).

4. Christ's resurrection is the sign and pledge of the resurrection of the body for all who are in Christ, and so determines the Christian's new attitude to death and transforms his hope (1 Cor. 15:12-58; *cf.* Acts 4:2; 26:23; Rom. 8:10, 11; 2 Cor. 4:14; 1 Pet. 1:3, 21).

5. Together with the ascension and exaltation, the resurrection completes the pattern of death-resurrection-exaltation which constitutes the spiritual initiation of believers in their identification with Christ. Like and with Christ, the convert becomes 'dead to sin' and 'alive to God', a passage from death to life that is sacramentally set forth in baptism. Consequently the appeal for sanctification becomes a summons to those who 'have been raised with Christ' to 'set their minds on things that are

above', and dying to self and living to God form the daily experience of the Christian (Rom. 6:3–11; 2 Cor. 4:10, 11; Eph. 2:4–6; Col. 3:1, 2).

6. The resurrection will always be foremost among the factors which attest the claim of the Christian revelation to be truly an 'unveiling of the divine mystery'. It removes the Christian faith from the sphere of philosophical speculation and moralism and establishes it as the action of God for the salvation of the human race.

b. Evidence for the Fact of the Resurrection

For a full discussion see a book on apologetics. The strongest arguments are associated with the following facts:

1. The revolutionary change in the attitude of the disciples. The minds of the majority were disposed not to believe it, and they had apparently failed to understand our Lord's prophecies concerning it.

2. The failure of the Jews to produce the body of Christ. The excuse of the 'stolen body' is ludicrous in view of the precautions taken by the authorities at the time of entombment. 'The silence of the Jews is as significant as the speech of the Christians' (Fairbairn).

3. The appearances to a successive series of individuals and groups of people, including one group numbering five hundred, at a variety of times during the day and in differing circumstances.

4. The survival and growth of the infant church and its impact on the world's civilizations. This has to be explained, especially in view of the fact that the human heart is intensely and universally resentful of some of its claims, and that it incurred opposition from the dominant religious leaders. Other religions and political theories which have made their bid for world power pander in some form to human cupidity and pride. Christianity is uncompromising in these respects.

c. Some Alternative Theories

On no subject has human ingenuity exerted itself more fully in providing other explanations than the obvious one. The detailed replies may be consulted in the appropriate reference books. A careful comparison of such alternative theories with the actual text of Scripture will do more to confirm the reader's faith than a great deal of marshalling of counter-arguments.

The chief attempts to explain away the Lord's resurrection are:

1. The 'swoon' theory, that is, that He was entombed in a state of coma, and subsequently revived.

2. The disciples saw a series of telepathic manifestations or visions, or were even the victims of hallucinations.

3. Their eager minds received a series of subjective sensations which may be described as resulting from some objective agency, but which were not the direct result of a physical resuscitation of our Lord's actual body.

4. It merely describes and represents a revival in the disappointed disciples of the power of our Lord's previous teaching.

5. It expresses in the form of 'myth' their conviction of the eternal significance of Jesus as something 'bigger than death' and transcending the passage of time.

On numerous occasions those who have set out critically to examine and to disprove the actuality of the resurrection have been forced to abandon the attempt and in some cases have been converted to Christ through the invulnerability of the evidence.

d. The Resurrection Body of our Lord

Here caution is needed. Scripture has already warned us that a complete understanding of the actual nature of the resurrection body is beyond the scope of human knowledge (1 Cor. 15:35-44), and this passage defines the limits within which human intelligence may make comparisons from other fields of human knowledge and experience.

As to the resurrection body of our Lord, the Gospel accounts undoubtedly indicate the following:

1. His body was not only real, but was the same body which had been entombed.

2. He Himself challenged the impression that He was purely spirit— 'A spirit has not flesh and bones' (Lk. 24:39-43). He partook of food, though whether of necessity is not clear. He also bore marks of the wounds He had received.

3. The resurrection body possessed certain characteristics which are not true of our bodies. For example, it was not restricted and impeded by external matter to the same extent as our present bodies; He passed through locked doors into the midst of the disciples, and suddenly vanished from the sight of two of them who had walked with Him on the road to Emmaus.

The truth appears to be that our Lord reoccupied the human body in which He suffered. But from the outset this resurrection body had different properties from the 'body of our humiliation' and the pre-resurrection body of our Lord. The arrangement of the clothes in the empty tomb suggests, if it does not prove, that our Lord passed through the swathing encumbrances and through the rock-hewn tomb. The rolling away of the stone appears to have been subsequent to the resurrection and an evidential addition rather than a necessary element in the process. St. Paul touches on this line of argument in 1 Corinthians 15: 'There are celestial bodies and there are terrestrial bodies.' But we must not allow ourselves to regard such evidence as destroying the distinction between body and spirit. A 'psychical' body is not composed of 'psyche' but expressive of it. A 'pneumatical' body *pari passu* is not composed of 'pneuma' but expressive of it. Nor is there any real evidence for actual ubiquity even in the resurrection body. When our Lord appeared to His disciples, He was, at all events during the period of His contact with earthly experience, subject to the law of space. It seems best to regard the evidence as teaching us that our Lord entered into a new existence in both body and spirit, but was capable of resuming such necessary relations to our present conditions as afforded unmistakable evidence of an actual resurrection without fully binding Him to the conditions of His previous humiliation. The heavenly life, invisible to human eyes, with a body adapted to this condition, was the normal experience of our Lord after His resurrection. The 'appearances' were the gracious condescensions to our need of 'many proofs'. The whole teaching of Scripture, however, points to a heavenly condition for completed man, body and spirit, rather than a denudation of the body which is more akin to Greek philosophy. It was 'the resurrection', not the survival of the soul, that constituted the stumbling-block to the Athenians.

In His state of exaltation our Lord still possesses His body, but in a spiritual, transfigured form. It is useless for the human mind to speculate on detail. The scriptural statements should be accepted in their simple grandeur. The peculiar character of the resurrection body is itself an evidence of the truth of the narrative.

f. The Ascension and Heavenly Session

The apostles taught that the ascension and present session at the right hand of God were the culmination of our Lord's work of redemption. No life of Christ is really complete which does not go on to indicate the reasons why our Lord left His disciples and the infant church in order to return to the throne of God, there to undertake His unseen ministry. This is the message of the Epistle to the Hebrews, which is unique among the books of the New Testament. It will well repay careful study and analysis. Among other things it tells us why it was necessary for our Lord to leave His disciples and why He has remained away so long. In the first place it was necessary for Him to enter into the 'holiest' by means of the merits of His atonement, to appear before God as the Forerunner of the redeemed race. Secondly, He is doing a vital work on behalf of His followers, both as the 'pioneer of their salvation' and mediatorially as their High Priest and Advocate.

Scriptures

a. The Resurrection

1. *The Facts and the Apostolic Testimony.*—Mt. 28; Mk. 16:1–8; Lk. 24; Jn. 20; 21; Acts 1:22; 2:14–36; 4:10, 33; 5:30, 32; 10:40–42; 13:34–39; 1 Cor. 9:1; 15:1–19.

2. Note *the emphasis placed on the resurrection* in the New Testament (i) by our Lord Himself (Mk. 8:31; 9:31; 10:34; Jn. 2:19; Acts 1:3) and (ii) by the apostles (St. Peter: Acts 2:24, 32, 36; 4:10; St. Paul: Acts 13:30–39; 17:31; 1 Cor. 15:1–4, 17; 2 Tim. 2:8).

3. *Its Significance for Salvation.*—See the verses listed on pp. 108, 109, and also Jn. 11:25, 26; Rom. 7:4; 8:34; 10:9; 14:9; 1 Cor. 6:13, 14; 2 Cor. 1:9; Eph. 1:18–20; Phil. 3:10, 11, 21; Col. 1:18; 2:12, 13; 1 Thes. 4:14; Heb. 13:20, 21; Rev. 20:4–6.

b. The Exaltation

1. *The Facts of the Ascension.*—Lk. 9:51; 24:51; Jn. 6:62; 20:17; Acts 1:2, 9–11.

2. *The Heavenly Session.*—Mk. 14:62; Lk. 22:69; Acts 5:31; 7:55, 56; Eph. 1:20, 21; Col. 3:1; Heb. 1:3; 6:19, 20; 8:1; 10:12; 12:2; 1 Pet. 3:22; Rev. 5:6; 7:17.

3. *The Gift of the Spirit.*—Jn. 7:38, 39; 14:25, 26; 16:7, 13; Acts. 2:33.

4. *The Significance of Christ's Exaltation and Heavenly Session.*—Jn. 14:2, 3, 12; Acts 2:34, 35; 3:21; Rom. 8:34; Eph. 1:3; 2:5, 6; 4:7–11; Phil. 2:9–11; Col. 3:1–4; 2 Tim. 2:12; Heb. 2:5–9 (*cf.* 1 Cor. 15:24–28); 4:14–16; 6:19, 20; 7:25; 8:1, 6; 9:24; 10:12, 13.

Questions

1. Discuss the assertion 'The faith of the apostles was pre-eminently one of the resurrection'.

2. Can you enumerate and disprove the theories which men have invented to explain away the resurrection?

3. Why did Jesus go away and leave His disciples to years of fierce persecution? Why does He stay away so long? Would it have been better for us if our Lord had not ascended, but had remained with His church?

BIBLIOGRAPHY

J. N. D. Anderson, *The Evidence for the Resurrection*, IVF, 1950.
G. R. Beasley-Murray, *Christ is Alive!*, Lutterworth Press, 1947.
Michael Green, *Man Alive!*, IVF, 1967.
H. Latham, *The Risen Master*, Deighton Bell, 1904.
W. Milligan, *The Ascension and Heavenly Priesthood of our Lord*, Macmillan, 1892.
W. Milligan, *The Resurrection of our Lord*, Macmillan, 1899.
F. Morison, *Who Moved the Stone?*, Faber, 1930.
C. F. D. Moule, *The Phenomenon of the New Testament*, SCM Press, 1967.
James Orr, *The Resurrection of Jesus*, Hodder and Stoughton, 1907.
A. M. Ramsey, *The Resurrection of Christ*, revised edn., Fontana, 1960.
S. D. F. Salmond, *The Christian Doctrine of Immortality*, T. and T. Clark, 1907.
A. M. Stibbs, *The Finished Work of Christ*, Tyndale Press, 1954.

8. The Threefold Work of Christ

One of the richest fields for devotional study is provided by an examination of the threefold office of Christ. The following are some of the leading thoughts which may profitably be followed out by the student himself collating Scriptures bearing on the subject and drawing his own conclusions with the aid of the Holy Spirit's illumination.

a. As Prophet

Scripture indicates the following:

1. Our Lord is the consummation of the line of Hebrew prophets. For example, see Deuteronomy 18:15; Acts 3:22, 26.

2. He spoke with *immediate* prophetic authority, replacing 'Thus says the Lord' by 'I say to you'. His ministry was characterized by direct authority, and also contained less of the predictive element than the messages of some of the earlier prophets. The other chief characteristics of His prophetic ministry were His incisive parabolic preaching to the common people, His eschatological pronouncements centring in the imminence of the kingdom of God, and His self-revelation as the Son of man through whose sufferings and exaltation the kingdom would come.

3. He confirmed His prophetic ministry by performing miracles of healing, *etc.*, such as had accompanied the beginnings of new epochs in the previous history of Israel.

4. He continues His prophetic office, in a *mediate* sense, through the apostles and in the gifts of ministry in the church.

b. As Priest

The New Testament clearly teaches that in the sacrificial office our Lord ministered in two ways:

1. *Actively*, by steadfastly setting His face to go up to Jerusalem (Lk. 9:51), voluntarily laying down His own life, and subsequently presenting Himself before the throne of God on behalf of the redeemed.

2. *Passively*, by submitting to crucifixion at the hands of men. He offered *Himself* as the sacrificial victim (see Heb. 9:14).

His present activity as High Priest consists in:

1. His mediation and suretyship of the new covenant.

2. His advocacy and intercession for His people at the throne of God.

3. His providing and ensuring the right of access into the presence of God to the humblest Christian.

There is no trace in Scripture of the erroneous teaching concerning our Lord's 'victim-state' by which He now perpetually offers Himself before God. The Epistle to the Hebrews states on more than one occasion, and states emphatically, that He has completed redemption by His one offering, which act of offering is said to have been 'once for all' (*cf.* Heb. 10:10 and similar statements in other chapters). Having obtained (completely) eternal redemption for us, He is viewed 'as seated at the right hand of God' (Heb. 8:1). There is no hint that our Lord can continually suffer on behalf of His people nor that He continually pleads His merits before the Father. His welcome by His Father has settled once for all the question of the acceptance of His work, and *His presence* (in itself) ensures testimony, mediation, and intercession on our behalf.

c. As King

1. The prophecies of the kingly Messiah find their fulfilment in Christ in two stages. They were *in principle* fulfilled in our Lord's first coming, when 'the time was fulfilled' for God's kingdom to be established among men. Through Christ's decisive victory God's reign was inaugurated, Satan and all the evil powers defeated, and the King Himself crowned in glory, whence He now dispenses the blessings of the kingdom which are summed up as 'eternal life'.

2. But the full realization of the kingdom that Christ won by His death and resurrection still awaits consummation. 'We do not yet see everything in subjection to him', and Satan continues to oppose His rule. Meanwhile, the kingdom still comes in the hearts of men as the gospel (which announces the enthronement of the king) secures ever-increasing allegiance. As Head of His body, Christ already reigns in reality over the church, but He waits until *all* His enemies are made His footstool, and His universal dominion over everything 'in heaven and on earth and under the earth' is revealed at His reappearing.

Scriptures

a. As Prophet

See Dt. 18:18, 19; Mt. 21:11; Lk. 4:24; 7:16; Jn. 4:19; 7:40, 52; Acts 7:37; Heb. 1:1, 2; and contrast Mt. 11:13.

For the *immediate* nature of His prophecy contrast Is. 6:5 with Mt. 17:5; 24; 25; Jn. 3:11. For the *mediate* see Jn. 15:26, 27; Acts 2:18; 1 Cor. 7:12, 25, 40; 12:10; 14:1, 24–32. *Cf.* too the book of Revelation; see 1:3, 10, 11; 19:10; 22:18, 19.

b. As Priest

1. *The Sacrificial Office.*—For His *active* work see Lk. 9:51; 22:39–44; Jn. 10:17, 18; Heb. 5:1–10; 6:20; 7:27; 10:12–14. For His *passive* work as the victim study the Old Testament sacrifices (see, *e.g.*, Ex. 12; Lv. 1–5 and 16) and note 1 Cor. 5:7, 8 (the Passover); Eph. 5:2 (the burnt-offering); Eph. 2:14–16 (the peace-offering); 2 Cor. 5:21 (the sin-offering); Heb. 10:1–22 (Day of Atonement); 1 Pet. 2:21–25; 3:18.

2. *His Present Activity.*—(i) As Mediator: 1 Tim. 2:5; Heb. 7:25; 8:6; 9:15; 12:24; 1 Jn. 2:1, 2. (ii) Giving access to God: Jn. 14:6; Rom. 5:2; Eph.2:13–18; Heb. 4:15, 16; 10:19–22. (iii) Intercession: Jn. 17; Rom. 8:34; Heb. 7:25; 1 Jn. 2:1. (iv) As Head of the church: Eph. 1:22, 23; 2:20–22; 4:4–16; 5:23–30; Col.1 :18; 2:19.

c. As King

1. *Old Testament Prophecies.*—Gn. 49:10; the Messianic Psalms such as 2; 45:6–7; 72; 110:1–4; Is. 9:6, 7; 11:1–5, 10; Je. 23:5, 6; Ezk. 37:24–28.

2. *Present Fulfilment.*—Mt. 12:28; 13:17; 21:1–9; 28:18; Mk. 1:15; Lk. 1:32; 4:18–21; 23:2; Jn. 18:36, 37; Rom. 14:17; Phil. 2:9; Col. 1:13; Heb. 1:3–9; 2:5–9.

3. *Future Consummation.*—Dn. 7:13, 14; Mt. 13:41; 19:28; 25:31–40; Lk. 1:33; 1 Cor. 15:24–28; Phil. 2:10, 11; 1 Tim. 6:15; Rev. 5:5, 7, 9, 10; 11:15; 12:10; 22:3.

Questions

a. As Prophet

1. 'Jesus was the greatest of the Jewish prophets.' Are you satisfied with this statement? In what relation does Jesus stand to the earlier prophets?

2. Did Jesus tell us anything new about God? In what respects does His teaching amplify or surpass that of the Old Testament?

3. How far did our Lord bear a prophetic relation to (*a*) His own generation, (*b*) posterity?

b. As Priest

1. Distinguish carefully between Christ's completed and continuing priestly service. What is the connection between the two?

2. Were *all* the characteristics and acts of the high priest of the Old Testament typical of Christ?

3. In what respects is our Lord superior to the Levitical priesthood? (See the Epistle to the Hebrews.)

c. As King

1. What do you understand by the term 'the kingdom' (of God or of heaven)? See, for instance, the NEB renderings of Lk. 19:11, 12, 15; 22:29; 23:42; Jn. 18:36; Rev. 1:9; 11:15; 12:10; 17:12. What is the relation of Jesus to 'the kingdom of God'?

2. Consider the inauguration of the kingdom in Christ's first advent and its future consummation at His second as two aspects of His *single* work of redemption, and show how the latter is the realization and unveiling of the former.

BIBLIOGRAPHY

J. Calvin, *Institutes*, Book II, chapters xv–xvi.
N. Dimock, *Our One Priest on High*, Longmans, 1910.
G. E. Ladd, *Jesus and the Kingdom*, SPCK, 1966.
H. B. Swete, *The Ascended Christ*, Macmillan, 1910.
A. J. Tait, *The Heavenly Session of our Lord*, Robert Scott, 1912.

THE DOCTRINE OF THE ATONEMENT

If the student has insufficient time for an attempt to master the other important sections of Christian doctrine, let him, at least, have a firm grasp of this, which is the very heart and core of the faith. Again the author would urge careful examination of the actual words of Scripture and a refusal to enter into any theorizing until these have been examined properly. Certain superficial views could never have gained currency had both theologians and the man in the pew read more fully and compared more carefully the actual words of Scripture. Some theories are false to the very genius of Christianity, and betray a sad lack of appreciation even of the actual teaching of the Jewish faith, which is supposed to explain many of the elements which the theorist wishes summarily to dismiss. On the other hand, truly devout and loyal minds have been guilty of inadequate illustrations of the profound truth behind the doctrine, and of exaggerated statements which are based on an equally superficial understanding of the immensity of the issues involved. In particular, much confusion exists concerning the nature of divine justice and the ethics of the redemptive act. Inconsequent police-court illustrations and thoughtless reiteration of certain phrases have given the impression, to those who have missed the profoundest truth which underlies the atoning sacrifice, that evangelical Christians have developed preposterous beliefs. It would be a mercy for Christendom if the phraseology of many enthusiasts could be purged of inaccuracy, so that the glory of the atoning sacrifice would not be prejudiced in the minds of many earnest seekers.

1. The Evangelical View Stated

The simplest expression of the evangelical view may be given in some such words as the following. The supreme mission of the Son of God was the redemption of man by a life of perfect obedience which culminated in 'one offering of himself once offered', and which constituted 'a full, perfect, and sufficient sacrifice, oblation, and satisfaction, for the sins of the whole world'.[1] While our Lord's death can and ought to be regarded as *exemplary*, that is, as the supreme example of obedience to the will of God, and *representative*, that is, as being that of the federal Head of the new race of men who, realizing their failure under the old covenant, find life and power in the new covenant given in His blood, yet no doctrine of the cross of Christ is adequate to the comprehensiveness of the full scriptural statement which does not present the even deeper fact that our Lord's death was in the nature of a *propitiation*. The adjectives usually applied to this further consideration (which is most clearly taught in Scripture) are those such as 'propitiatory', 'vicarious', 'substitutionary'.

The terms which are used in reproach of this doctrine, such as 'the penal view', are in themselves too ambiguous to clarify the issues on the subject, and frequently reveal a misunderstanding of what is being suggested by those who believe in propitiation. At the same time it is only

---

[1] From the Communion Service, Book of Common Prayer.

fair to state that, in rejecting the evangelical view, numerous modern theologians are aware that there is much still unaccounted for by their theories of the death of Christ, and that this 'something' which 'is in some way connected with human sin' is often acknowledged, whatever alternative phraseology may be used.

Evangelical Christians have the right fearlessly to contend that 'this something', this deeper mystery of the Saviour's death, is the crowning wonder of the grace of God, the most superb gesture of the Godhead to men, and the very heart of Christianity. To them their Saviour's death offered to God a complete satisfaction and atonement for their sin and alone could open the way for the reconciliation which has transformed their lives.

> Jesus, the sinner's Friend,
>   We hide ourselves in Thee;
> God looks upon Thy sprinkled blood,
>   It is our only plea.
>
> He hears Thy precious name;
>   We claim it as our own.
> The Father must accept and bless
>   His well-beloved Son.

2. Scriptural Illustrations

Before attempting to construct any theory, the reader is requested to observe the constant plea of this book to examine the expressions in Scripture and its own illustrations of the doctrine. If this be done with the help, for example, of the section on Scripture references, little support will be found for such shallow contentions as that the evangelical view of the atonement is found only in the Pauline Epistles. It will also shatter the objection that no trace of it is found in our Lord's own teaching.

a. New Testament Terms

The terms employed in the New Testament concerning the priestly office of our Lord are stated without interpretation, and it is a legitimate inference that words such as 'sacrifice', 'shedding of blood', 'propitiation', 'ransom' are to be construed consistently with those of the Old Testament. It is a well-known rule of interpretation, often neglected in practice, that the best explanation of a writer's meaning is found in the literary and religious atmosphere in which he had been trained. It is this fact, apart from any theory of inspiration, that makes the Old Testament so important in interpreting the New Testament.

b. Old Testament Illustrations

In Genesis and Exodus biographical descriptions are provided, many of which have as their turning-points the building of an altar and acts of sacrifice. Similarly, Israel was delivered from Egypt by a method which seems clearly to suggest a symbolism attaching to the Passover.

Two conceptions are plainly discernible. First, redemption is connected with the shedding of blood, and secondly, there is a form of substitution in the use of animal victims. These conceptions are worked out in fuller detail in the book of Leviticus, and are extensively illustrated in the instructions for the sacrifices and priesthood. Most of the subsequent Old Testament books have references and sometimes whole passages based upon these two principles. They are fundamental to the whole volume.

Our Lord plainly intended His teaching to be consistent with them (see the Scripture references below), and the Epistles, not only of Paul, but also those of John and Peter and the Epistle to the Hebrews, declare that our Lord's death was the consummation and fulfilment of the Old Testament teaching of the sacrifices.

3. The Meaning of the Word 'Atonement'

The English word 'atonement' is not a strict translation of the Hebrew word used in the Old Testament, which means 'to cover'. The Middle English words 'atone' and 'atonement' have been borrowed, bringing with them the idea of 'reconciliation', a thought which has been developed by Christian usage into a fuller conception, which may be described as 're-conciliation with God in Jesus Christ'. Trench, in his book *Synonyms of the New Testament*,[1] has very valuable remarks on this point.

Adhering strictly to the Hebrew usage, the Old Testament teaching through the words used may be given as: 'The animal sacrifices, if accompanied by faith in the offerer, made a *covering* for sin', that is, sin was covered from God's sight so that it no longer invited the reaction of His wrath. Both Old Testament and New Testament state plainly that God had no real pleasure in animal sacrifices, except in so far as they were to the penitent sinner who brought them a true symbol of his faith in the pardoning love of God. It must be considered that the prophets who spoke so much against a mere external observance of sacrifice were themselves observers of the customary ritual. Some of them were priests. This is often overlooked.

In the New Testament the chief Greek words used are *thysia* (sacrifice); *hilasmos* (propitiation); *katallagē* (reconciliation); *prosphora* (offering); *apolytrōsis* (redemption); *lytron* (ransom). The Bible student should examine them carefully in their contexts. Those who have no knowledge

[1] R. C. Trench, *Synonyms of the New Testament* (Macmillan, 1871).

of the original language may do this by means of Young's *Analytical Concordance*. The appropriate sections in James Denney's *The Death of Christ* and Leon Morris's *The Apostolic Preaching of the Cross* should also be studied.

Even after taking into full consideration the usages of several of these words in classical Greek, and giving full weight to all objections regarding what may be 'read into' them, it is difficult to escape the conviction that the New Testament authors were fundamentally unanimous in their views of the importance of the death of Christ. It may, surely, be claimed that our Lord's own teaching and the apostolic view fully endorse the two Old Testament conceptions which we have already noticed. Remission of sin has as its basis the shedding of blood (*our Lord's own blood*) and there is need for propitiation; there is also a process of substitution whereby our Lord acts on our behalf in the transaction of our redemption. It is significant that our Lord was born into a nation possessing this elaborate sacrificial conception purified from ancient Semitic perversions.

4. The Theology of the Atonement

There is a tendency for man in approaching a divine provision to regard it entirely from his own standpoint and to lose sight of the fact that God has His sovereign claims in all matters concerning man and the world. It is easy to forget the Godward side of the atonement.[1]

a. The Godward Aspect

1. Towards God, the atonement is the supreme event in the world's history. It has for Him a special significance which may be described as giving Him 'pleasure'. In this connection the emphasis is chiefly on the perfect obedience of Christ—even 'to the death of the cross'. It was the first time that God's will had in entirety been 'done on earth as it is in heaven'.

2. It demonstrated God's attributes of righteousness and love. It is not always fully observed that the Scriptures give no hint of conflict between God's attributes. His justice and His love are not in any way opposed. The remission of sins is as much derived from His *justice* as His love. At Calvary 'Mercy and truth are met together; righteousness and peace have kissed each other' (Ps. 85:10, A v).

3. It vindicated God as the Lawgiver. The moral wrong committed by the sinner in defiance of the law is a stain on the honour of the Lawgiver. Our Lord's perfect obedience, extending even to voluntary sub-

---

[1] The writer would earnestly advise the student to read at least one book dealing with this aspect, such as *The Death of Christ*, by James Denney (ed. R. V. G. Tasker, Tyndale Press, 1951); *The Atonement*, by R. W. Dale (Congregational Union, 1878); or *Why the Cross?* by H. E. Guillebaud (IVF, 1946).

mission to death, vindicated the Lawgiver. At the cross He assumed our 'legal liability', and gave full satisfaction to the Upholder of the moral laws of the universe.

4. It secured a satisfactory basis for the remission of sins. Those who ask for a pardoning mercy in God, apart from a completely satisfying basis for such pardon, can have little understanding either of the nature of God's holiness or of the heinousness of sin. Any view of the atonement which omits to indicate that the work of Christ was in the nature of a satisfaction which fully met all God's claims against the sinner is inadequate when compared with scriptural descriptions.

It is necessary to be accurate concerning the nature of this 'satisfaction'. The work of Christ is not merely a substitute for an equivalent unfulfilled work of the sinner. It has in itself an intrinsic value which, when once God has accepted it on behalf of a sinner, entirely removes his legal liability. The value of Christ's sacrifice consisted in the infinite worth of His own Person. The scriptural view is not satisfied by mere descriptions of the 'innocent suffering for the guilty' and similar half-truths on which the true doctrine of the atonement has often been rejected. It is nearer to Scripture (whilst guarding against patripassianism[1]) to say that, in view of the nearness to God of the beloved Son, the atonement was God *accepting in His own person* the result of man's wrong-doing (Heb. 9:13, 14). The law's claims being fully satisfied, He will not bring the justified man into judgment for those same offences. This view is abundantly supported and illustrated in the Old Testament sacrifices, *etc.*

b. The Manward Aspect

Many of the views expressed by writers who approach the subject from the manward aspect are inadequate, if they are to be accepted as the full explanation. The view that our Lord went to the cross in order to demonstrate in the most striking of ways the supremacy of God's love is true to the Scriptures, but does not begin to explain the vast bulk of scriptural references, which alone portray that demonstration in its true character. It has been remarked by the critics of an unbalanced presentation of this fact that a demonstration of love, such as a heedless rushing into the same danger by a would-be rescuer, does not effect anything, save to awaken a sentimental reaction in the onlookers. In any case, the problem of sin and guilt remains unrelieved.

The only subjective view which Scripture fully supports is that this supreme demonstration of God's love towards us should lead to a realization of the intense loathing which the holy nature of God has for sin. It

[1] A form of modalism (*i.e.*, the belief that the Father, Son and Holy Spirit are all modes or aspects of the one God) which taught that it was God *the Father* who *suffered* on the cross, for 'the Father' and 'the Son'are just two names for one Person.

should result in repentance towards God and faith towards our Lord Jesus Christ.

c. The Exegetical Approach

Those who have access to a copy of Hodge's *Systematic Theology* should take the time to study this doctrine by means of the grouping and careful exegesis of the relevant Scriptures which the author gives. He suggests three groups, and the following leading ideas:

1. *Christ saves men as a Priest*. See the Epistle to the Hebrews and similar passages.

(i) A priest is a representative and substitute acting on behalf of men. He is authorized to secure reconciliation between God and men.

(ii) This reconciliation can be effected only by means of an expiation for sin.

(iii) The expiation in the Old Testament was by means of a substituted victim.

(iv) But God had no pleasure in the animal sacrifices; they were but temporary illustrations of the one true sacrifice.

(v) Christ became man in order to be our High Priest and to effect reconciliation for the sins of the people.

(vi) He did not offer the mere blood of animals, but His own most precious blood. He was a substitutionary victim of infinite moral worth.

(vii) By this one sacrifice He has perfected for ever them that are sanctified. This sacrifice has superseded all others. No other is needed; and no other is possible (Heb. 10:14).

2. *Christ saves men as a Sacrifice*. See the book of Leviticus, Isaiah 53, and the references to sacrifice in the New Testament (*e.g.*, Rom. 3:25). It would seem to be clear that:

(i) The design of such offerings was to propitiate God.

(ii) This propitiation was secured by the expiation of guilt. (In the Old Testament the sin was 'covered' from justice.)

(iii) This expiation was effected by vicarious punishment, the victim being substituted for the offender.

(iv) The effect of such sin offerings was the pardon of the offender and his restoration.

It can scarcely be disputed on exegetical grounds that the plain teaching of the New Testament is that the death of Christ was a sacrifice and offering for sin in the fullest sense of the above remarks.

3. *Christ saves men as a Redeemer*. Compare, for example, the Epistles to the Galatians and Romans and the kinsman-redeemer passages of the Old Testament. Christ is said to redeem from:

(i) The penalty of the law (*e.g.*, Gal. 3:13).
(ii) Even the law's obligations (*e.g.*, Gal. 4:4, 5, and Rom. 6:14).
(iii) The power of sin (*e.g.*, Tit. 2:14; 1 Pet. 1:18, 19).
(iv) The power of Satan (*e.g.*, Acts 26:18; Heb. 2:14, 15).
(v) The wrath to come (1 Thes. 1:10).

The thought of 'buying back' from under bondage is prominent in many Scriptures.

5. Objections to the Doctrine

Briefly, the objections which have been raised against the above views of the atonement may be divided into three categories:

a. Ethical

The 'ethics' of the atonement have been called in question. Some have gone so far as to call God's permitting our Lord to die for sin, with all that is connected with the word 'substitute', an 'immoral act' on His part. This is frequently based on a crude and inaccurate paraphrase of the doctrine under some such description as 'the innocent suffering for the guilty'. While the phrase is correct on any theory, yet the element of necessary connection between the innocent and the guilty is too frequently overlooked. The Sufferer must have a double connection between God and Himself on the one hand and the sinner and Himself on the other. The term 'legal fiction', so often heard, ignores this factor in the scriptural approach.

Some critical arguments betray the shallowest possible conception of the nature of sin, and others a quite grotesque misunderstanding of the actual constituents of the evangelical view (yet sometimes, unfortunately, based on the careless use of inadequate illustrations by well-meaning but ill-instructed Christians). In stating these views, certain words are unfairly employed which stigmatize the evangelical doctrine at the start with asserting what, in point of fact, it does not assert.

It may be well to point out that the ethic of sacrifice always involves the innocent in some sense suffering for the guilty.

The only objections which can properly be made to the evangelical doctrine, as stated above, are those which are exegetical in origin. If an alternative interpretation can be given which fully satisfies the groups of scriptural passages referred to above, it must be carefully examined. In practice, the critics approach from the direction of their preconceived notions of what God *ought to have done* and their own superficial ethical standards.

b. Theological

Some theological writers have glossed over the atonement and substituted other doctrines and other points in our Lord's life as the centre of Christianity. For example, in spite of the 'sacrifice' of the Mass, the incarnation is in practice the pivot of the Roman Catholic system of teaching. It is also the central point in much of modern Protestant teaching. The objection is raised that the facts of the atonement were overemphasized by the divines of the past three centuries, and that Evangelicals have exalted it out of all proportion to its place in the scheme of biblical doctrine.

The reader is invited to examine the relative frequency of mention of the cardinal doctrines and the space which they occupy in the pages of Scripture. It is unassailable that the death of Christ is the very heart of Christianity.

c. Scientific

The two chief objections from this source are:

1. Man is so small, and the universe so vast, that it is inconceivable that God's Son should die for such insignificant creatures. The Psalmist voiced the same wonder: 'What is man that thou art mindful of him, and the son of man that thou dost care for him?' It is easily demonstrable that size is not a final criterion of value, even in the affairs of men.

The truth of the statement stands, or falls, with the truth of the whole Christian revelation, which, viewed from any standpoint, is a source of wonder to the mind of man. In the words of the children's hymn:

> It is a thing most wonderful,
>   Almost too wonderful to be,
> That God's own Son should come from heaven
>   And die to save a child like me.

> And yet we know that it is true:
>   He came to this poor world below,
> And wept, and toiled, and mourned, and died,
>   Only because He loved us so.

2. If certain evolutionary hypotheses are true, the Christian absolutes of right and wrong have no basis in fact, and there is no such thing as the guilt of sin necessitating an atonement. This reasoning is very curious. In the first place, such evolutionary hypotheses in the sphere of man's moral and theological values are not based on a shred of fact. They are as abstract and as much the product of philosophy as the above objection suggests the Christian claim to be. Even supposing the hypotheses were supported by accurately observed scientific facts, it in no way follows that God could not have instituted an absolute standard at some period of human development. 'The law-giving of Sinai could quite well have taken

place as soon as man was first able to perceive between right and wrong. In fact, this contention might legitimately be taken to increase man's responsibility—for, if man has evolved to the point of acknowledging law, he is responsible to attain, or nearly to attain, unto it, and since he is not handicapped by the results of a fall, there seems no excuse for his not doing so.' This, however, really amounts to saying that there has been an evolution of law, but that there never was any law to evolve. It is thus self-contradictory.

6. Some Further Problems

a. Penal Suffering

It is often objected that our Lord's sufferings cannot be described as 'penal' —i.e., partaking of the nature of punishment. In the sense of suffering for His own sins His sufferings cannot, of course, be termed penal. But in the sense of His taking upon Himself the results of the infringed 'legal liabilities' of those for whom He has rendered satisfaction they were penal. While the word 'penal' must be used with care, the scriptural references to 'bearing sin', the Lord 'laying on him our chastisement', Christ being 'made sin', must receive adequate recognition.

b. Equivalence of Punishment

A friend of the author's was astounded at a meeting of Christian students to hear the view propounded that our Lord had received the fullest (i.e., numerically or in intensity) equivalent of punishment for all the actual sins of men from the first man till the end of time!

It should be clearly grasped that it is the *qualitative*, not *quantitative*, values with which Scripture is concerned in its presentation of this subject. Those who fail to understand the infinite value to God of our Lord's mediatorial work must, surely, have a very low opinion of the instrinsic worth of the Son to the Father and a very small appreciation of the stupendous nature of His work.

c. The Limits of the Scope of the Atonement

In other words, 'For whom did Christ die?' For the whole world, or actually only for His church? There has been much theological discussion upon this subject. The Augustinian school of thought (though not St. Augustine himself) suggests that, since God's decrees have been settled from eternity, our Lord's coming and His work had special reference only to the elect. 'Christ loved the church and gave himself up for her.' The opposite school claims that the work of our Lord has equal application to the needs of all mankind.

The question does not concern the nature and efficacy of the atonement. It concerns *the purpose* of His sufferings, the restrictive view claiming that, while His merit was equal to the needs of the whole world, He had definitely in view only those who would believe and receive Him.

It should also be noticed that the problem should not affect the preaching of the gospel. The Augustinian (in his ignorance of those whom God may call) must equally earnestly offer the fruits of the gospel to all to whom he may preach. On the other hand, 'the Anti-Augustinians leave out of view the clearly revealed special love of God to His people; the union of Christ with His chosen; the representative character He assumed as their Substitute; the certain efficacy of His sacrifice in virtue of the covenant of redemption; and the necessary connection between the gift of Christ and the gift of the Holy Spirit' (Hodge).

7. Historical Survey

There have been three main phases in the church's teaching on the atonement:

a. The Early Church

The view chiefly appreciated and enforced by the Fathers was that of man's moral and spiritual renovation by the sacrifice of Christ. They were interested rather in its results than with discussion of its theoretical basis or mode of operation. The more orthodox of the Fathers laid stress on the value of our Lord's divinity in association with His human suffering and death and the unique value of His offering.

On the other hand, in discussing the question of ransom, the curious doctrine of our Lord's paying the ransom-price to the devil was promulgated—*i.e.*, that the sacrifice of our Lord had an element which was in the nature of a discharge of a debt due to the devil before removing man from his thraldom. Dorner gives exhaustive references to this view in his *History of the Doctrine of the Person of Christ*,[1] and decides that it was 'never more than an excrescence' on even patristic theology. Some modern writers both distort and exaggerate it. The rational basis for the theory is that through sin even the devil, as an accuser, has claims on men only discharged fully in view of the sacrifice of Christ.

b. Anselm and the Middle Ages

Anselm's book *Cur Deus Homo* constitutes a landmark in the development of this doctrine. He introduced the idea of the Lord's voluntary discharge of man's obligation to God. He saw that our Lord's death offered to God the full satisfaction of obedience to the divine law and that our Lord's

[1] J. A. Dorner, *History of the Development of the Doctrine of the Person of Christ*, 5 vols. (T. and T. Clark, 1861–63).

merit was more than equal to any obligation which man can possibly incur towards God. Hence, the emphasis came to be placed on man's debt to the Lawgiver, and the guilt of sin came to be measured by the dignity of the Lawgiver.

c. The Reformation

The Reformers were chiefly interested in the legal aspects of the atonement and its relation to their central teaching of justification by faith. Hence, the emphasis was largely on forensic aspects as given in the Epistle to the Romans—*viz.*, since Christ has made propitiation and discharged all our legal liabilities, 'who shall bring any charge against God's elect?'

d. The Modern Period

In recent years there have been many conflicting theories, and some which have sought to explain away the necessity for an expiatory or substitutionary view.

The student is earnestly counselled to be careful not to restrict himself to any one view of so great a subject. There are many facets of truth in this the very heart and genius of the Christian faith. But he is further warned that no grasp of the doctrine is adequate which does not include the following (quoted from Griffith Thomas):

1. The representation of the sinner before God;
2. The substitution of the Saviour for the sinner;
3. The identification of the sinner with his Saviour;
4. The revelation of God in Christ to the sinner.

Scriptures

a. Illustrations and Statements in the Old Testament

1. The Hebrew word *kipper* derives from a root which probably means 'to cover'. But with its cognates it is used figuratively in a similar sense to New Testament words meaning 'to make atonement'. See, *e.g.*, Ex. 30:10, 15; Lv. 1:4; 16:17, 30, 34, *etc.* The word 'atonement' originally meant 'reconciliation' (*cf.* Rom. 5:11, AV), but in modern theology it is used comprehensively of 'man's restoration to God through the sacrificial death of Christ'.

2. Illustrations such as the Passover (Ex. 12:1–28. *Cf.* 1 Cor. 5:6, 7 and 1 Pet. 1:18, 19); the offering of Isaac (Gn. 22); the brazen serpent (Nu. 21:8, 9); kinsman-redeemer (Ru. 3:12, 13; Lv. 25:47–55); ransom (Nu. 3:49. *Cf.* Jb. 33:24).

3. The sacrifices. See Leviticus, the Messianic Psalms (*e.g.*, 22; 40; 69; 118) and such passages as Is. 53; 59:20.

b. The New Testament Statements

Modern theology has tended unnecessarily to contrast the statements in the Epistles with those of the Gospels. There is no opposition, in actual fact, between the two groups of statements. But there is, of necessity, a greater expansion of all doctrines in the Epistles, as our Lord Himself had prophesied (Jn. 16:12).

1. *Gospels and Acts.*—Mt. 1:21; 16:21; 26:26–29; Mk. 9:12, 31; 10:33, 34, 45; 14:22–25; Lk. 1:77; 2:11; 4:18, 19; 9:31, 44; the illustrations of 15; 22:14–22; 24:6–8, 21, 25–27, 44–47; Jn. 1:29; 2:19–22; 3:14–17; 6:33, 48–58; 10:11–18; 12:23–25 and 31–33; 14:30, 31; Acts 2:23; 3:14–19; 13:32–39; 20:28.

2. *Epistles.*—Rom. 3:24–26; 4:25; 5:6–11; 8:3, 32, 34; 14:9, 15; 15:3; 1 Cor. 6:20; 11:23–26; 15:3; 2 Cor. 5:14–21; Gal. 1:3, 4; 2:20; 3:13; 4:4, 5; Eph. 1:7; 5:2, 25; Col. 1:14, 20–22; 2:14, 15; 1 Thes. 5:9, 10; 1 Tim. 1:15; 2:6; Tit. 2:14; Heb. 1:3; 7:27; 9:12–15, 26–28; 1 Pet. 1:18, 19; 2:24; 3:18; 1 Jn. 1:7; 2:2; 3:5; 4:10.

3. *Revelation.*—1:5, 18; 5:6, 9, 12; 7:14; 12:11; 13:8; 22:14.

c. *The New Testament Words*
   (Look up other references for each of these.)
   Offering.—Heb. 10:10, 14.
   Reconciliation.—2 Cor. 5:18, 19; Col. 1:20–22.
   Sacrifice.—1 Cor. 5:7; Heb. 10:12.
   Propitiation.—Rom. 3:25; 1 Jn. 4:10 (AV or RV for both).
   Ransom.—Mt. 20:28; 1 Tim. 2:6.
   Redemption.—Rom. 3:24; Eph. 1:7; Col. 1:14.

The student is recommended, where possible, to study the Greek equivalents of the words given here.

Questions

1. Was the death of Christ an absolute necessity if men are to be saved? Do you think there is any other way of deliverance for man? Give reasons for your answer.

2. Demonstrate from the New Testament that the death of Christ was considered by the apostles of paramount importance in their teaching about Christ.

3. Of what 'theories' of the atonement do you know? Where do you set the limit between what is adequate and what is inadequate?

4. How would you answer the charge that the idea of propitiation divides the Persons of the Trinity?

5. Can we rely on God's compassion apart from the death of Christ? Give your reasons for your answer.

6. Are the words 'propitiation' and 'reconciliation' synonymous? If not, what are the differences in meaning?

7. What types of illustration of the death of Christ are legitimate? Which are not pertinent? Discuss the question as to whether the atonement can be represented adequately in one or more illustrations.

BIBLIOGRAPHY

G. C. Berkouwer, *The Work of Christ*, Eerdmans, 1956.

E. Brunner, *The Mediator*, Lutterworth Press, 1946.

R. W. Dale, *The Atonement*, Congregational Union, 1878.

James Denney, *The Christian Doctrine of Reconciliation*, James Clarke, 1959.

James Denney, *The Death of Christ*, ed. R. V. G. Tasker, Tyndale Press, 1951.

P. T. Forsyth, *The Cruciality of the Cross*, Independent Press, 1948.

R. S. Franks, *The Work of Christ*, Nelson, 1962.

L. Morris, *The Apostolic Preaching of the Cross*, Tyndale Press, 1965.

L. Morris, *The Cross in the New Testament*, Eerdmans, 1964.

A. M. Stibbs, *The Meaning of the Word 'Blood' in Scripture*, Tyndale Press, 1954.

PART FIVE

THE PERSON OF THE HOLY SPIRIT

1. His Personal Being

Subject to the limitations in the uses of the word, which were discussed under the section on the Being of God, 'personality' is to be attributed to the Holy Spirit. Much current theological writing conveys the impression that the author subconsciously views the Holy Spirit merely as a diffuse 'influence' in the church. The terms which are used concerning Him imply a vagueness of thought and a lack of appreciation of the unique blessings to be derived from our Lord's gift of His Spirit which seem inexcusable. It may be true that the mediaeval theologians did not give this immense subject the attention which it deserves, but that provides little explanation for the modern neglect and misunderstanding of the divine Spirit's nature and work.

Some writers have taken the view that the Spirit is a divine 'mode of action'—i.e., that scriptural references to 'the Spirit' may be simply symbolic expressions for an action of God in a spiritually creative manner. The Greek word translated 'Spirit' is the same as that for 'breath', and its gender is neuter. On this and similar considerations are based the views of the impersonality of the Holy Spirit. Those contexts of the Old Testament references to the Spirit where His work, rather than His Person, is the object of the writer's allusions are further claimed to support these views.

On the other hand, it is difficult to explain some of the New Testament references (among them some very direct ones by our Lord Himself) on any basis other than that of equality in His personal nature with the Father and the Son. Consider the following:

1. The titles given to Him, such as 'the Spirit of God'; 'the Holy Spirit of God'; 'the Holy Spirit whom you have from God'; 'the Spirit of his Son'; 'the Spirit of Christ'.

2. While His work and influence, being the result of His presence, are not rigidly separated in Scripture, there appears to be a definiteness implied by emphatic uses of the article, *the Spirit*, and at other times with the accompanying adjective 'Holy' (see Acts 2:4). His influences are more usually expressed symbolically—fire, water, oil, anointing and sealing.

3. The key passage is that of our Lord's discourse recorded in John

14-16. Here is given the Holy Spirit's most prominent official title, 'the Paraclete' ('Advocate'—so NEB). Having described His own intercessory work, our Lord promises 'another Advocate', and the context unmistakably demonstrates that this Advocate is a Person. In 14:26 and 15:26 our Lord's use of the masculine personal pronoun ('He', *ekeinos*) can scarcely describe a mere influence. See also 16:7-15.

4. Elsewhere in the New Testament we find references to 'lying against' the Holy Spirit and 'grieving' the Holy Spirit, *etc.*, which clearly indicate a personal Being (Acts 5:3; Eph. 4:30).

5. The descriptions of His work, His relation to us, and references to His manifestations all imply intelligence, will, individual subsistence, *etc.*—in short, all the characteristics of personal Being.

2. His Deity

The chief reasons for belief in the proper deity of the Spirit of God are:

1. In the Old Testament, all that is implied of the Being of Jehovah is also implied of the One who is called the 'Spirit of Jehovah'.

2. In the New Testament, words which are quoted from Old Testament contexts which describe the speaker as 'Jehovah' are cited as having been said by the Spirit.

3. Our Lord speaks of an 'unpardonable sin', which consists in dishonouring, and blasphemy spoken against, the Holy Spirit. It is asserted that this is even a worse form of blasphemy than 'blasphemy against the Son of man', a strong evidence that it is regarded as the act of discrediting a divine Person.

4. The New Testament references to the Spirit would be equally befitting of the other Persons of the Trinity. For example, He is the source of enlightenment, the teacher, the sanctifier and an object of worship. In the baptismal formula He is on an equality with Father and Son. The Christian's body is described as a 'temple' for the Spirit.

There has been comparatively little divergence of opinion upon the subject of the Spirit's deity. The early church for several centuries was undisturbed by discussions of the subject until there arose the Pneumatomachi ('fighters against the Spirit') in the second half of the fourth century. Their denials of the divinity of the Holy Spirit were countered in the expanded form of the Nicene Creed, in which the following was added to the credal statements concerning the Holy Spirit:

'The Lord, the Life-Giver, that proceeds from the Father, that with the Father and Son is together worshipped and together glorified.'

This formula was finally adopted by the Council of Chalcedon. It will be helpful to examine closely the words used.

a. 'The Lord, the Life-Giver'

This title from the Nicene Creed, one of the most beautiful descriptions of the Spirit, is not actually in the words of Scripture. But the truth expressed can be abundantly supported from Scripture which on numerous occasions indicates that creative activity and the convicting and awakening of the soul which is dead in sin are the work of the Spirit, and that the implanting of the new life in Christ is an operation of the Spirit. Notice, for example, such phrases as 'born of the Spirit' (Jn. 3:5–8) and 'live by the Spirit' (Gal. 5:25).

It is important, however, to notice that the Spirit of God is the imparter of the life and not the life Himself. Scripture makes it very clear that life for the sinner is to be found in Christ alone and it is the reception of Christ which brings him life eternal. But it is equally clear that the act of regeneration and the constant mediation of the new life in Christ is the work of the Holy Spirit.

b. 'Proceeds from the Father . . .'

The phrase comes from John 15:26, which has given rise to the definition of the Spirit's relationship to the Father (and the Son; see below) as 'procession' (cf. the 'generation' of the Son). The fact of the Spirit's procession is implicit rather than explicit in Scripture, but verses which speak of the Spirit as sent from or by the Father and/or the Son (Jn. 14:16, 26; 15:26; 16:7; 20:22; Acts 2:33; Gal. 4:4, 6) imply the subordination of the Spirit to the Father and the Son expressed by these words. We must remember that both 'generation' and 'procession' denote not a coming into being but an *eternal relationship* within the Trinity. This subordinate relation appears mostly when the Spirit's function is depicted in terms of serving the Father and the Son.

c. '. . . Filioque'

The addition of the word *Filioque* ('and from the Son') to the Nicene Creed at the Council of Toledo (AD 589) has been the occasion of much controversy. The Western church (largely through the influence of Augustine) made the insertion, in order to prevent the loss of the plain scriptural teaching that the Spirit is as much the 'Spirit of Christ' (which is one of His scriptural titles) as of the Father. The Eastern church has consistently refused this insertion because it is considered to weaken the doctrine of subordination, to which reference has already been made, constituting our Lord a separate 'fount of deity'. (The Greek word would be *Archē*.) Also the Greek church refers to the decision of Ephesus that no addition to the Nicene Creed is permissible. But in reply to this latter objection it is pointed out that our present Nicene Creed differs in several important points from the Creed to which reference is made in the decree of Ephesus. The union of Father and Son in 'sending' the Spirit really makes against any idea of differentiation which would mar the inner harmony of the divine Triad. The Spirit is the unifying bond proceeding alike from Father and Son. It is in accordance with this conception that He becomes also the bond between Christ and His church and between individual believers, knitting them together into 'the mystical body'.

Scripture seems clearly to state that, while the Spirit proceeds from the Father, He was also 'given' by the Son to His church and that He is as much the Spirit of Christ as the Spirit of God. (See the Scripture references below.)

3. The Scriptural Names for the Spirit

It is only from the Christian revelation that knowledge can be derived on this subject, and only revelation from God can make it at all intelligible to us. It is necessary to adhere closely to Scripture in all thought and discussion concerning the Persons of the Holy Trinity.

The student should consider whether importance is to be attached to the differences of title which are to be found chiefly in the New Testament. We have, for example, 'Spirit' (*pneuma*), without the article, chiefly used of the operation of the Spirit; 'the Spirit' (*to pneuma*), with the article, a more personal designation; and 'the Holy Spirit'. This latter phrase appears to imply a clearly personal Being. In the Old Testament we have such titles as 'the Spirit of Jehovah', 'the Spirit of God' and 'the Spirit of wisdom'.

In the New Testament such titles as 'the Spirit of Christ', 'the Spirit of the living God', 'the Spirit of truth', 'the eternal Spirit', 'the Holy Spirit of promise', 'the Spirit of grace' and 'of glory', *etc.* appear. His distinctive official title is 'the Paraclete' (or 'Advocate'). Note also the symbols used in connection with His Person and ministry.

The main aspects of scriptural teaching about the Spirit relate to His personal Being, His deity, His intimacy with the Person of our Lord, and His office as the Executor of the Godhead. The student should notice in this connection that the Creeds include the church and the forgiveness of sins, *etc.*, in the clause concerning the Holy Spirit. See pp. 133ff.

4. Historical Survey

a. The Early Church

There was generally a simple belief in the plain scriptural statements. But theological writers show many inconsistencies in their writing on the nature and operations of the Spirit. What seems to have caused them most difficulty was the scriptural practice of ascribing the same operations sometimes to the Father, sometimes to the Son, and then to the Spirit. For instance, the Spirit is sometimes confused with the Son of God prior to His incarnation.

The Arians regarded the Spirit as a created being, and divine only by virtue of His having been willed into existence by the Son. This partly explains the repugnance of the Eastern church to the 'Filioque' clause.

b. From the Council of Nicaea to the Council of Toledo

The Council of Nicaea was primarily concerned with the doctrine of the second Person of the Trinity. Athanasius subsequently taught more fully concerning the third Person, particularly as to His personal nature. The heresy of the Pneumatomachi (and perhaps others, opponents of Athanasius) at length necessitated more explicit statements in the Nicene Creed concerning the deity of the Spirit (see pp. 129f.). These rulings were confirmed by the Council of Chalcedon.

As described above (pp. 130f.), the Western church at Toledo added to the Latin Creed the 'Filioque' clause—viz., that the Spirit proceeds from the Son as well as from the Father, but this seems to have been at first an error in reading.

c. The Reformation

The rediscovery of the unique and essential work of the Holy Spirit in the church and in the individual was one of the greatest bequests of the Reformation divines. The emphasis was, if anything, on His work rather than upon abstract problems concerning His Person. The chief controversy of the period centred around His operation upon the individual in the application of the gospel (His 'effectual call', in relation to a man's 'freedom'). This problem is still unsolved.[1]

d. Modern Period

In modern times there have been two opposite tendencies. Among the more liberal schools of thought (e.g., in Germany) there has been widespread teaching which regards the Spirit as impersonal, 'the Christian consciousness', or 'mind', in spiritual matters. On the conservative side there have been movements (sometimes, in untrained hands, going to unbalanced extremes) to re-emphasize the fact of the Spirit's personal Being and to awaken the church to a practical experience of His work, particularly that of sanctification.

There is a special need today for attention to His function as the Interpreter of the sacred Scriptures.

[1] See the section on 'God's Eternal Purpose and Human Freedom', pp. 86ff.

Scriptures

1. *Deity.*—The principal passages are Mt. 28:19 and 2 Cor. 13:14, where the Spirit is associated with the other Persons of the Trinity. For further indirect evidence see Mt. 12:31, 32; Acts 5:3, 4, 9; 1 Cor. 2:9–11; 2 Cor. 3:18; Eph. 4:4–6.

2. *Procession.*—In addition to the verses listed on p. 56, *cf.* the implications of Lk. 24:49; Jn. 16:13–15; Acts 16:6, 7; Rom. 8:9; Phil. 1:19; 1 Pet. 1:11, 12.

3. *He is a Person.*—Jn. 14:26; Acts 11:12; Rom. 8:16; Gal. 4:6; 1 Pet. 1:11. Only a person can be spoken of as 'saying' (Acts 8:29, *etc.*), 'forbidding' and 'not allowing' (Acts 16:6, 7), 'making' (*i.e.*, appointing; Acts 20:28), *etc.*

4. *Scriptural Designations.*—Rom. 8:26, 27; 1 Jn. 5:6–8. He is called 'the Spirit' (1 Cor. 2:10), 'the Spirit of God' (Rom. 8:14), 'the Spirit of Christ' (Rom. 8:9), 'the Spirit of the Son of God' (Gal. 4:6), 'the Holy Spirit' ('Paraclete') (Lk. 11:13; Jn. 14:26).

Questions

1. What in your judgment, are the principal grounds for believing (*a*) in the 'personality' of the Holy Spirit and (*b*) in His deity?

2. Have you any reason for differentiating between 'the Spirit of God' in the Old Testament and 'the Holy Spirit' of the New Testament? What is the meaning of John 7:39?

3. Summarize our Lord's teaching about the Holy Spirit in John 14–16.

4. Are there any differences from, or additions to, what our Lord taught concerning the Holy Spirit in (*a*) the Acts of the Apostles, (*b*) the Pauline Epistles?

BIBLIOGRAPHY

James Buchanan, *The Office and Work of the Holy Spirit*, Banner of Truth, 1966.

A. Kuyper, *The Work of the Holy Spirit*, Funk and Wagnalls, 1900.

G. Campbell Morgan, *The Spirit of God*, H. E. Walter, 1953.

L. Morris, *Spirit of the Living God*, IVF, 1960.

G. Smeaton, *The Doctrine of the Holy Spirit*, Banner of Truth, 1959.

A. M. Stibbs and J. I. Packer, *The Spirit Within You*, Hodder, 1967.

H. B. Swete, *The Holy Spirit in the New Testament*, Macmillan, 1909.

W. H. Griffith Thomas, *The Holy Spirit of God*, Eerdmans, 1955.

THE WORK OF THE HOLY SPIRIT

1. The Divine Executor

The importance of a correct view of the work of the Holy Spirit may become apparent to the reader from the following review of His functions. For all practical purposes the individual Christian needs to learn to regard the Spirit as the Executor of the counsels and purposes of the Godhead. In other words, whatever God may purpose to do, He completes through the Spirit's agency.

The functions as the divine Executor are as follows:

a. In Relation to Christ

1. He is revealed in the New Testament as 'the Spirit of Christ'.

2. He mediates Christ to the church and to the individual—*i.e.*, He is instrumental in the manifestation of Christ to men (Jn. 16:14).

b. In Relation to the Scriptures

1. He is the Inspirer of the Scriptures (see Acts 1:16; 2 Tim. 3:16; 1 Pet. 1:11; and other references below). And since He has been active in the production of the Scriptures, we may also trace His providential care in the preservation of the biblical books in the history of the church.

2. He is the Interpreter of Scripture to the Christian understanding. In this sense, He gives them a contemporary voice, as it were, and helps us to apply them to our need each time we reverently seek His aid. Care must be taken, however, to avoid the mistake of assuming that 'an inward illumination' can do violence to grammatical and historical consistency. The Spirit makes plain the meaning that is already in the Word.

c. In Relation to Nature and the World of Men

1. The control of the material universe and of the ordinary processes of nature, and the source of all natural life are ascribed to the Spirit (Ps. 104:29, 30; *cf.* Is. 32:14, 15).

2. He is responsible for witnessing of Christ to the world and 'convincing of sin, righteousness, and judgment' (Jn. 16:8–11).

d. In Relation to the Church

1. He is the true '*vicarius Christi*' (to use Tertullian's phrase) in the church.

2. He imparts and controls the exercise of our Lord's gifts to His church.

3. He is the Dynamic of the church, supplying the divine energies which alone enable the church to fulfil her mission.

e. In Relation to the Individual

1. 'The Lord the Life-Giver' awakens the sinner's sleeping conscience, gives 'the effectual call', imparts 'saving faith', and is the divine Agent in the whole process of his regeneration.

2. The Christian's communion with God and power for prayer are dependent upon the Spirit of God (*e.g.*, see Rom. 8:26, 27).

3. He is the Agent in the transformation of character and in the sanctification of the individual and the church (see Rom. 8).

Scriptures

The Divine Executor (vitally concerned in the life, death and resurrection of Christ): Mt. 12:28; Lk. 1:35; 2:25–27; 3:21, 22; 4:1, 14, 18, 19; Rom. 1:4; Heb. 9:14.

a. In Relation to Christ

1. The gift dependent upon the ascension and glorification of Christ: Jn. 7:39; 16:7; Acts 2:33.

2. He glorifies Christ: Jn. 15:26; 16:8–11, 14; Acts 5:32; 1 Cor. 12:3; 1 Jn. 4:2; 5:6–8.

3. He is the 'Spirit of Christ': Gal. 4:6; 1 Pet. 1:11.

b. In Relation to Scripture

1. Inspirer: Acts 4:25; Heb. 3:7; 10:15; 2 Pet. 1:21. *Cf.* Lk. 1:41, 42, 67, *etc.*

2. Interpreter: *cf.* Jn. 14:17; 16:12–15; 1 Cor. 2:9–13; Heb. 9:8; 2 Pet. 1:20, 21.

c. In Relation to the World

1. The Creator: Gn. 1:2; Jb. 33:4; Ps. 104:30.

2. Convicts men: Jn. 16:8–11.

d. In Relation to the church

1. The constitution of the church: Acts 2:1–4, 18; 4:31–33; 1 Cor. 3:16; 12:12, 13; Eph. 2:22.

2. Author of the gifts in the church: 1 Cor. 12:4–13; Eph. 4:3, 4; Heb. 2:4.

e. In Relation to the Individual Christian

1. New birth: Jn. 3:5, 6, 8; Rom. 8:9–11; 1 Cor. 12:13; Tit. 3:5. *Cf.* 1 Cor. 12:3.

2. He imparts revelation and faith: 1 Cor. 2:9–14; Eph. 3:5. *Cf.* 1 Cor. 2:4, 5.

3. Sanctification: see, *e.g.*, Rom. 8:2–4, 13; 1 Cor. 6:11; Gal. 5:16–25; 2 Thes. 2:13.

4. Guidance: Acts 8:29; 10:19; 11:12; 16:6, 7; Rom. 8:14; Gal. 5:18.

5. Intercession: Rom. 8:26, 27; Eph. 6:18.

(Note the various symbols used by Scripture of the Spirit of God—*e.g.*, 'Oil', 'Fire'.)

Questions

1. How far do you see the Holy Spirit functioning in the church life of today as He did in the days of the apostles? Does He still bestow all His 'gifts' (1 Cor. 12:4–11) in the church? Give careful reasons for your answer.

2. Does the Holy Spirit remain with or in the Christian, or does He visit him intermittently? Give Scripture for your reply.

3. How may the Holy Spirit be 'grieved' (Eph. 4:30)?

4. In what sense is the Holy Spirit our Lord's 'deputy' or 'representative'? What is the meaning of the word 'Paraclete' in Jn. 14:16, 26; 15:26; 16:7?

2. God's Approach to the Sinner

a. The Need of Grace

In the words of Article X of the Church of England, 'The condition of man after the fall of Adam is such, that he cannot turn and prepare himself, by his own natural strength and good works, to faith and calling upon God.' This represents the Augustinian view.[1] Put into other words, the Article teaches that while man is regarded as possessing freedom, he yet lacks the power to perform God's will. The same thought is expressed in the collects. 'We have no power of ourselves to help ourselves' and therefore 'without Thee we are unable to please Thee'. This would appear to be in conformity with the scriptural presentation of the subject.

Much controversy has raged around the question of whether a man can prepare himself to approach God and can co-operate with Him in the process of his redemption, or whether the initiative must always be on the side of God. The Pelagians, Semi-Pelagians, and similar schools of thought in more modern times have placed their emphasis on the human free will and, as a result, taught that man was free to turn to God when he so chose. The chief mediaeval development of this view was the doctrine of grace *de congruo*, which was, briefly, that man was free to turn to God and that this effort to please God made it congruous with His divine nature to afford the necessary assistance to enable the sinner to turn to Him. This assistance was not actually merited, but, as it were, invited as a feature of God's goodness and hence was called 'congruous grace'.[2] Augustine (wholly) and Thomas Aquinas (mostly) opposed these views and insisted that the human will needed wholly unmerited grace from God before it could make any movement back towards God. The Reformation divines were almost unanimous in support of this latter doctrine and uncompromisingly stated their conviction of the need of 'prevenient grace' from God.

It is often objected that the usual view of man's freedom is impaired by this latter doctrine and that it ultimately leads to a type of fatalism. For example, an opponent may object that if no man is able to turn and prepare himself to seek after God, then the onus of taking initiative rests upon God and a man cannot be accounted responsible for continuing in his corruption. No complete reconciliation can be attained by the human mind between the divine sovereignty and human freedom, but certain considerations are of importance in connection with this subject. Among them are the following:

1. Under no pretence can man's will be considered 'free' in certain respects. He has always been circumscribed by the limitations of his own nature.

[1] See above, p. 92.   [2] See below, p. 149.

2. When he was unfallen, his will, while being free, was perpetually inclined to do God's will. But since the Fall, man's will has been inclined to self-pleasing.

3. Man's will is vitally bound up with his own nature and he has now come into bondage in his nature.

4. The grace of God will never compel a man to holiness, but God is able to take the initiative and, lifting him above the bondage of his evil nature, to incline his will towards Him, leaving his freedom unimpaired but now directed by the impulse of a new nature. The intent of God's intervening grace is that 'we may have a good will'.[1] The reader is advised to consult a larger work for a full discussion of this difficult yet important subject.

b. 'Prevenient Grace'

'Prevenient' means 'anticipating, predisposing' (compare the older sense of 'prevent'; see Ps. 59:10, AV), and is used by theologians of the grace that 'precedes and prepares' any Godward inclination in man. It describes a special work of the Spirit of God whereby, before there is any human will to good, the Holy Spirit recreates in a man the desire to be reconciled to God and to do His will. Human co-operation is demanded at each subsequent phase of this preparation.

There is a measure in which, on the basis of the atoning sacrifice of Christ, the Holy Spirit strives with all men, restraining the disobedient and attracting the obedient. Man's responsibility now appears chiefly centred in the obligation not to 'quench the Spirit' and to resist His strivings, but freely to co-operate with these divine promptings.

The importance of this doctrine consists in its acknowledgment that redemption from beginning to end is the work of God and that He has in all things taken the initiative in approaching man. 'For God is at work in you, both to will and to work for his good pleasure' (Phil. 2:13).

c. The Effectual Call

It is a matter of common experience that when the Word of God is preached it does not appear to have uniformly the same influence. Some hear and obey, others in varying proportions do not. There are two views as to the reason for this. Some hold that it is to be sought in the hearers themselves, others that there is a difference in the intensity of the accompanying divine influence. The latter view is the Augustinian (Calvinist) position and the one which is commonly held in the English-speaking world. The title given to it is 'the effectual call'. The Augustinian view is

---

[1] If the will could not be redirected through good influences and wider knowledge, then the whole theory of education is destroyed. Freedom is not a movement of heart and mind *in vacuo*.

sometimes represented as if it assigned 'the grounds' on which God's call is based. As a matter of fact, it declines to do this. God's counsel is 'secret to us'. The difference in the hearers may be a condition, but cannot be the complete explanation of the different results of God's call. 'It depends not upon man's will or exertion.'

There is what may be called 'the external call' which is addressed to everyone when the word of God is preached to a congregation. 'Many are called, but few are chosen.' It is plain from the Scriptures that God 'commands all men everywhere to repent', and His invitation in Christ is 'Come to me, *all* who labour and are heavy laden'. No views of the subject of the purposes and decrees of God should hamper the fullest and widest offer of the gospel to everyone. If they do, they are most certainly wrong. In any case, the preacher has no knowledge of who are God's elect and he is simply responsible to preach His message. There is 'common grace' which the Spirit of God exercises in His own way and according to God's inscrutable purposes on the hearts of all men.

In addition to these operations of the divine Spirit there is a special and efficacious influence which is certain in its results on the hearts of men. In the words of the Westminster Confession, 'All those whom God hath predestinated unto life, and those only, He is pleased, in His appointed and accepted time, effectually to call ... renewing their wills, and by His almighty power determining them to that which is good; and effectually drawing them to Jesus Christ; yet so as they come most freely, being made willing by His grace.' This 'effectual calling' is the result of 'the almighty power and grace of God'. That Scripture teaches this, as clearly as it does the fact of 'the eternal purpose' and 'common grace', will be made clear by reference to such verses as Romans 8:30; I Corinthians 1:26–28; 2 Tim. 1:9; Hebrews 3:1; *etc.*

To summarize, we may say that, while Scripture teaches that there is a common call which extends to all mankind and to which man has a responsibility to respond, on the other hand, it also reveals clearly man's need of 'prevenient grace' and of 'the effectual call'. The responsibility of the Christian preacher and personal worker is to 'sow bountifully', for he does 'not know which will prosper, this or that'. These issues God has kept in His own power, leaving to the church the responsibility of preaching the message world-wide and holding individuals who hear it responsible to accept the gospel.

d. Repentance

The process of the awakening and the regeneration of the sinner may be said to take place in three phases.

1. There is a prior movement on the part of God's Holy Spirit. He takes the initiative and gives the call (see above).

2. The operation of the Spirit leads to repentance towards God and saving faith in Christ.

3. The Spirit causes the *new birth* of the individual.

Repentance may be defined as a conviction of guilt brought about by the application by the Holy Spirit of the divine standards resulting in a change of attitude towards God, which proceeds to a change of conduct. Compare John 16:8, He will convict 'the world of sin and of righteousness and of judgment'; 2 Corinthians 7:10, 'Godly grief produces a repentance that leads to salvation'; and Luke 3:8 'Bear fruits that befit repentance.'

True repentance may be regarded as midway between a state of nature and a state of grace. It is a turning from sin and leads on to an act of faith. Faith is to be regarded as the instrument whereby God's provision is made actual in the individual's experience. But there is also in repentance already an element of faith. The sinner believes God's testimony concerning himself. The new element which emerges in 'faith towards our Lord Jesus Christ' is the appropriation of God's saving mercy revealed in His Son.

e. Conversion, Regeneration and New Birth

After repentance and the act of faith (or before them, according to a common view of the initiating work of the Spirit) comes the birth of new life in Christ, though we must not think of a sequence of clearly separated happenings. All may take place very quickly, but it is necessary to be quite clear as to the actual nature of the change from the 'state of nature' to the 'state of grace'.

With regard to the new birth, Christians have come to employ certain terms as synonymous which were originally confined to technical uses. In particular, the word 'regeneration' is frequently the cause of unnecessary debate from its difference of connotation when used by different people.

Even the language of the theological schools has tended to mix the three terms 'conversion', 'regeneration', and 'new birth'. But at certain stages in the history of dogma an attempt has been made to clarify the terms, and this has occasioned further difficulty! Such attempts are represented by the distinctions made between 'conversion' and 'regeneration' and 'regeneration' and 'renovation'. Some regard conversion as the subjective side and regeneration as the objective side of new birth. The first is connected with repentance, that is, with what a man is called upon to do: the second is what God does for him. Others—Waterland, for example—in explaining their doctrine of 'baptismal regeneration', use the term regeneration to indicate the bringing of the child within the sphere of the blessings of the visible church, and the word 'renovation' to describe the essential change when faith is consciously exercised to appropriate the Christian's covenant blessings in Christ.

For the purposes of this volume, the essential points to consider are the necessity for and the nature of the new birth. As for the first, our Lord Himself is conclusive in His discourse to Nicodemus and elsewhere. See, *e.g.*, Matthew 18:3, 'Unless you turn and become like children ...' This necessary transformation is variously described in Scripture: 'You turned to God from idols, to serve a living and true God', 'to all who received him ... he gave power to become children of God', *etc.* The conscious experience differs widely and the time between a definite reception of Christ and its manifestations may vary. It is possible (but not the normal experience) for a man to be converted and to go through life without a conscious act of reception of Christ or a self-conscious manifestation of the fruits of conversion. We should, however, expect and work for a normal experience in any individual.

As regards the nature of the new birth, much has been written and said against the evangelical view of conversion on the ground that it represents a mere psychological change. It may be well to discuss its nature. It is not:

1. A change in the essential substance of the soul.

2. A free action explicable solely by reference to the inherent powers of the soul itself.

3. A mere change in any one faculty of the soul.

4. A psychological change, understanding by that term a revulsion in habit due to the operation of merely natural mental experiences.

But it is an act of God, whereby a soul, previously dead to Him, experiences a spiritual resurrection into a new sphere of life, in which he is alive to God and united to Him in Christ. God has implanted in the new-born soul a totally *new principle* of life. If any man be in Christ he is a member of a new order in creation. Conversion on this interpretation is the natural and inevitable expression, whether completely conscious or not, of the new nature communicated by the Spirit of God. 'God turns us and we turn.'

Scriptures

1. *The Need of Grace.*—Ps. 51:5; Is. 53:6; Je. 17:9; Mt. 15:19; Jn. 3:3; Rom. 3:19, 23; 8:5–8; 1 Cor. 2:14; 2 Cor. 4:4; Eph. 2:1–3, 12; Tit. 3:3.

2. *Prevenient Grace.*—Jn. 6: 44; Acts 16: 14; 1 Cor. 15:9, 10; Gal. 1: 15, 16.

3. *Effectual Call and Choice.*—Jn. 6:36, 37; 10:16; Acts 13:47, 48; Rom. 1:5–7; 8:28–34; 1 Cor. 1:9; Phil. 2:12, 13; 1 Thes. 1:4, 5; Rev. 17:14.

4. *Conversion, Regeneration and New Birth.*—Je. 31:33, 34; Ezk. 33:11; Mt. 3:11; 16:24; 18:3; Jn. 3:1–12 (the classic passage); 5:24; Acts 3:19; 26:20; Rom. 10:9, 10; 2 Cor. 5:17; Eph. 2:10, 12, 13; Tit. 3:5; Jas. 5:20; 1 Pet. 2:24, 25; 2 Pet. 1:4; 1 Jn. 5:10–12.

Questions

1. What scriptural evidence is there for and against the assertion that every right movement on the part of man is always in response to a prior act of God?

2. What do you understand by the phrase 'effectual call'? What is its relation to 'the external call'?

3. Does regeneration precede or follow repentance and faith?

4. Name some of the evidences that new birth has taken place.

BIBLIOGRAPHY

B. Citron, *The New Birth*, Edinburgh University Press, 1951.

T. C. Hammond, *The New Creation*, Marshall, Morgan and Scott, 1953.

James Orr, article on 'Regeneration', *Hasting's Dictionary of the Bible*, T. and T. Clark, 1963.

3. The Remission of Sins and Justification

This doctrine was the grand discovery and genius of the Reformation and Protestant theology. It deserves the most careful study.

a. The Basis

The Bible is unequivocal in its claim that the remission of sins and the justification of a soul before God are entirely on the basis of our Lord's atoning sacrifice. This, if properly held, is in direct conflict with any view which attributes the pardon of sin solely to an external rite or the mechanical working of a sacrament. The extreme *ex opere operato*[1] claim for the sacraments, put forward, for example, by the Roman church, is inconsistent with the teaching of Scripture.

b. Forgiveness and Justification

The modern plea that God can overlook sin because He is a God of love and unable to refuse any but the most extreme rebels of humanity is not consistent with a true scriptural exegesis, nor indeed, if the full implicates are considered, with a true doctrine of love itself. A more strictly accurate translation of the Greek equivalent for our word 'forgive' would be the word 'remit'. 'If we confess our sins, he is faithful and just, and will remit our sins and cleanse us from all unrighteousness', *i.e.*, there is a basis on which He can be consistent with His justice and yet cancel the guilt of sin. The word 'forgive' should never be used loosely, but as far as possible always in this association with a righteous basis for the forgiveness.

Justification may be defined as 'an act of God's free grace, wherein He pardoneth all our sins, and accepteth us as righteous in His sight, only for

---

[1] *Ex opere operato*, 'by virtue of the act performed', is the theory that sacraments possess in themselves an inherent power of producing the spiritual grace which they signify, provided no obstacle is offered to the natural working of the sacramental virtue. See also pp. 170, 171.

the righteousness of Christ imputed to us, and received by faith alone'.[1]
The man who has had his will liberated from the downward pull of his
own nature, and has been re-created into a new order of life in Christ,
needs a change in his legal standing in the sight of the Lawgiver. Hence, the
doctrine of justification is primarily concerned with 'legal status'. The
Greek term (translated by the ecclesiastical Latin *justificare*) is borrowed
from the language of the law courts and in its classical usage indicates that
a course of action or state is 'legally proper'. The whole imagery which
surrounds the word is that of the law courts and it signifies, primarily, a
declaration. In his uses of the term Paul makes it abundantly clear that
justification is to be taken as indicating the sense that God has pronounced
judgment in favour of redeemed men. The word is not intended to
convey the idea of a bestowal of virtue.

In short, justification means our 'being accounted righteous before
God'. It does not mean that God pronounces the ungodly to be godly (this
would be to enact a falsehood), but He states that, though man is totally
unworthy, He is willing to account him as holy on the ground of Christ's
infinitely acceptable work on his behalf. In other words, the relationship
to God which man lost by the Fall is restored to him. As has well been
pointed out by Christian writers, the divisive factors are removed. The
penalty of sin has been borne by the Lamb of God; its guilt has been ex-
piated by His atoning death; and forgiveness of sin awaits the penitent and
he can be restored to communion with God. Justification differs from
forgiveness in that whereas the latter merely removes the penalty, the
former declares a new status of righteousness. Hodge has the following
summary (abbreviated). Justification is:

1. An act of grace to the sinner whereby a guilty sinner is declared
free. (Contrast sanctification, which is progressive.)

2. As regards the *nature* of the act, it is not an act of power (*i.e.*, it does
not produce any subjective change in the individual). Nor is it a mere
executive act of a sovereign, such as pardoning a criminal. Rather it is a
forensic act, the act of a judge, wherein the sinner is declared free from
the claims of justice and entitled to receive the reward due to righteousness.

3. The meritorious ground of justification is not faith (faith is not
considered as a virtue), but the sacrifice of Christ, associated with His
perfect obedience to the law and enduring of the penalty of the law on our
behalf.

4. A status of righteousness is imputed to the Christian. So far as the
legal position is concerned, it is a bequest of Christ, which may be treated
as belonging to the Christian by inheritance.

[1] The Shorter Catechism. *Cf.* Article XI of the Church of England.

5. Faith is the *condition* of justification. God does not impute righteousness to the sinner until (and unless) he receives the work of Christ.

The following distinctions and contrasts between forgiveness and justification and justification and sanctification are suggested by Griffith Thomas:

Forgiveness	*Justification*
An act, followed by a succession of such acts.	An act, followed by an attitude.
Repeated throughout life.	Complete and never repeated.
Negative, removing condemnation.	Positive, the bestowal of a proper standing before God.
Does not of itself alter formal status.	A reinstatement.

It is well for us to keep distinct in our thinking the process of sanctification ('to make righteous'). This latter follows on justification and is the working out of righteousness in the practical experience of the person who is declared to be righteous before God. (See also pp. 145ff.)

Justification	*Sanctification*
Standing before God	Actual state
The position of the Christian	The condition of the Christian
Relationship to God	Fellowship with God
The foundation of peace and assurance—'Christ for us'	The foundation of practical righteousness—'Christ in us'
It has no degrees—it is complete and eternal	It has degrees (But see below)
God's work alone	Man co-operates with God

c. The Roman Catholic Doctrine

Roman Catholic teaching has confused justification and sanctification and has infused the Pelagian idea of man's obtaining righteousness by meritorious works. This shows itself in many ways. While it is granted that there is no good in fallen man, and that so far as grace is concerned the new life comes only through the merits of Christ, this new life is said to be imparted at baptism. Subsequent to this original infusion of righteousness, good works done by the faithful partake of the nature of merit. In the last analysis the ground of acceptance before God becomes the state in grace and meritorious acts of the baptized. (Recent attempts by Roman Catholic theologians to demonstrate that their church's doctrine of justification is the Bible's and the Reformers' one have—not surprisingly—failed to carry their point.)

In point of fact the gulf between the Roman and Protestant views is wider than the official statements would show. In practice abuses abound, and there seems no limit to the possibilities of further divergence, as, for example, when the teaching of degrees of justification has as its final result the doctrine of purgatory.

Nothing is more needed today than that Christians should be fully aware of the supreme importance of a right conception of the place of Christ in human redemption. The doctrine of justification is the ground of our assurance of acceptance with God and also the source of all true spiritual liberty. Luther called it 'the criterion of a standing or a falling church'.

d. The Place of Good Works

The taunt is often hurled at evangelical Christians that because of their overemphasis on justification by faith they belittle the value of good works and moral effort. Nothing is more unjust and untrue to facts. If an empirical test has any value any true evangelical community would compare very favourably in the matter of 'works' with any of those of its critics. The antinomianism which was prophesied has not inevitably followed among the succeeding generations of the Reformation churches. There has never been any desire on the part of Protestant divines to teach the neglect of good works, but they were anxious to leave no doubt as to the ground of justification and to put works in their proper and secondary place.

The legal system introduced by Roman theology tends to check the spontaneity of love and to introduce the concept of a bargain with God. James in his *Varieties of Religious Experience* points out the psychological value of Luther's sweeping away of 'a profit and loss account with God'.

Scriptures

1. *Forgiveness.*—In Old Testament times the penitent was 'covered' in view of our Lord's full atonement, and 'separated' from his sin. (See section on 'atonement', pp. 115ff., and Lv. 16:21, 22; Pss. 51; 103:8–13.) In the New Testament we find the phrase 'the forgiveness (or remission) of sins'. See Mt. 6:14, 15; 26:28; Mk. 1:4; Eph. 1:7; Col. 1:14; 1 Jn. 1:8–10; 2:12, *etc.*

2. *Justification.*—Lk. 18:13, 14; Rom. 3:20–31; 4; 5:9, 16–18; Gal. 2:15–21; 3:24–26; Tit. 3:4–7.

3. *The Basis of Assurance.*—Jn. 3:36; 5:24; Rom. 8:16, 28–39; Gal. 4:4–6; 2 Tim. 1:12; 4:7, 8; Heb. 10:19–22; 11:1; 1 Jn. 3:1, 2; 5:9–13, 19, 20.

4. *Good Works.*—Rom. 12; Gal. 6:1–10; Eph. 2:10; 4:22–5:17; 1 Thes. 4:1; 2 Thes. 3:13; 2 Tim. 2:19–21; 3:14–17; Heb. 10:24; 13:16, 20, 21; Jas. 2:14–26.

Questions

1. Consider the three terms in Rom. 3:24, 28; 5:9; 'justified by grace', 'justified by faith', 'justified by his blood'. What aspect of justification does each emphasize?

2. How would you meet the objection that the doctrine of justification rests upon a 'legal fiction'?

3. What connections does the New Testament establish between faith and works?
4. How is justification related to assurance?

BIBLIOGRAPHY

G. C. Berkouwer, *Faith and Justification*, Eerdmans, 1954.
James Buchanan, *The Doctrine of Justification*, Banner of Truth, 1961.
Leon Morris, *The Apostolic Preaching of the Cross*, Tyndale Press, 1965, chapters 7, 8.
Commentaries on *Romans* 3 by C. Hodge (Eerdmans),W. Sanday and A. C. Headlam
(T. and T. Clark), A. Nygren (SCM Press) and J. Murray (Marshall, Morgan and
Scott).

4. Union with Christ and Sanctification

a. Sanctification

The Shorter Catechism defines it as 'the work of God's free grace, whereby we are renewed in the whole man after the image of God, and are
enabled more and more to die unto sin, and live unto righteousness' (*cf.*
Articles XII, XIII and XIV of the Church of England). The ultimate aim
of redemption is that the redeemed man might attain to perfect communion with God and complete conformity to His likeness.

The various terms used in the Old Testament, such as 'sanctification'
('setting apart' or 'making holy'—in a wide range of senses), 'holiness',
'purification' and 'consecration', are invested in the New Testament with
a deeper meaning in connection with the work of Christ and the operation of the Holy Spirit in the believer. The third Person of the Trinity is
specially connected by Scripture with the work of sanctification. The
leading ideas in the Old Testament words were 'separation from sin' and
'living in obedience to God'. These are expressed in the New Testament
in such verses as 'Consider yourselves dead to sin and alive to God in Christ
Jesus', 'If you have been raised with Christ, seek the things that are above'.
The separation from sin is associated with the Christian's identification
with the death of Christ, and his living to God through his union with
Christ in resurrection.

Sanctification may be viewed in two ways, from the side of (1) God's
provision in Christ, and (2) the Christian's appropriation of this provision.
There always remains a gap between the two.

1. *God's Provision.*—So far as the work of God for our sanctification is
concerned, it must be regarded as complete. He has made Christ 'our
sanctification', and therefore our union with Him imparts to us complete
sanctification. We are given the status of 'those sanctified in Christ Jesus'
or 'by the Spirit'. Paul says of the Corinthians, 'You were washed, you
were sanctified, you were justified . . .', and Hebrews states that 'we have
been sanctified through the offering of the body of Jesus Christ *once for all*'
(Acts 26:18; 1 Cor. 1:2; 6:11; Heb. 10:10; 1 Pet. 1:2). The designation

of Christians as 'the saints' conveys the same idea, which is not only that of being 'set apart' or 'consecrated' as God's servants, but also that of the achievement of our sanctification in the cross and resurrection. *In principle* our sanctification is a reality in Christ, who on the cross 'crucified our old self' and by His resurrection raised us to 'newness of life' (see Rom. 6:1–14).

2. *Man's Experience*.—From the side of the Christian, sanctification is the process of becoming in practice what he already is 'in Christ'. This inevitably takes the form of a gradual transformation of our character until it is 'like Christ', a work which God will complete at our Lord's reappearing when even 'our lowly body' will be made 'like his glorious body' (Phil. 3:21). Our glorification will be the crowning act in our sanctification.

Meanwhile, unless the old nature is totally eradicated by some such method as the physical death of the Christian (which incidentally, is not all that is required for its removal), it lingers on to obstruct the growth of the new nature, which is imparted in Christ at conversion. The divine method of dealing with this old nature, which is called by Scripture 'the old man' or 'the flesh', constitutes the practical side of sanctification.

Scripture brings this subject before us in three different ways:

1. There are passages which present what we may call a forensic view of the possession of true righteousness and holiness. For example, 'Christ Jesus, whom God made . . . our righteousness and sanctification'; 'Yield your members to righteousness for sanctification' (1 Cor. 1:30; Rom. 6:19; *cf*. 22). Such verses appear to teach two things:

(i) The righteousness of the Christian is to be regarded as based solely upon the obedience and atoning work of Christ. This alone is 'righteousness' in the sense of our standing before God. It is described as 'the righteousness of God which depends on faith'.

(ii) The indwelling Christ works out in us by His Spirit a copy of His own righteousness. The unaided strivings of the Christian would frequently miss the pattern. His realized righteousness is the result of a continual operation of the divine Spirit. In other words, the Lord Jesus is both the Ground of our righteousness in relation to God and the Source of our righteousness in daily living. God's requirement of a life of practical righteousness is made abundantly clear—*e.g.*, Titus 2:12.

2. Other Scripture passages present sanctification as the putting off of the old and putting on of the new nature (see, *e.g.*, Eph. 4:22–24). This teaching states clearly that there is perpetual strife between the old principles of evil and death which used to be supreme in mind and heart and the new principles of righteousness and life in Jesus Christ (*cf*. Rom.

6:6; Eph. 4:22 and Col. 3:9). The doctrine of the Pauline Epistles may be summed up as follows:

(i) The old nature is to be regarded as having been sentenced to death. God refuses to acknowledge it, and it has no right to obstruct the Christian's progress.

(ii) This being so, the Christian is invited to live in daily enjoyment of his potential freedom—that is, to discard the old principles of life like an outworn garment and to 'put on the new nature'.

3. Finally there are Scripture passages which present sanctification as the result of the Christian's union with Christ and identification with Him in His death and resurrection—e.g., Romans 6:11 ('So you also must consider yourselves dead to sin and alive to God in Christ Jesus'; cf. Gal. 2:20; Col. 3:3.) This is an even deeper approach. Scripture encourages us to regard our union with Christ as being as real, and as close, as our Lord's relationship with the Father. 'He who is united to the Lord becomes one spirit with him.' See also the unity referred to in John 17:21-23.

In other words, the Christian is to regard himself as 'crucified with Christ' (the death of the old nature) and 'risen with him' (that is, walking in a new sphere of life). This is the meaning of phrases such as 'brought from death to life'; 'If then you have been raised with Christ . . . set your minds on things that are above.' There is surely no antinomianism attaching to such doctrines, but the most powerful possible appeal to a life of holiness!

b. The Practical Means

The keystone in the doctrine of sanctification is provided by a right understanding of the office of the Holy Spirit. His indwelling of the believer is for the express purpose of rendering God's provision for a life of holiness operative and effectual in the life of the individual. There is nothing vague about the scriptural views on this matter. The source of power and victory over sin resides in the resurrection life of Christ mediated to the Christian by the Holy Spirit.

For a full discussion see one of the volumes on the ministrations of the Spirit.[1] The production of 'righteousness' in a man's life, the ability to exchange the old life for the new, and the practical demonstration of the 'resurrection life' in Christ are operations of the Holy Spirit. The law of sin relentlessly working in our members is counteracted by the law of the Spirit, which persistently operates to abrogate its power over the will. The Christian is called upon continually to maintain the attitude in which his liberated will makes its choice to take sides with the Holy Spirit. This attitude of absolute confidence in the liberating, uplifting and empower-

[1] For example, *The Holy Spirit of God*, by W. H. Griffith Thomas (Eerdmans, 1955).

ing control of the Holy Spirit spells victory and a life of holiness for the Christian.

c. *Practical Difficulties*

1. *Crisis or Process*.—There is difference of opinion amongst evangelical Christians themselves concerning the method by which their sanctification becomes a practical reality. To some it is a crisis, which may be accompanied by emotional results as intense as those accompanying conversion. To others it is a process of gradual enlightenment, until at length they awaken to the realities of the operations of the Holy Spirit.

The following considerations should be borne in mind:

(i) If the most advanced and fullest experiences of a truly sanctified life were found only in those who belong to one school, there might be some justification for the sweeping assertions which have sometimes been made. But the fact remains that equally enlightened, equally devoted, and apparently equally sanctified lives are found in the best representatives of each of the schools of thought.

(ii) Comparing the realization of these truths with what happens at conversion, it is a matter of common observation that some are unable to indicate the day on which they became fully conscious of the meaning either of conversion or of the purpose of the Spirit's indwelling. Others, however, awakened suddenly to one or the other, or both. The fact which matters is whether each adult Christian is living in the full blessedness of both. If he is not, then it is legitimate to bring the matter urgently to his notice, and this often results in a sudden and dramatic change in his whole Christian life.

2. *'Fullness'*.—The use of the word 'fullness' and 'fully' in connection with this subject is legitimate in reference to a Christian's heritage in Christ. But it is misleading if applied to a man's practical experience. Experience has shown, times without number, that the excesses of those who make claim to 'full sanctification' may be far more dishonouring to Christ than the lack of attainment which they condemn in others.

3. *Sinlessness*.—Christ alone was without sin. Scripture lends no support either to the Roman claim for the sinlessness of the Lord's mother or to the claim to 'sinless perfection' made by some Christians. 'If we say we have no sin, we deceive ourselves, and the truth is not in us.' But this is vastly different from saying that the Christian cannot know 'freedom from sin', both as regards its penalty and its unlawful thraldom in our innermost being. The Christian may, and should, know freedom from 'the habitual practice of sin', and he can, and should, experience victory over besetting sins and over his sinful desires. Constant victory, yes; but inabil-

ity to sin again, no. Victory over conscious sin is a blessed possibility, but even then there remain 'the hidden faults' of which the psalmist speaks (Ps. 19:12). The Christian should walk humbly and warily always.

4. *'De Congruo'*.—The mediaeval doctrine with regard to 'meritorious works' has presented itself again in several subtle modern forms. Originally, it was dependent on the view that the essential loss at the Fall was of a supernatural gift and that man's natural powers still enabled him to approach God and to invite grace. That is to say, if a man wills to use his natural powers properly he may become a recipient of divine grace. The addressing of himself to the task of doing right in itself invites grace (*meritum de congruo*), and if he uses his will aright he can acquire an habitual gift of grace which may result in merit of a further and higher kind based on divine justice (*meritum de condigno*). The effect is to make it a consequence that God will eventually justify the man so meriting grace. The Roman church similarly contends for the value of works anterior to justification. One modern form of this doctrine is widespread. It is argued that it is a man's manner of life and morality which count and not his beliefs. In other words, the criterion is one of *conduct* and not of faith in Christ. It is even stated in a more positive form: 'Those who do not pretend to religion often live better and more honourable lives than those who habitually go to church.' It is implied that God, therefore, thinks more highly of the former and will overlook their lack of belief. It is forgotten that God's original and chief quarrel with man was, and is, the wrong use of his will rather than his method of living. A first-class morality, to assume for a moment the impossible, if proceeding from rebellious self-will which refuses to acknowledge God and to receive Christ, can have little intrinsic value to God. To live righteously is what a man ought to do—merely his duty. Motive, as well as the actual mode of life itself, must be taken into consideration.

d. The Three Views Concerning Practical Sanctification

There are three chief schools of thought on the practical application of the doctrine of sanctification.

1. *Eradication*.—Some hold that the evil principle of sin is eradicated by the Holy Spirit. Both Scripture and common experience are against this view.

2. *Suppression*.—Others go to the other extreme and leave man to fight a long and hopeless battle for the mastery of the law of sin. This view does scant justice to the power and function of the Holy Spirit. It is inadequate to account for the claims of some of the New Testament passages (*e.g.*, Rom. 6-8).

3. *Counteraction*.—The view which seems to be most in accord with

Scripture is that through the force of the 'law of the Spirit' sin is no longer inevitable, and the Christian has no legitimate excuse for the habitual practice of sin. He should not make allowance for it, but if he should fall there is a Helper to plead his cause. 'I am writing this to you so that you may not sin; but if any one does sin, we have an advocate with the Father' (1 Jn. 2:1).

e. Final Perseverance

This doctrine is in theological writing usually referred to as 'the final perseverance of the saints'. It is rather God's perseverance with the salvation of His saints, or 'final preservation'.

The problem is one which has caused much heart-burning and controversy among Christians. It has been a source of difficulty in all ages of the church. The question of final security was one of the chief disagreements which caused the separation of Whitefield from Wesley. The former believed that once a man had been justified and eternal life had been imparted, it was impossible for that man finally to perish. 'He who began a good work in you will bring it to completion at the day of Jesus Christ' (Phil. 1:6). Wesley, on the other hand, placing his emphasis on certain other passages of Scripture, continually warned his followers that they must give heed to themselves lest they should 'fall from grace'. He was quite certain that God, on His side, was both able to complete the process of redemption and was willing to do so. But he held that a man could sell his birthright and deliberately commit what amounts to spiritual suicide. The process might start in an insidious way by lack of watchfulness and a dilly-dallying with sin which might almost imperceptibly increase to deliberate apostasy from God. See Hebrews 6:4–6 and 10:26, 27.

It will at once be seen that it is a matter which is soon determined for a student who belongs to the Calvinist school. His very principles forbid any suggestion of the final loss of one who, 'elect of God', has received the effectual call and has been justified (Rom. 8:29–39).

On the other hand, those whose system leads them to place their emphasis in these matters upon the response of the human will, rather than upon the decrees of God, will tend to leave open the possibility of failure in the human object of divine mercy to continue the Christian pilgrimage.[1]

There are two sets of relevant Scriptures:

1. Those emphatically asserting the eternal security of the Christian, such as Jn. 6:37; 10:28, 29; Rom. 5:9, 10; 8:29–39; Eph. 1:13, 14; 4:30; Phil. 1:6; 2 Tim. 1:12; 4:18; 1 Pet. 1:3–5.

---

[1] There are many other theological problems which are connected with this one, e.g., the 'unpardonable sin'. For these see books of reference.

2. Those which give warnings about the results of trifling with divine things and of the neglect of spiritual privileges, such as 1 Cor. 8:11; Heb. 2:1–3; 6:4–6; 10:26, 27, 38, 39; 2 Pet. 1:10; Jude 5.

A great deal depends upon how we approach the subject. 'When we start from divine sovereignty, we cannot help believing in preservation, and it is only when we start from human freedom that we contemplate the possibility of falling from grace' (Griffith Thomas). A careful collation of the various Scriptures on both sides leaves no doubt concerning the side on which Scripture places its authority. There is a greater number of allusions and far more positive statements on the side of eternal security. It should be also noted that the Scriptures on the other side are mostly negative and in the nature of warnings not to presume. As for Hebrews 6:4–6 and 10: 26–27, they are both hypothetical cases, stated for the purposes of argument. 'If they fall away . . . what would be the expected result?' Further, the fact of falling away from given grace is admitted by all, but two questions arise. Is it saving grace? Is it a final fall?

'It is as if the positive side conveyed a ruling spiritual principle—the negative, a warning not to distort it; the positive, an assurance for the *Christian* as such—the negative, a caution to the *man* not to delude himself as to his Christianity, above all, not to allow anything to palliate a moment's sin' (H. C. G. Moule).

Scriptures

1. *The Indwelling Christ.*—Jn. 14:20; 15:4–7; 17:23, 26; Rom. 8:10, 11; 1 Cor. 6:17; 2 Cor. 13:5; Gal. 2:20; Eph. 2:5, 6; 3:17; Col. 1:27; 3:3, 4.

2. *The Believer's Righteousness.*—(i) The Beginning: Rom. 6:1–11; 1 Cor. 1:30; Eph. 1:13, 14; 2:10; 4:24; Phil. 3:4–9; Heb. 9:14; 10: 10, 14; 1 Pet. 1:2, 16. (ii) The Process: Jn. 17:17; Acts 20:32; Rom. 6:11–22; 8:2, 4, 5; 12:1, 2; 1 Cor. 6:19, 20; 2 Cor. 3:18; 7:1; Gal. 5:16–25; Eph. 3:15, 16; Col. 2:20–3:2; 1 Thes. 5:23, 24.

Questions

1. What are the connections and differences between justification and sanctification?

2. What part is played, according to Scripture, by the three Persons of the Godhead respectively in the work of sanctification?

3. If sanctification means negatively separation from sin and positively living in obedience to God, how are these effected in the life of the Christian? By what agencies and means are they accomplished?

4. 'You have put off the old nature' (Col. 3:9); 'Put off your old nature' (Eph. 4:22). How do you integrate these two statements in the light of the rest of the New Testament? Collect other instances of declarations concerning our sanctification that appear to conflict in this manner.

5. Make a list of the terms that describe man's part in his sanctification (*e.g.*, 'yield', 'seek', *etc.*), and observe their over-all emphases.

BIBLIOGRAPHY

Steven Barabas, *So Great Salvation: The History and Message of the Keswick Convention*, Marshall, Morgan and Scott, 1952.

G. C. Berkouwer, *Faith and Perseverance*, Eerdmans, 1958.

G. C. Berkouwer, *Faith and Sanctification*, Eerdmans, 1952.

Evan H. Hopkins, *The Law of Liberty in the Spiritual Life*, Marshall, Morgan and Scott, 1952.

D. Martyn Lloyd-Jones, *Christ our Sanctification*, IVF, 1948.

K. F. W. Prior, *The Way of Holiness*, IVF, 1967.

J. C. Ryle, *Holiness*, James Clarke, 1952.

Jeremy Taylor, *Holy Living*, 1650 (many editions).

R. S. Wallace, *Calvin's Doctrine of the Christian Life*, Oliver and Boyd, 1959.

John Wesley, *A Plain Account o Christian Perfection*, Epworth Press, 1952.

PART SIX

THE CHRISTIAN IN THE CHURCH

This section covers a field in which there have been many conflicting opinions and occasions for fratricidal strife. There is, however, no inherent reason why it should necessarily be so. In an interdenominational community such as that to which this volume is primarily addressed, much may be learned by an earnest inquiry into the nature of primitive Christianity, the essential principles on which our Lord founded the government of His church, and the reasons for some of the wide divergences of the present day. There are, however, certain principles and cautions which need to be observed.

1. Every Christian should have settled convictions as to God's will for him in the matter of his association with some community in the visible church of Christ. Young people, especially, should beware of impatience with the traditional forms (remembering their great influence in the past) and of hasty judgments in matters of this kind. All things considered, it is a wise general rule for them not to attempt experiments. They should remember their duty to the parents who have trained them in what they sincerely believe to be the most pure forms of Christianity. The only conditions under which this general rule must be disregarded is where the conscience of the individual is greatly exercised on any problem. In such circumstances he must, at all costs, search the Scriptures and determine for himself their teaching, and follow it.

2. Much harm has been done by those who dogmatically assert, not that their way is 'one true way', but that it is 'the *only* true way'. It has sometimes brought its own nemesis. By a strange irony those who have set out to obtain a purer community have sometimes ended by securing a larger 'mixed multitude', and those who have disavowed what they considered to be abuses have themselves become the most addicted to them, under other names!

3. The points on which emphasis is needed are those which concern our common evangelical Protestant position in contradistinction to liberalism and sacerdotalism and other perversions of the apostolic tradition.

1. The Church

In its fullest sense, the church must be described as the 'company of all true believers', and this includes those who have passed to their rest, as well as true believers who are still living. 'The Church is the universal society of all the faithful whom God has predestinated from eternity to everlasting life' (Nowell's Catechism). For purposes of more detailed description, the church may be divided into the church triumphant (*i.e.*, all those who have 'died in the Lord') and the church militant here on earth. Or a more usual distinction is between the 'church visible' (as seen by men, ecclesiastically organized) and the 'church invisible' (as known to God alone, *i.e.*, comprising only those who are truly Christ's, whether thought of in terms of the true believers within the church visible, or as including past and future believers as well).[1]

The Greek word is *ekklēsia*, which was used of the citizens 'summoned' together as the sovereign 'assembly' of the people (*cf.* Acts 19:39), and so means 'the assembled congregation' of God's people. In its New Testament setting it was always applied to a community of people and never to a building.

a. The Purpose of the Church

1. The supreme object of the church (the church invisible) must be related to the eternal purposes of God. It is stated to have a peculiar and special value to our Lord Jesus (Eph. 5:25-27).

2. So far as its immediate purpose (the church visible) is concerned, it is:

(i) A company of redeemed men, who meet for a common worship of God and for mutual edification. The underlying idea is that of a close fellowship. Notice the illustrations in Scripture of a body and its members, and of a building compacted of living stones.

(ii) A centre of witness, through which the gospel might be preserved and propagated to other men. Since the ministrations of the gospel have been committed to the church, and not to angelic beings, the church is actually of first importance in the affairs of men. It exists to make Christ real to them.

b. The Nature of the Church

It cannot be too strongly emphasized that the church is an organism rather than an organization. It is for this reason that elaborate instructions, comparable with those of Leviticus, are absent in the New Testament. Much latitude is left for national or local differences, and uniformity is not enjoined. If the student confines himself to direct statements and injunctions, the rules for the church are found to be a series of principles to safeguard certain vital necessities, but do not themselves comprise a

---

[1] This is Nowell's distinction. The Convocation which approved the Thirty-Nine Articles, 1563, also revised Nowell's Catechism.

complete system. The distinguishing features of the apostolic ecclesiastical traditions were simplicity and adaptability.

In using the terms 'visible' and 'invisible' of the church, it is necessary to add that the visible church is never co-extensive with the church invisible here on earth, because there are often attached to communities of professing Christians those who do not really belong to them (1 Jn. 2:19). There may thus be membership in the visible church which does not secure membership in the invisible. Scripture recognizes that the local communities of Christians may become 'mixed' with those who are not true Christians. While they are plainly to aim at the highest possible standards, the extent of their attainment will be always variable. But, on the other hand, 'the body of Christ', 'the temple of God', 'the bride of Christ', descriptive of the invisible church, represents something perfect and complete in the purposes of God. Yet, once again, the terms 'visible' and 'invisible' must not be represented as denoting quite separate communities. The visible church is the body of Christ in action in the world, though never in its ideal character, but beset with the limitations of time, space and human infirmity.

In the context of continuing controversies, we see the disastrous results of attempting to identify the visible with the invisible. For example, the church of Rome still claims to be co-extensive with the body of Christ and all outsiders are seriously defective.[1] By putting the emphasis on visibility more is lost than appears at first sight. There is a consequent loss of spiritual standards and sinking to mechanical methods, which lower the conception of the church to that of a mere hierarchy or organization. The New Testament places its emphasis upon union with Christ in a life 'hidden in God' and looks for the outward manifestation of that inward spiritual life in seeking to determine the extent of the visible church.

c. The Characteristics of the True Church

The ecclesiastical term is 'Notes of the Church'. There are certain attributes which declare it to be the body of which Christ is the Head. These are usually described as four: unity, sanctity, catholicity and apostolicity. 'I believe in one holy catholic apostolic church.'

1. *Unity.*—The unity of the church was never shown (even in apostolic times) by a unity of organization, nor was there uniformity of usage, nor a complete unanimity in doctrine. The essential unity of the church is in its Headship—'All one in Christ Jesus.' There is 'one Lord, one faith, one baptism, one God and Father of all'. It is not that the church is united in its

---

[1] Since Vatican II there has been a much greater readiness on the part of the Roman church to acknowledge the members of other 'communions' as in some sense 'Christians', albeit 'separated' ones.

worship, government and methods of service, but that there is one church composed of all who love our Lord Jesus in sincerity. 'No external organization can supersede the original relation in which the society stands to its Founder.'

2. *Sanctity.*—The church is separate and holy unto God. This is confined to those who are in Christ and are manifesting the fruits of the Spirit. Their existence in the church visible and the measure of their influence in life and expressed doctrine upon it are the grounds for attributing sanctity to the visible church, which is therefore more or less holy in proportion to the sanctity of the lives of its members. The church is also 'the temple of the Holy Spirit'.

3. *Catholicity.*—The original meaning of the word was that of *universality*. The church differed from the Jewish religion by being open to all nations on an equal basis, and did not have the local character of the churches in the various cities. The universality consists also in the applicability of the message to all races. Later use tended to identify catholicity more with the preservation of the wholeness of the universally held doctrines of the Faith.

4. *Apostolicity.*—This consists in its being 'built upon the foundation of the apostles and prophets' and in the perpetual adherence of its members to the apostolic teaching as recorded in the New Testament. 'They devoted themselves to the apostles' doctrine' (Acts 2:42).

What it *certainly does not* mean is a continuous succession of leadership preserved in a regular transmission of 'orders' from bishops who can trace a lineage back to the apostles. This is disproved by Scripture and by history, which shows serious interruptions in any reconstruction of an 'apostolic succession' which may be attempted. There is a succession of leadership and order, but not of the kind indicated in the above addition to the scriptural provisions.

The true church of Christ is to be found everywhere where He and the Holy Spirit are enthroned in men's hearts. Hence the true church is 'the whole congregation of Christian people dispersed throughout the world'.

'The Church is *One* because it is united to Christ, and it is so, notwithstanding the impossibility of outward unity of earthly government. The Church is *Holy* because it is possessed by the Spirit of God. The Church is *Catholic* because Christ is proclaimed everywhere and its life is independent of place or time. The Church is *Apostolic* because it is true to the New Testament Apostolic teaching. Thus every "note" is associated with Christ, and the One Holy Catholic Apostolic Church is neither a mere aggregate of visible Churches nor a simple invisible community of individuals. It is none the less real because its life is in Christ and its character is spiritual. The Church of the New Testament is that Body of Christ which consists of all the faithful in Him, and every separate community of such people is a true visible Church'.[1]

d. The Relation of the Individual to the Church

The above definition of the church places its emphasis upon the relation of the individual Christian to Christ. This is where Scripture itself places it. Nothing must supersede or divert the Christian's direct communion with the Head. The indwelling Spirit supplies the humblest Christian with guidance which is unfailing when rightly used. It is *possible* for an individual Christian to be cut off from external and visible means of grace for long periods at a time and yet to maintain the vigour of his new life in Christ through his right of access to the Head of the church Himself. This gives a dignity to the individual's judgment in matters of faith which no theory of church discipline should lightly override.

On the other hand, Scripture clearly teaches that it is not normal for a Christian to live to himself. He gains much from fellowship with other Christians, in particular the exercise of the 'gifts' which are in the church. He also derives special benefit through the means of grace. No words can express strongly enough the risk of serious loss which dogs the steps of the Christian who has no time for a spiritual 'home' in a local community of Christian men. He may pride himself on being 'unattached', but he can ill afford to live a detached kind of life in a world which necessitates the use of all the provided means of grace if he is to be a successful disciple of Jesus Christ.

e. The Authority of the Church

As previously discussed (p. 40), the evangelical Protestant position is that the Scriptures are the supreme rule of faith. The church has authority only in a secondary sense. But in view of the persistence of the claims of the church of Rome to supreme authority in matters of faith and conduct, and over the individual, it may be well to consider the extent of church authority.

To quote Article XX of the Church of England formularies: 'It is not lawful for the Church to ordain any thing that is contrary to God's Word written, neither may it so expound one place of Scripture, that it be repugnant to another ... besides the same ought it not to enforce any thing to be believed for necessity of Salvation.' Church authority may be described as limited in the following ways. Its ordinances must be censored by the written Word of God, and in its teaching it must expound the Word of God without adding to or taking from the statements there made.

---

[1] W. H. Griffith Thomas, *The Principles of Theology* (Church Book Room Press, 1956), p. 278.

On the other hand, the church has authority in the following respects:

1. It has the full right to determine points of procedure and ceremonial (subject to the above limitations).

2. It exercises a corrective influence upon the doctrine and practice of the individual by means of its standards. A Christian's private judgment greatly benefits from a comparison with the views of his fellow-members of the body of Christ.

3. There is a disciplinary authority in the case of immorality and certain misdemeanours of its members.

As we have seen, the Roman church claims infallibility for its decisions and makes them binding over its followers. But the doctrine of an infallible church is untenable for the following reasons:

1. It is contrary to Scripture. Matthew 16:13–20, in any case, refers to Peter only and makes no hint of a succession.[1]

2. No early Councils acknowledge the supremacy of the Roman bishops, who were not even presiding at any of them.

3. The statement 'The church gave us the Bible' is only partially true. The Word of God, spoken and written, created the church, and not vice versa (1 Cor. 14:36; 2 Thes. 2:15). Even though the *early* church, in the person of the apostles, *etc.*, can be said to have attended to its transcription in the books of the New Testament, and the *later* church to their transmission and preservation, it does not follow that the church *of today* has authority over the *message* of these books. We must distinguish between the production and collection of the biblical books *qua* books, and the authority of their teaching as the Word of God, between 'The church gave us the Bible', and 'The Word of God gave us the church'. See pp. 28, 39.

f. Unity and Uniformity

The mind of man in all ages has been prone to attach a greater importance to uniformity than unity. There have been many examples of misguided attempts on the part of a strong community to enforce uniformity of worship and uniformity of government upon neighbouring communities. The results have in some cases been a common decadence and in others bitter divisions which have marred church history.

Unity is deeper than uniformity. Although the human mind has much difficulty in believing the truth of the assertion, a spiritual unity such as that of a common loyalty to the gospel and the Person of Christ, even though

---

[1] It must be regarded as virtually certain that Peter did get to Rome and was martyred there not long after his arrival, but this has no bearing on the question of papal supremacy and infallibility.

diversely expressed, is ultimately far more influential than any merely external form of amalgamation or uniformity of procedure.

Among evangelical Christians today there are in general two attitudes to church unity:

1. Many believe that *the spiritual unity of all true Christians* in the body of Christ is sufficient, and that there is no need to form a single visible church. So long as we are united in essentials as revealed in God's Word, and above all in a real spiritual communion based on loyalty to the one true Head of the church, our separate denominations and our differences over baptism, church polity, *etc.*, are matters of indifference. The advocates of this view stress the proper meaning of such passages as John 17:20–23 and Ephesians 4:3–6, and the informal unity of the apostolic churches, and point to the dangers of compromise with error and the institutional stifling of life and vigour in any all-embracing ecclesiastical structure.

2. Others feel that this *spiritual unity of the one body of Christ demands visible expression* in a single church within each locality. They maintain that the New Testament provides no justification for our present de-nominational divisions, and that to a lesser or greater extent they hinder the efficient fulfilment of the church's task of evangelism (remembering that the ecumenical movement of the twentieth century grew largely out of missionary concern). The advocates of visible unity do not see it as involving a rigid uniformity, or as modifying in any way the requirement of a biblical basis for the church. Within this second attitude there are differences of emphasis depending on whether a 'mixed' or 'pure' view of the church is more dominant.

Scriptures

1. *The Purpose of the Church.*—Eph. 1:3–14; 2:22; 3:8–11; 1 Pet. 2:5, 9; Rev. 21:2, 3.

2. *Its Nature and Characteristics.*—Mt. 16: 16–18; Jn. 10:16; Acts 2:42; 7:38; 1 Cor. 10:17; 12:12, 13; Gal. 6:16; Eph. 1:22, 23; 2:19–22; 4:11–16; Col. 1:18, 24; Heb. 12:22, 23; Rev. 5:9, 10.

3. *Its Authority and Government.*—1 Cor. 12:28; Eph. 1:22, 23; 4:3–6, 11; 5:23, 24; Col. 1:18–24.

4. *The Individual's Relation to the Church.*—Mt. 18:15–17; Acts 2:44–47; Rom. 12:4–8; 1 Cor. 10:32; 11:29; 12:14–27; Eph. 4:15, 16; Heb. 10:25; 13:17; Jas. 5:14.

Questions

1. Give a list of the various descriptions of the church given in the New Testament. What were God's purposes in bringing it into being?

2. What is meant by our Lord's prayer 'that they all may be one' (Jn. 17:21)? What does the 'unity' of the church consist in, and how should it be expressed? What is the relationship between 'uniformity' and 'unity'?

3. Is the holiness of the church consistent with the sinfulness of its members?

BIBLIOGRAPHY

Roland Allen, *Missionary Methods: St Paul's or Ours?*, World Dominion Press, 1960.
G. C. Berkouwer, *The Conflict with Rome*, Baker Book House, 1958.
E. Best, *One Body in Christ*, SPCK, 1955.
E. Brunner, *The Misunderstanding of the Church*, Lutterworth Press, 1952.
H. M. Carson, *Roman Catholicism Today*, IVF, 1964.
J. D. Douglas (ed.), *Evangelicals and Unity*, Marcham Manor Press, 1964.
C. H. Hodge, *The Church and its Polity*, Nelson, 1879.
F. J. A. Hort, *The Christian Ecclesia*, Macmillan, 1908.
T. M. Lindsay, *A History of the Reformation*, T. and T. Clark, 1907-8.
D. Martyn Lloyd-Jones, *The Basis of Christian Unity*, IVF, 1962.
J. I. Packer (ed.), *All in Each Place*, Marcham Manor Press, 1965.
G. Salmon, *The Infallibility of the Church*, 1890; abridged edn. ed. H. F. Woodhouse, Murray, 1952.
A. M. Stibbs, *God's Church*, IVF, 1959.
W. Walker, *A History of the Christian Church*, T. and T. Clark, 1960.

2. The Ministry

In this section, points on which there is not common agreement amongst evangelical Christians have been omitted. The student will be well advised to concentrate upon the important distinctions between evangelical and sacerdotal views. There is much which is being overlooked and undervalued today. The true conception of the ministry is in danger of being weakened, and in some cases lost.

a. The Ministerial Office

While elaborate instructions, comparable to those provided for the Levitical priesthood, are not found in the New Testament, yet there is sufficient to indicate definitely the nature of the ministerial office. See the relevant Scriptures.

There is common agreement upon the following points:

1. Our Lord has provided 'gifts' for His church (Eph. 4:11, 12), including those who have special ability for serving the people of God in various ways, of which the chief is power in the exposition of the Word of God, in giving instruction in the faith, and in witnessing to the unconverted.

2. The verses referred to in Ephesians and other passages make it clear that the primary object of the ministry is the edification of Christians and leadership in the evangelization of others.

3. The Word of God does not support the two false elements which crept into the mediaeval doctrine of the ministry and have remained influential ever since. These two alien conceptions are the confining of the power of government over the church to an hierarchical order (the New Testament treats church 'government' in the context of *service*) and the

assigning to ministers of a mediatorial work as priests. Scripture asserts that Christians as a whole constitute a priesthood (1 Pet. 2:5). Scholars are agreed that a sacerdotal ministry does not appear in Christian writers until the close of the second century. 'Sacrifice is no part of the Christian ministry' (Hooker).

4. The idea of a distinction between the ministry and other Christians, leading to the setting up of a clerical 'caste', is unknown to Scripture. Ministers are not differentiated from the rest of the *laos* or 'people' of God (hence our use of 'laity' is clearly misleading). This is not the same as to say that the church has no 'gifts' of individuals who are called to exercise government among Christian people and that the church is to be considered as an unguided democracy with a claim to self-determination. Those called to the ministry (as the very name implies) were 'servants' of the church and not its governors.

5. The essential safeguards imposed by Scripture must be preserved at all costs. These are:

(i) The person undertaking to serve the church in the capacity of a Christian minister should be one who has received the necessary 'gift' from the Head of the church and should be as certain of his call to this ministry as he who undertakes to carry the gospel to heathen lands.

(ii) The representatives of the church are responsible to recognize whether he has the necessary formal qualifications for the proper exercise of 'the gift', and to be satisfied concerning his spirituality and exemplary conduct.

(iii) Ordination is not to any *power* over the church; it is an official recognition, commendation and setting apart of one whom God has previously endowed.[1]

b. Development

It is often said that the scriptural references were to the 'temporary', 'embryonic' ministry beginning to emerge at the time of the apostles and that subsequently further developments were bound to arise. This is undoubtedly true to a limited extent. But it seems inconceivable that while being clear on so many other matters, Scripture should have omitted or made slight reference to any matters which were to prove of vital importance in the eventual development, progress and government of the church. It seems a justifiable claim that principles are laid down which are sufficient for the church in all ages, and that, whatever local conditions may render expedient or necessary in other ways, no plain principle of Scripture should be infringed by such developments.

[1] See J. B. Lightfoot's *Essay on the Christian Ministry* (Macmillan, 1901) for a scholarly examination of scriptural passages which bear on this subject.

A brief historical sketch may help to clarify the position.

1. The New Testament recognizes three periods:

(i) Our Lord's ministry, together with that of the seventy directly commissioned by Him.

(ii) The apostles were delegated with special authority by our Lord, having been chosen for the purpose of authoritative leadership in the infant church following Pentecost.

(iii) The Holy Spirit directed the apostles in further measures, and afterwards controlled and developed their work. They appointed 'deacons' to attend to the temporal business of the church. Note that these needed spiritual qualifications in addition to their natural aptitude. They ordained 'elders' or 'bishops', who united in conferences which were the germ of the later General Councils of the church. They recorded the apostolic teaching and practice in a permanent form. The three Pastoral Epistles, for example, contain the principles of the office of the ministry.

2. *The Transitional Ministry.*—During most of the lifetime of the apostles, and until the New Testament had been circulated to the various Christian communities, there were special gifts, for example of 'prophecy', in the church. The object of these was to enable the local community to receive the elements of the New Testament revelation of Christ direct from the Spirit of God. When the apostles had completed their work some of the 'gifts' ceased. For instance, there was not a continued succession of apostles and prophets. Compare Ephesians 2:20; 3:5; 4:11.

3. *The Permanent Ministry.*—The Pastoral Epistles indicate two 'orders' of ministry:

(i) 'Deacons' to fulfil a service of which no details are given.

(ii) 'Elders' or 'bishops' responsible for the regular ministry of the church. They were ordained by the 'laying on of hands' of their fellow 'presbyters'. Their functions and the necessary spiritual qualifications are clearly delineated. They were responsible for the conduct of the worship and services of the church, for teaching from Scripture, and for the discipline of the local members of the church.

Scripture, while never encouraging ideas of mere democracy or communism in spiritual affairs and definitely discouraging unnecessary individualism, makes it clear that the elders were directly responsible to the Head of the church for the conduct of the work. They were His stewards. While being responsible to see that all things were in order, they had no right to legislate for their fellow-Christians. All mediaeval and modern developments which have impaired the chief principles underlying the plain teaching of the Pastoral Epistles are to be deplored. The ministry is responsible to uphold the rule of Holy Scripture in the church and not to impose demands which add to or detract from Scripture. Most of all is it to be deplored that one elder (the pope) should have arrogated to himself the claim to supreme spiritual territorial jurisdiction and to have power to make additional spiritual laws equally binding with the New Testament principles on all the faithful.

c. Historical Survey

The chief historical divisions in procedure have been:

1. *The Latin Church.*—The system of metropolitan bishops exercising a certain measure of control over the bishops within their area appears in the third century. From about this time, the bishop in Rome began to lay claim to authority over all other bishops, and within a few centuries this claim attained universal recognition in the Western church. With it went the development of a sacerdotal system. The claim of papal supremacy has continued to undergo refinement and elaboration into modern times.

2. *The Eastern Church* (*Greek Orthodox*) has persistently refused to acknowledge papal supremacy and has continued under its patriarchs. It regards the Roman position as one of schism. (The term 'Eastern church' is here adopted for convenience; in fact, there is a loose federation of several existent churches in the East.)

3. *The Anglican Reformation* rejected papal authority, while retaining the episcopal form of government. It restored the lost conception of 'the priesthood of all believers' and the conception of ordination to the ministry as the official recognition of a prior gift of the Spirit (see above).

4. *The Reformed Churches* on the continent (and in Scotland), under the influence of Calvin, instituted a form of government which is, briefly, based on the authority of the elders from the smallest community to the General Assembly. A distinction is made between teaching elders and ruling elders on the basis of 1 Timothy 5:17.

5. *The Society of Friends* and a few other communities of Christians either regard the orders of ministry (also to some extent the sacraments) as intended for the early transitional period in the church or deny the authority of any of the present forms of ministry. Several of the latter have no external means of ratifying or commending these gifts. They consider that they should prove themselves when being exercised.

d. Variations from Scriptural Standards

The following four abuses of the order of the ministry will be but briefly considered. For a fuller discussion reference books should be consulted.

1. *Ordination.*—*The method* is of comparatively little importance. But the conception of the nature of ordination may have profound consequences. It will be found that the germ of many of the abuses of the

Christian ministry lies here. The chief divergence is the unwarranted claim of certain churches to bestow on Christian ministers those powers of priesthood which belong solely to our Lord Jesus Christ (Heb. 7:24). Any view of the Christian ministry which makes ordination the occasion for the supposed bestowal of powers of mediation, sacrifice and special judicial powers over sinners is false to Holy Scripture. There is no occasion in the New Testament where the Christian minister is termed 'priest'.

2. *Apostolic Succession and 'the Power of the Keys'*.—The claim frequently made to apostolic succession rests on a very flimsy basis. Rome makes a double claim:

(i) That 'the power of the keys' (*i.e.*, authority in ecclesiastical matters) was delegated to St. Peter (Mt. 16:19) and by him to the succeeding bishops in Rome. The power of 'binding and loosing' in the matter of the forgiveness of sin is associated with this authority. (This must be distinguished from the ministerial power of the keys, which involves the right to impose censure and to excommunicate for grave offences, and which is acknowledged and practised by many Christians outside the Roman communion.)

(ii) That certain sacraments of the church are fully performed only by members of the priesthood who are in the apostolic succession, which is claimed to be an unbroken succession of the laying on of hands from the time of the apostles.

As for (i), there is no evidence that St. Peter did or could transfer any special authority which was given him. (In fact the other apostles were given the same authority as he was. See Mt. 16:19; 18:18; Jn. 20:22, 23.) In an issue of this importance, we are justified in demanding greater clarity than is afforded by the decidedly sketchy evidence relating to Peter's sojourn in Rome. It is clear that papal claims developed slowly (Mt. 16:18, 19 were not invoked till the third century) out of the prominence enjoyed by the Roman church as the church of the capital of the Empire, where the two chief apostles, Peter and Paul, were martyred.

With regard to (ii), Scripture clearly teaches the desirability of a succession of godly ministers (2 Tim. 2:2), and the presence of such a succession has great influence on the stability of the church. But this is vastly different from the Roman claims. Archbishop Whately emphatically stated that so far as historical evidence goes not a single cleric can demonstrate his succession from the apostles. There is no evidence that the apostles had exclusive sacerdotal authority, or, if they had, that they were empowered to transmit it. Nor is there any indication that their immediate successors claimed or used such authority.

The rigid theory of apostolic succession developed in the third century out of a healthy stress on the external historical continuity of the churches founded by the apostles, and of the ministries within those churches. In its time this emphasis played a valuable part in the defence of the faith against heretical innovations claiming apostolic authority.

3. *Sacerdotalism.*—The idea that the Christian minister is in any sense a mediator between God and man is 'repugnant to holy Scripture'. He may be a channel (or medium) through whom God speaks to His people. But there is no hint in Scripture that he is an indispensable link between an individual Christian and his God. There is no trace of the doctrine of the Mass whereby the Christian minister becomes a *sacerdos* in the sense of a sacrificing priest. Not once in the New Testament is the word used of the ministry.[1]

The same perversion may be present in subtler forms. The Christian must beware of any obtrusion on the part of a ministry which in any way weakens the glory of our Lord's High Priestly work (see the Epistles) or arrogates to itself any power which Scripture claims belongs solely to Him or the Holy Spirit. While he ought to magnify the office of those commissioned to 'feed the flock of God', he must also hold firmly to his own privileges as a member of the 'royal priesthood' of redeemed sinners.

Scriptures

a. *The Ministerial Office*

See especially Paul's Epistles to Timothy and Titus.

1. *The Gifts to the Church.*—I Cor. 12:28; Eph. 4:11, 12. The gifts which receive considerable emphasis are:

(i) Apostles and prophets: Eph. 2:20; 3:5; 4:11. These seem to have ceased, at least in their New Testament form, at the completion of the foundation of the church (see Rev. 21:14), and after committing the apostolic faith to writing.

(ii) Evangelists: Acts 8:5, 35; 21:8; Eph, 4:11; 2 Tim. 4:5.

(iii) Teachers: Acts 13:1; Rom. 12:7; 1 Cor. 12:28; Eph. 4:11.

(iv) Pastors (lit., shepherds): Eph. 4:11. *Cf.* Acts 20:28; I Pet. 5:2–4.

2. *Permanent Ministry*

(i) Characteristics of Officers: Acts 20:17–35; 1 Tim. 3:1–13; 4; 5; 2 Tim. 2–4.

(ii) Elders or Bishops: Acts 14:23; 20:17, 28; Phil. 1:1; 1 Tim. 3:1–7; 4:14; 5:17, 19; Tit. 1:5–9; 1 Pet. 5:1–4.

(iii) Deacons: Acts 6:1–7; Rom. 16:1; Phil. 1:1; 1 Tim. 3:8–13.

b. *Rule in the Church*

1. *Our Lord's Primacy.*—Eph. 1:22; 4:15, 16; Col. 2:19; Heb. 13:20; I Pet. 5:4.

2. *Evidence of Government within the Church.*—Mt. 16:18; 1 Cor. 12:28; 16:15, 16; 1 Thes. 5:12, 13; 1 Tim. 5:17; Tit. 1:9; Heb. 13:7, 17, 24.

---

[1] Bishop Westcott used to claim this absence of the term 'priest' (in view of the constant Jewish and Roman usage with which the apostles were familiar) as the strongest point in favour of verbal inspiration. Etymologically neither the word *hiereus* nor *sacerdos* has a sacrificial import. Usage has invested the words with this significance. Tertullian uses *sacerdos* freely, but it would be precarious to import modern sacrificial implicates into all of his uses.

3. *Association of Churches.*—Acts 15:2; 20:17; Rom. 15:26; I Cor. 11:16; 2 Cor. 8:1, 18, 19, 23–9:2; Col. 4:16; Tit. 1:5.

c. *Priesthood*

1. *Our Lord Alone High Priest.*—Heb. 9:28; 10:11, 12; 13:10–16. (*Cf.* Heb. 7: 1–28.)

2. *All Believers Priests* (in spiritual sense).—I Pet. 2:9; Rev. 1:6; 5:9, 10.

Questions

1. What preparation did our Lord make during His life on earth for the government and ministry of His church?

2. How far are the functions of 'bishop', 'elder' and 'deacon', as depicted in the New Testament, synonymous, and how far are they to be differentiated?

3. Is there a proper form of 'apostolic succession'? If so, what does it consist of? *Cf.* I Tim. 1:18; 6:20; 2 Tim. 1:14; 2:2.

4. What is meant by 'the priesthood of all believers', and what does it not mean?

BIBLIOGRAPHY

N. Dimock, *The Christian Doctrine of the Sacerdotium*, Longmans, 1910.

E. M. B. Green, *Called to Serve*, Hodder and Stoughton, 1964.

J. B. Lightfoot, *Essay on the Christian Ministry*, Macmillan, 1901.

T. W. Manson, *The Church's Ministry*, Hodder and Stoughton, 1948.

T. W. Manson, *Ministry and Priesthood: Christ's and Ours*, Epworth Press, 1958.

L. Morris, *Ministers of God*, IVF, 1964.

3. The Means of Grace

By 'means of grace' is meant all the ordinances of God whereby we receive His covenanted blessings. There are many easily obtainable booklets on these subjects. The student should take into careful consideration the teaching of his ministers and parents, but clearly what is most needed is a knowledge of what Scripture actually says. The following notes will indicate the points needing emphasis and where twentieth-century Christianity is tending to forget the lessons of the past.

a. Prayer

The nature of prayer is very far from being generally understood. To many Christians it is merely an instrument for obtaining deliverance from awkward situations or the obtaining of something which is desired. It does not seem to be clear to them that it is one of the chief means of grace and the one in which the soul may come to know God in a way fuller and deeper than perhaps any other. It is the result of our Lord's High Priestly work that the individual Christian has now the right of direct access to the throne of God. This in itself should give a dignity and value to all prayer which other exercises of the soul may lack.

The Christian should study carefully the scriptural injunctions and examples of prayer from this point of view. The following points should be especially noted:

1. It is primarily the communion and free converse of the soul with God. Compare the communion between God and unfallen man.

2. It is the form of exercise of the soul which brings us into line with God's own will. It is impossible properly to pray when under the dominion of self-will, and nothing dispels our own desires so rapidly as prayer. It is also the place where we learn to share God's views of Christ and become occupied with His interests in the world.

3. It is the opportunity for direct request to God on our own or someone else's behalf.

It should also be noticed that the other means of grace are ineffectual unless connected with prayer, and that God has connected special blessing with the united prayer of the church.

b. Bible Reading

Again, in relation to the work of the Holy Spirit, the habit of daily Bible reading takes on a new importance and dignity. How many Christians habitually go to their Bibles with a full realization that the revelation of God is displayed before them and that they already possess within them the illumination supplied by the authorized Interpreter? It is as they peruse His portrait and sayings that the living Christ is mediated in their daily experience.

Note also that the Word of God is the means of grace in three ways:

1. It is the medium through which God makes Himself known when it is read either privately or publicly.

2. In Christian preaching it is the instrument God normally uses to produce conviction of sin, saving faith and sanctification.

3. It is connected closely with all the other means of grace. Compare the use of prayer.

c. The Ministry of the Word of God

While the Holy Spirit is the true Giver of full understanding, the individual Christian's capacity for the reception of divine teaching is limited. One of the means provided by God for increase in the capacity for reception and in the knowledge of divine things is the spoken ministry of the Word of God. By means of the 'gifts' in the ministry of the church the individual is led to compare his grasp of truth with the standards of another and is led into new spiritual pasturage through the differing viewpoint of another. Preaching is 'truth expressed through personality' and too much emphasis cannot be laid on the value to the Christian of the stimulus to deeper study supplied by the wider experience of the true Christian minister. We neglect any of God's spiritual provisions at our peril.

d. Worship

It is often truly said that the Christian can worship in his home or where-ever he is. But, having said this, there lurks in some minds a curious in-ability to see God's side of the question. Scripture informs us that pleasure is given to God when a community of redeemed men meet for the express purpose of doing honour to Christ. This was one of the earliest forms of Christian activity. Descriptions such as that in Pliny's letter to Trajan reveal the simple nature of the worship of the early Christians. 'They sing a hymn to Christ as to God.'

A wealth of meaning underlies such a statement.

Quite apart from its uplifting and transforming influence on the Christian himself, to do honour to the ever adorable Trinity from whom they have received such incalculable blessing is, surely, to be regarded as the highest object to which redeemed men can turn their powers. Men meet for purposes of mutual enjoyment and for doing honour to their fellows. It is a surpassing mystery that Christians should need persuading to assemble for the corporate worship of God. The cause, more often than not, is a flagrant neglect of the other means of grace.

e. The Sacraments

In recoiling from mediaeval abuses in the teaching and administration of the divine ordinances, the Reformation churches duly emphasized the right of direct access and the all-importance of personal faith in Christ. Their modern descendants have reiterated their emphasis, but sometimes have lost sight of their practice and the importance they attached to the means of grace. There is a danger today that in resisting the claims of sacerdotalism some of the most important provisions of God for the health of the Christian may become undervalued or neglected. It is difficult to understand how keen and devoted Christians can read a passage such as 1 Corinthians 11:23-26 without attaching more than ordinary importance to the Communion service.

1. *Definition.*—The term is derived from *sacramentum*, the Latin equivalent of the Greek word *mystērion*, which meant 'a secret now revealed', and so 'something of mystical significance', 'a symbol'. Its Latin equivalent applied to a soldier's oath on entering the army, and also to a solemn engagement or pledge of a religious nature.

By the third century the word had come to have a more specialized meaning in ecclesiastical Latin and was confined to the more sacred acts pertaining to the Christian ministry. The Church of England Catechism defines the meaning of the word as 'an outward and visible sign of an inward and spiritual grace'. The Westminster Shorter Catechism says: 'A sacrament is an holy ordinance instituted by Christ; wherein, by sensible signs, Christ and the benefits of the new covenant are represented, sealed, and applied to believers.' For a full discussion of the development of the modern usages of the word see larger books.

2. *Number*.—The Reformed churches have confined the number of the sacraments to two, limiting the use of the word to those ordinances which were instituted by the Lord Himself and making this requirement a further part of the definition of a sacrament. The only two symbolic acts commanded by Christ Himself are Baptism and the Lord's Supper. The Roman church recognizes seven sacraments, adding to the above—confirmation, penance, orders (authority given to the priest), matrimony and extreme unction.

3. *Nature*.—*Externally* they are to be regarded as visible tokens ('badges and seals') of God's grace. Compare circumcision and the Jewish feasts such as the Passover. Hence, their observance is an outward sign of the Christian's profession to the world around him. *Internally* they are to the Christian himself a pledge of the certainty of God's covenanted grace. Hence, they are both outward 'signs' whereby God declares the fact of His operation on behalf of the recipient and 'seals' in which He pledges the verity of His promises to the one participating. In this latter sense of a 'seal' the sacrament, for example, of the Lord's Supper, is God's signature and token that He will assuredly complete all that He has promised under the covenant of redemption (this is implied in 'You proclaim the Lord's death until he comes'), and that He is actually operating in fulfilment of these covenant promises.

Hence, the three requirements for a sacrament (in the evangelical sense) are that it must be by Christ's own appointment, it must have a visible sign or emblem, and it must be associated with an inward grace. (See below.)

4. *Efficacy*.—There have been two tendencies away from the true view of the value of the sacraments. In the first place, there has been an overvaluation. The mediaeval church became a community in which the 'mysteries' of religion were performed with increasing ritual observances. A type of Christianity was produced which consisted in the laity's paying the clergy to perform on their behalf rites which they did not understand and to which they superstitiously attributed an unfailing efficacy which absolved them from the heart-service of God. A sacrament was provided for each main requirement of life. This reduced the practice of religion to mere attendance on the sacraments.

On the other hand, there have been those who have undervalued the sacraments. Zwingli is reported, but not correctly, to have taught that they were but external signs and that the grace attached to them was derived solely from the spiritual concepts in the minds of those partaking of the sacrament. The mystics spiritualized their meaning and tended to regard the use of the signs as almost unspiritual, saying that the Christian's faith should be strong enough not to need them. The Society of Friends took the view that the two sacraments were intended merely for the infant church and were not destined to continue when true religion had become strong.

In approaching the subject as to how the two sacraments are to be regarded as 'means of grace', it is necessary to be certain what we mean by 'grace'. It is easy to state what it is *not*. It is not a vague, indefinable divine influence. It is not a 'commodity' which can be distributed at will in the manner of the material of which the symbols are composed. It is not something different from what we understand of the grace of God elsewhere. 'Grace' is God's constant approach in unmerited favour towards men, which has displayed itself in the giving of His Son and in His continued working for human redemption. By using the words 'means of grace' we do not intend to imply that there is a special type of favour to be obtained from God in their use, but that they are means through which God's constant activity towards us becomes more fully known and His favour is definitely apprehended.

The chief views of the efficacy of the sacraments may be described as follows:

(i) The Roman Catholic doctrine, as expressed in its official formulas of the Council of Trent, states: 'If anyone shall say that grace is not conferred *ex opere operato* (*i.e.*, 'by the act performed'), but that belief in the divine promise alone suffices to obtain grace, let him be anathema.' The mediaeval *ex opere operato* view may be briefly stated as follows: Grace is objectively conveyed in a sacrament by virtue of the execution of the sacramental action, and this holds true so long as the participants are not in a state of mortal sin and the administrator's 'intention' is in conformity with that of the church. This mechanical view was accompanied by the equally unscriptural doctrine of 'intention'. This taught that, on the one hand, the grace conferred was independent of the administrator's mode of life and, on the other, that he was necessary to the due performance in that it has no efficacy apart from the minister's ability to perform the ceremony according to the correct 'intention' of the church. In matrimony the contracting parties are regarded as ministers of the sacrament.

(ii) The Lutheran doctrine agrees with the Roman in its strong objective emphasis and has also been called an *ex opere operato* view, but differs in ascribing the sacrament's efficacy to the Word of God associated with the sacramental action. Luther further insists that the absence of faith creates an obstacle to the reception of blessing rather than the presence of 'mortal sin' as in the Roman teaching. Most Lutherans object to being charged with the *ex opere operato* view. They maintain that where the stress is laid upon faith and God's Word it is impossible to regard the sacrament as effective merely by the performance of the sacramental action, whatever view is held of the sacrament in other respects.

(iii) The Calvinistic view, with which the Anglican agrees, insists on 'worthy reception', and attributes the effect to God working in us, so that the sacraments become 'sure witnesses', and pledges of God's favour to us. The emphasis is moved from an inherent power in the sacrament to the direct work of God in the believing soul.

(iv) Zwingli's (alleged) teaching states that the sacraments represent man's pledges of loyalty to God, rather than of God's favour to men.

The emphasis must surely be on faith and on 'worthy reception'. 'Without faith it is impossible to please God.' In all God's operations in the hearts of men, His Agent is the Holy Spirit, and the instrument whereby man receives Him is faith. On the other hand, faith does not transform the nature of a sacrament. It merely enables a man to appropriate God's prior provision for him. The sacraments represent God's approach to men in the form of special covenant pledges, and man's attitude in return should be one of faith.

The suggestion of grace *ex opere operato* must be refused in any form; there is no shred of evidence for it in Scripture, and it is directly opposed to the whole scheme of God's dealings with men on the basis of faith.

f. Baptism

In view of the divergent opinions which are held as to the mode and subjects of baptism, it would be unprofitable for us to discuss these in the present studies. 'Let everyone be fully convinced in his own mind.' Attention will, therefore, be focused upon certain important principles upon which all Christians should be quite clear, and there should be no difficulty if, for these purposes, the considerations be confined to adults. Let the reader imagine himself in a foreign country where a number of adults have been converted to Christ from pure paganism. Certain qualifications will be required in the candidate. There must be a definite profession of faith in Christ and an avowal of allegiance to Him; a certain knowledge of Christian doctrine (at least a few fundamentals), for no missionary would baptize a completely uninstructed convert; a renunciation of the old life and old allegiances—in other words, the intention to 'walk in newness of life' under the control of his new Master.

Baptism, as we have seen, is 'the outward and visible sign of an inward and spiritual grace'. In the case of the new convert referred to above, he became inwardly a member of the church by virtue of his reception of Christ by faith. He was *declared* to be a member of the church openly by the sacrament of baptism. Hence baptism is a *sign* of his new membership in the body of Christ and, to the man himself, a *seal* of his union with Christ and his covenant relationship with God. The apostle appeals upon the basis of baptism for a 'reckoning' that henceforth the man's old life has been crucified and buried with Christ and that he is now risen to a new life in which he is exhorted 'to walk in newness of life'. He is vividly assured of the benefits which are his by virtue of his union with his new Owner.

Needless to say, there is an obligation resting upon all Christians to observe this sacrament, and it is neglected to the definite loss of the persons or communities who undervalue it.

In conclusion, it may be helpful to summarize the three most usually held views:

1. The Roman Catholic doctrine of baptism is again largely devoid of scriptural support, and is in accordance with the view of *opus operatum* in general. In effect, the mechanical application of the rite of baptism by a member of the priesthood, or even a layman or woman, removes the disabilities of original sin and results in the subject's justification. The emphasis is upon the right administration when the grace is automatically conferred. The Reformers placed their emphasis on right reception and insisted on the fact of faith accompanying.

2. In the case of adults the main body of Protestant communities require the qualifications described above. On the question of infant baptism, it ought to be emphasized that the common evangelical view has never been that through baptism the child of Christian parents is 'regenerated'[1] (in the sense of 'renovation') and thereby becomes a member of the body of Christ, but that when brought in faith by believing parents and baptized he is brought into the visible church and thus brought within the sphere of the covenanted mercies of God. The sacrament is a sign and a pledge that he is within the circle which is in enjoyment of the privileges bestowed by the Christian covenant. 'The promise is to you and to your children.' But the child is yet responsible himself to receive Christ by faith and voluntarily to enter into the covenant union with Christ. The early administration of baptism does not remove the requirement of faith either in the parents who bring the child or in the child himself who must exercise it, on coming to years of discretion, to claim his inheritance. Nor does it relieve the parents of the duty of careful instruction in the things of God. Compare circumcision, which was the pledge and sign of the coven-

---

[1] The use of the word 'regeneration' in connection with baptism follows the principle laid down by Augustine that the sign is spoken of in the terms of the thing signified. Thus the bread in Holy Communion is called 'the body of the Lord'. The invariable spiritual regeneration of all infants in baptism cannot be deduced simply from the use of the term 'regenerate' or 'regeneration'.

ant with Israel. The Jewish child was still responsible to retain his birth-right and to take for himself the Lord Jehovah as his God. Personal faith is invariably the requirement and the instrument whereby man claims and receives God's grace and provision.

3. The view of the Baptists and several other communities is that baptism should be confined to those who at the time of the rite possess the qualifications outlined at the beginning of this section.

For the various considerations upon which these two latter schools base their teaching see larger books.

g. Holy Communion

With few exceptions, the church has been agreed as to the obligation resting upon the followers of Christ to observe the sacrament which is so clearly stated in Scripture to have been instituted by the Lord Himself. The mode of administration differs little among the Protestant communities, and all are agreed as to the qualifications required in the person desiring to participate. There is also a deep appreciation of the value of this sacrament on the part of the majority of evangelical Christians. Students, however, particularly those who are in residential universities, need to be even more on their guard against the neglect of Holy Communion than of public worship in general. A careful study of the Scriptures which apply to this profound subject will abundantly repay the time and any pains spent upon it.[1]

In connection with the New Testament account of the institution, compare the observance by the Jewish people of the Passover. The latter represented a memorial of deliverance from bondage and a perpetual sign of and renewal of the covenant. By the fact of His instituting the Com-munion service in connection with the Passover feast, our Lord replaced the observance of the Passover by that of Holy Communion. To the Christian the Holy Communion is a memorial of the death of Christ; avows and ensures his participation in the body and blood of Christ; signifies his acceptance of the new covenant, which was sealed by the blood of Christ; and represents and effects the union of Christians. 'We who are many are one bread.'

The chief controversies concern the Protestant refusal of the Roman divergences from the teaching of Holy Scripture and in particular: Communion 'in one kind', the doctrine of the Mass, and the doctrine of the 'real presence'.

1. *Communion 'in one kind'*.—The Council of Trent has emphatically stated that the Roman church has 'just reasons' for withholding the cup

[1] See the three Gospel accounts of the institution and 1 Cor. 10:15-17 and 11: 23-29.

from the laity, and 'if anyone shall deny that Christ, whole and entire . . . is received under the one species of bread, because, as some falsely assert, He is not received according to the institution of Christ Himself under both kinds: let him be anathema.'

This is probably the most patent of Rome's perverse divergences from the plain teaching of Holy Scripture. Nothing is more clear from the accounts of our Lord's institution of the sacrament than that He intended the cup, equally with the bread, to be offered to each participant. The rulings of the Council of Trent are, on clear historical evidence, contradictory of fifth-century papal decrees, and as late as the twelfth century there is an instance of a pope (Pope Paschal II in 1118) deprecating the practice of 'Communion in one kind'.

The Reformers, claiming that the representatives of the church have no authority for amending a divine commandment, restored the cup to the laity.

2. *The Doctrine of the Mass.*—The Reformers equally rejected the doctrine of sacrifice, which is the ultimate blasphemy of the Roman teaching. 'If anyone shall say that in the Mass a true and proper sacrifice is not offered to God, let him be accursed.'

The Reformers utterly rejected the doctrine that the Roman priests had power to 'recrucify' Christ on their altars and to repeat the one sacrifice of Christ. They regarded it as a most intolerable slight upon the efficacy of the one, full and perfect satisfaction for sins made by our Lord on Calvary. 'The offering of Christ once made is that perfect redemption, propitiation, and satisfaction, for all the sins of the whole world, both original and actual; and there is none other satisfaction for sin, but that alone.'[1]

For a full discussion refer to the appropriate books. A survey of the evidence will reveal that in regard to the Roman Catholic doctrine there is no scriptural support whatever, but emphatically the reverse (*cf.* Heb. 7:27; 9:12, 26; 10:10). In Hebrews 6:6 the blasphemy of recrucifying Christ (if it were possible) is plainly deprecated. We shall also find that the use of sacerdotal words, such as 'altar' and 'sacrifice', was not developed until the end of the second century. Cyprian is the first to refer unambiguously to such a sacrifice connected with the Holy Communion. 'In this first stage of Christian literature there is not only no example of the application of the word "altar" to any concrete, material object as the Holy Table, but there is no room for such an application' (Westcott).

The student is advised to read carefully the Epistle to the Hebrews, which ought to leave him in no possible doubt on this matter. 'So far as the Atonement in relation to God is spoken of in any terms of time, the

[1] Article XXXI of the Church of England.

Bible seems to me to teach us to think of it as lying entirely in the past—a thing done "once for all" ' (Hort).

Included in the Roman Catholic doctrines of the Mass are those concerning the supposed changes in the essence of the material bread and wine, resulting in the claim that our Lord is present in a way which differs in character from that of His presence with Christians met for worship.

Historically, the stages in the development of this 'advanced' doctrine concerning the nature of the sacrament were as follows:

The Holy Communion was always, it seems, the central act of Christian worship, and its position of prominence led in the early centuries to its being invested with an almost superstitious significance and virtue.

The next stage consisted in changing the nature of the service from one chiefly of memorial and pledge to a visible repetition of the sacrifice of our Lord. Consequently, the material substance of the emblems was soon claimed as changed into the actual substance of the victim to be sacrified.

By an easy step the emblem of sacrifice was claimed actually to be the 'host' (from *hostia*, 'a sacrifice') and offered for adoration and worship by the faithful. A further stage of departure from the simple institution of our Lord was the offering of masses for the departed in order to aid in their escape from purgatorial fires.

The two chief elements of the official Roman teaching are:

(i) That in the Mass there is a transubstantiation or change of substance which is as much a miracle as our Lord's incarnation.

(ii) That the actual substance of the bread and wine thus changed into the substance of the actual body and blood of Christ is offered to God the Father for sins and offences through the medium of the priest. The accidents (appearance, taste, *etc.*, of bread and wine) remain. These changes take place (provided the administrator's 'intention' is that of the church) with unfailing regularity and efficacy, and the offered body and blood of our Lord are available for the sins of the living and the dead.

The chief opposing views are:

(i) *The Lutheran.*—That our Lord is really present, but without change in the substance of the emblems. This view, known as *consubstantiation* (in contrast with transubstantiation), may best be defined as the real Christ *with* the unchanged substance of the bread. The communicant partakes of the glorified body at the same time as the bread. The word 'consubstantia- tion' is not always accepted by Lutherans as clearly indicative of their doctrine. They prefer to say 'in, with, or under' the bread and wine.

(ii) *The So-called Zwinglian.*—That the sacrament is only symbolical, and the partaking of the emblems a memorial only.

(iii) *The Calvinist.*—That while our Lord's actual glorified body is not partaken by the communicant and the substance of the emblems is unchanged, yet the communicant by faith enters into a special spiritual union of his soul with the glorified Christ. It presents the view of a 'spiritual reception' of Christ by faith. This is the most general view in English-speaking countries. Many, however, prefer to associate the Communion with Christ crucified, and to teach a spiritual union with the crucified Lord.

(iv) *The Doctrine of the Real Presence.*—A more subtle view, which is apt to deceive unwary Christians by its plausibility, is the doctrine of the 'real presence', which comes between transubstantiation and consubstantiation. This holds that the priesthood has power so to consecrate the elements that the Lord becomes conjoined with the elements in a real manner (the *praesentia realis*). This presence is not only a spiritual one and is not merely accompanying the elements. It is a modified form of transubstantiation which hesitates to say that the substance of the elements is changed, and yet would like to do so. It comes from an undue emphasis upon the words 'This is my body'. The Lutherans stoutly rejected any form of adoration of the elements and insisted that the body of our Lord is present only for purposes of communion and at the moment of use. The mediating view given above recognizes no such limitations, and in that particular approximates more closely to the Roman Catholic doctrine.

Scriptures

a. Prayer

1. *Private.*—Mt. 9:38; 26:41; Mk. 9:29; Lk. 11:1–3; Jn. 14:13, 14; 15:7; 16:24; Rom. 8:26, 27; Phil. 4:6; Col. 4:3; Jas. 5:16–18; 1 Jn. 3:22; 5:14–16.

2. *Corporate.*—Mt. 6:9–13; Acts 1:24; 2:42; 3:1; 4:23–31; 12:5, 12; 13:3; 16:13; 21:5; 1 Tim. 2:1, 2, 8; Heb. 10:19–25.

b. Bible Reading

Jos. 1:8; Pss. 1:2; 19:7–11; 119; Is. 34:16; Dn. 9:2; Jn. 5:39; Acts 17:11; 2 Tim. 3:14, 15.

c. Ministry of the Word

1. *Primary Duty.*—Mt. 28:19, 20; Lk. 24:44–48; Acts 5:20; 10:42; Rom. 10:11–17; 2 Cor. 5:19, 20.

2. *The Emphasis of the Apostles.*—Acts 2:14–40; 3:12–26; 4:29; 5:28, 42; 6:4; 8:4, 5; 1 Cor. 1:17; Col. 4:16; 2 Thes. 3:1; 1 Tim. 4:13, 16; 2 Tim. 2:2; 4:2.

3. *The Benefits.*—Jn. 8:31, 32; 15:3; 16:13–15; 20:30, 31; Rom. 15:4; 1 Cor. 10:6–11; Eph. 6:17; Phil. 2:16; Col. 3:16; 2 Tim. 3:15–17; Heb. 5:11–14; Jas. 1:21, 22.

d. Worship

1. *Individual.*—Ex. 34:5–8; Jos. 5:14; Pss. 103:1–5; 138:2; Mt. 4:10; Lk. 18:10–14; Acts 22:17–21; Rom. 12:1, 2; 1 Cor. 6:19, 20; Heb. 13:15, 16; Rev. 1:10–18.

2. *Public.*—Jn. 4:19–24; Acts 2:46, 47; 3:1; 13:2; 14:27; 15:12; 20:7–12; 1 Cor. 11:18, 20; 14:23–40; Eph. 5:19, 20; Phil. 3:3; Col. 3:16; Heb. 10:25; Jas. 2:1–4.

e. The Nature and Efficacy of Sacraments

Apart from faith they have no virtue in themselves: Acts 8: 13–24; Rom. 2:28, 29 (cf. Heb. 4:2); 4:9–12; 1 Cor. 10:1–6; 11:27–29; 1 Pet. 3:21.

f. Holy Baptism

1. *Obligation.*—Mt. 28:19; Acts 2:38; 8:36; 10:47, 48; 16:33; 22:16.

2. *Meaning.*—Acts 11:15–17 (with 10:47, 48); 19:1–6; Rom. 6:1–4; 1 Cor. 12: 13; Gal. 3:27; Eph. 4:5; Col. 2:11, 12; Tit. 3:5; 1 Pet. 3:20, 21.

3. *Subjects.*—Acts 2:39; 8:12. 'Baptists' restrict the subject of baptism to 'adult' believers. 'Paedobaptists' believe that believers and their children are proper subjects of the sacrament. The two texts are given as illustrating both views.

g. Holy Communion

1. *Institution.*—Mt. 26:26–29; Mk. 14:22–25; Lk. 22:14–20; 1 Cor. 11:23–29.

2. *Examples in the New Testament.*—Lk. 24:30, 35; Acts 2:42, 46; 20:7, 11; 1 Cor. 10:21: 11:20.

3. *Significance.*—1 Cor. 5:7, 8; 10:16–23; 11:20–34. See also Jn. 6:44–58, which, although not referring directly to the Lord's Supper, teaches truths which find visible expression in that sacrament.

Questions

Students are urged to gain a clear grasp of the nature of, and obligations connected with, the sacraments. They should not allow themselves to be side-tracked by debating the diversities of administration.

1. How do you understand the relation (a) between personal prayer and Bible reading, and (b) between intercessory prayer and the will of God? See Romans 8:26, 27.

2. Show how both Baptism and Holy Communion are 'sacraments of the gospel', and show further how Holy Communion is related to the past, present and future aspects of Christ's work of salvation.

3. Do the sacraments have any significance or value for the spiritual life over and above the blessings of the Word through faith? If not, why did Christ ordain them?

4. How should the ministry of the Word and the ministry of the sacraments be connected in the life of the church?

BIBLIOGRAPHY

R. Abba, *Principles of Christian Worship*, OUP, 1957.
G. R. Beasley-Murray, *Baptism in the New Testament*, Macmillan, 1962.
E. M. Bounds, *Power through Prayer*, Marshall, Morgan and Scott, 1954.
G. W. Bromiley, *The Baptism of Infants*, Church Book Room Press, 1955.
Robert Bruce, *The Mystery of the Lord's Supper*, James Clarke, 1958.
E. P. Clowney, *Preaching and Biblical Theology*, Tyndale Press, 1962.
N. Dimock, *The Doctrine of the Sacraments*, Longmans, 1908.
O. Hallesby, *Prayer*, IVF, 1961.
A. J. B. Higgins, *The Lord's Supper in the New Testament*, SCM Press, 1952.
C. H. Hodge, 'The Sacraments', *Systematic Theology*, James Clarke, 1960.
G. W. H. Lampe, *The Seal of the Spirit*, Longmans, 1951.
A. J. MacDonald (ed.), *The Evangelical Doctrine of Holy Communion*, SPCK, 1930.
P. C. Marcel, *The Biblical Doctrine of Infant Baptism*, James Clarke, 1953.
R. P. Martin, *Worship in the Early Church*, Marshall, Morgan and Scott, 1964.

Handley Moule, 'Pastoral Charge', *Letters to my Younger Brethren*, Hodder and Stoughton, 1892.

C. F. D. Moule, *Worship in the New Testament*, Lutterworth Press, 1961.

R. H. Mounce, *The Essential Nature of New Testament Preaching*, Eerdmans, 1960.

J. Murray, *Christian Baptism*, PRPC, 1952.

W. Niesel, sections in *Reformed Symbolics*, Oliver and Boyd, 1962.

J. I. Packer (ed.), *Eucharistic Sacrifice*, Church Book Room Press, 1962.

J. C. Ryle, *Knots Untied*, James Clarke, 1954.

J. C. Ryle, *Practical Religion*, ed. J. I. Packer, James Clarke, 1960.

J. C. Ryle, *Principles for Churchmen*, Thynne, 1884.

C. H. Spurgeon, *Lectures to my Students*, Marshall, Morgan and Scott, 1954.

J. S. Stewart, *Heralds of God*, Hodder and Stoughton, 1946.

A. M. Stibbs, *Expounding God's Word*, IVF, 1960.

A. M. Stibbs, *Obeying God's Word*, IVF, 1955.

A. M. Stibbs, *Understanding God's Word*, IVF, 1950.

A. M. Stibbs, *Sacrament, Sacrifice and Eucharist*, Tyndale Press, 1961.

J. R. W. Stott, *The Preacher's Portrait*, Tyndale Press, 1961.

R. A. Torrey, *How to Pray*, Oliphants, 1955.

J. Warns, *Baptism: its History and Significance*, Paternoster Press, 1958.

PART SEVEN

THE LAST THINGS

It is of the utmost importance that Christians who address themselves to the study of the problems of the future should be extremely cautious about their sources. Holy Scripture is the only utterly reliable guide, and even here, since God has seen fit to give us but brief statements on certain matters, care in the interpretation of isolated texts is clearly necessary. Much harm has been done by well-meaning but incautious zealots who have allowed their enthusiasm to run riot in wild and dogmatic assertions upon points where dogmatism is impossible. Still more harm has been done by those who have seized upon certain isolated texts and woven around them doctrines which are inconsistent with the rest of Scripture. Any theory of the hereafter which modifies or weakens any doctrine plainly stated elsewhere in Scripture is to be held suspect. In no field of study is it more vital to observe the rule of comparing Scripture with Scripture and remembering that none of the prophecies of Scripture is 'a matter of one's own (*i.e.*, private or esoteric) interpretation' (2 Pet. 1:20).

1. The Second Coming of Christ

a. *The Fact*

On the fact of a second coming of Christ there is common agreement amongst evangelical Christians. There can be no possible doubt that the Bible holds out to the Christian the 'blessed hope' of the second coming of our Lord Jesus Christ as the outstanding landmark of his spiritual horizon. Proof of this, if it be needed, may be found in a careful examination of the Scripture references. If frequency of mention is to be regarded as indicative of the importance of a doctrine (which of course does not necessarily follow), then there is an overwhelming case for the doctrine of the second coming. In any case, there are a sufficient number of references to make it a matter which cannot lightly be dismissed.

It has been found that the doctrine is referred to some three hundred times (or an average of once in every fifteen verses of the New Testament). In comparison with the fact that Holy Communion is mentioned on but four clear occasions and only one Epistle has an explicit reference, it is hard to understand why, if prominence be given to the one, neglect should be shown to the other by many Christians.

The student should concentrate on the *fact* of the coming and notice the scriptural applications of the subject. It should be one of our chief incentives to holy living and diligence in Christ's service.

b. Its Nature

As to the *mode* of the coming (except that it is 'in the same way as' the ascension) and the *time-factor* (except that the duration of church history is declared to be relatively short in God's reckoning), it is not wise to debate, and, in any case, Scripture does not supply sufficient data to justify rigidity. The one outstanding fact is that Christ has promised to return (Jn. 14:3 and Acts 1:11) and that this (not the physical change of death) is the event which the Christian awaits.

This applies equally to the generations of Christians who 'fell asleep' in Christ in the early stages of history. The coming of Christ is the event which will complete their salvation just as it will ours. They also await the final change into the promised conformity with Christ's glorified body, and even creation is said to 'groan in travail' awaiting 'the revealing of the sons of God'.

The Christian should be clear in his own mind regarding the following:

1. The phraseology of the Scripture references is not adequately interpreted by certain limitations of the doctrine such as that 'Christ comes at death'. It is gloriously true that Christ receives His own at the dissolution of their mortal bodies, but Scripture goes much further than that. Acts 1:11 and 1 Thessalonians 4:13–18 can, on no exegetical grounds, be made to mean anything but a coming in Person, such that the church as a whole (the completed company of the redeemed) will be aware of and benefit by it. Our Lord Himself implies a distinction between death and His coming (Jn. 21:23).

2. The fact of the *personal* nature of the Lord's return is the keystone of the doctrine. Whatever else the coming may not be and may not accomplish, Scripture unequivocally asserts that it will effect a union between Christ and all true believers. It will mean, at least, that they will see Him in a manner comparable to that of natural sight, and be made like unto Him in a (spiritual) form comparable to that of similarity in stature and character among men.

3. This doctrine is not intended to be merely for intellectual satisfaction. It should so be taught among Christians that they may be diligent in their stewardship ('Trade till I come'), righteous in their conduct ('Every one who thus hopes in him, purifies himself'), filled with joyous anticipation in all circumstances, and shown how all prophecy and the promises of God (including the glorification of the church and their own salvation) will be fulfilled.

c. Its Purposes

The chief purposes of the coming may be listed as follows:

1. *The final vindication of Jesus Christ as Lord and King*. There will be a complete realization of what His first advent achieved—the triumph of His death and resurrection and the establishment of the kingdom. The return will be the *apokalypsis* ('unveiling' or 'disclosure') of Christ and His glory (I Cor. 1:7; Tit. 2:13; I Pet. 1:7, 13; 5:1). See Mk. 14:62; I Cor. 15:23–28, 54, 55 (*cf.* Heb. 2:5–8, 14, 15); 2 Tim. 4:1; Heb. 9:28; Rev. 12:10.

2. *The completion and glorification of the church*. (The Epistles are primarily concerned with this part of the purpose.) This will include the salvation of the people of Israel (Rom. 11:25–32). See Mt. 24:31; Rom. 8:19, 23; I Thes. 4:15–17; 2 Thes. 2:1.

3. *The righteous judgment of the living and the dead*. For Christians, this will be in the nature of an assessment of their stewardship and the giving of rewards for faithfulness (Rom. 14:10–12; I Cor. 3:9–15; 4:5). For those who have rejected Christ there will be irretrievable loss (Mt. 13:41, 42, 49, 50; 2 Thes. 1:7–9; Rev. 20:11–15).

The judgment is preceded by the general resurrection of the dead (Dn. 12:2; Jn. 5:28, 29; Acts 24:15).

4. *The final overthrow of all powers of evil*. See I Corinthians 15:23–28 and 2 Thessalonians 2:3–10. At least parts of the central chapters of Revelation depict this ultimate conflict, though the detailed imagery is of uncertain significance.

5. *The establishment of 'a new heaven and a new earth'*. See below, pp. 191, 192.

It is important to realize that the New Testament, in the majority of cases, states bare facts concerning the consummation of the various unfulfilled prophecies. It does not, as a general rule, encourage speculation as to the times and the modes of these events. Every Christian should benefit from the glorious affirmations concerning the 'blessed hope' of Christ's personal return and from the repeated warnings associated with it. He may well be given deeper insight into, and gain more inspiration from, detailed study. But a rigid systematization of 'times and seasons', dependent upon veiled allusions, which are also capable of meanings other than that which is arbitrarily selected to fit the theory, is to be discouraged.

d. Historical Survey

1. *Our Lord*, while stating that He would certainly return, indicates that His coming would follow a necessary interval (Mt. 24:3, 14, 30, 31) and that many Christians would pass through death (*e.g.*, Jn. 6:44, 54; 21:18). But the *certainty* of His return as the final unfolding of His prospective victory on the cross naturally found expression in sayings that suggest it is imminent.

2. *The Apostles.*—It is by no means so certain as some would have us believe that St. Paul was convinced that our Lord would return during his lifetime. It is true that from time to time his words give the impression of an imminent expectation of Christ's coming, but other aspects of his writings make it clear that this is the way he expresses his urgent conviction of its certainty and his desire for its speedy accomplishment. Thus in numerous passages he discusses the effects of death and indicates that he himself expected to die and be raised at the coming. See Philippians 1:23; 3:11; *cf.* 2 Thessalonians 2:2. His missionary plan was conceived strategically to secure the effective evangelization of the whole Roman world.

3. *The Second and Third Centuries.*—There was much difference of opinion among Christian writers, varying from that of a final climax to the world's history by a general resurrection and great white throne of judgment to that of an earthly reign of Christ for one thousand years following the coming.

4. *Augustine* and a number of others were convinced that the powers of darkness had been annulled (Heb. 2:14) in the fullest degree and rendered powerless from the time of the death of our Lord. This implied that the millennium had already begun. He further believed that the verses in the Revelation which referred to further manifestations would be fulfilled at the close of the millennium. Due chiefly to the above teaching, there was widespread belief as the year AD 1000 approached that the close of the world's history was at hand.

5. *At the time of the Reformation*, many of the leaders believed themselves to be in the time of final catastrophe and that they were striving against antichrist in the form of Roman Catholicism.

6. *In modern times* there have been two schools of thought amongst evangelical Christians, which are dependent upon the view taken of Daniel and the Revelation (particularly of the latter).

(i) *The Historicists* believe that the major part of the prophecies of Daniel and Revelation have been already fulfilled, but that there still awaits a final climax to the strife of the evil powers against the dominion of our Lord, which will end in the complete overthrow of the former.

There is much to be said in favour of this view. That the 'mystery of lawlessness' was already at work is proved by Paul's second Epistle to the Thessalonians, and Luther contended that the symbolism of 'the scarlet woman' of the Revelation was an accurate delineation of papal Rome. But obviously there still remain some as yet unfulfilled events described in the Revelation.

(ii) *Futurist.*—Others take the view that most, if not all, of the prophecies subsequent to the end of chapter 3 of the Revelation as yet apply to the future.

The truth appears to be that much that has already happened in history (and the Reformers and other loyal souls in all ages of the church have rightly applied the instructions of Revelation to their own times) will be 'summed up' in the climactic and conclusive events of the end.

For a consideration of the views of a pre- and post-millennial advent see the appropriate books.

e. Fundamental Principles

The all-important nucleus of truth which should be firmly held irrespective of all divergences on matters of detail consists of:

1. The promise of a literal personal return of Christ.

2. The final glorification of the church—at last triumphant—and the irretrievable loss of the Christ-rejecters.

3. The doctrine of the coming must be preserved both from undue spiritualizing (for example, that Pentecost was the fulfilment) and from undue literalism (for example, that which presses the phraseology so that the conception of our Lord's final universal reign becomes lowered to that of the world conquest of an earthly emperor).

Finally, Dr. James Orr has pointed out that there are three very well-marked principles running through the scriptural references to this subject:

1. Scripture is neglectful of the date-element. Events which are apparently separated by a long duration of time become telescoped, and one verse may contain allusions to three prolonged and successive stages of divine operation.

2. The coming of Christ is so presented that it would appear to be a *process* (with several stages) rather than a single event.

3. The time of the coming seems to be conditional. Had more Christians remained faithful and the church completed her task the Lord might have come already. In the counsel and foreknowledge of the Father the date of our Lord's coming is indeed fixed. Yet (in an antinomy) the church is called upon to 'hasten' the coming, for example, by carrying the gospel to all nations, and is held responsible for any neglect.

Scriptures

The Second Coming

1. *Personal.*—Mt. 24:30; 26:64; Lk. 17:24; Jn. 14:3; Acts 1:11; 1 Cor. 15:23; Col. 3:4; 1 Thes. 4:16; 1 Tim. 6:14; Tit. 2:13; Heb. 9:28; 1 Pet. 5:4; Rev. 1:7; 22:20.

2. *Blessing and Judgment are prophesied.*—2 Cor. 5:10. (i) Blessing: Mt. 13:43; 25:34; Lk. 22:29, 30; Rom. 8:18–23; Col. 3:4; 2 Tim. 4:8; Rev. 3:11; 22:3, 4. (ii) Judgment: Mk. 8:38; Jn. 5:26–29; Acts 17:31; Rom. 2:16; 2 Thes. 1:7–9.

Questions

1. What Scriptures in your judgment most clearly teach the personal return of Christ? What are the purposes of His return?

2. What do you understand by the phrase 'The resurrection as applied to Christians'?

3. What results should the hope of Christ's return produce in the lives of Christians?

BIBLIOGRAPHY

David Brown, *Christ's Second Coming*, T. and T. Clark, 1882, for the post-millennial view.
W. J. Grier, *The Momentous Event*, Evangelical Bookshop, Belfast, 1945.
W. Hendriksen, *More than Conquerors*, Tyndale Press, 1947.
G. E. Ladd, *The Blessed Hope*, Eerdmans, 1956, for the pre-millennial view.
G. T. Manley, *The Return of Jesus Christ*, IVF, 1960.
Article on 'Eschatology', *The New Bible Dictionary*, IVF, 1962.

2. Human Destiny

Men still repeat the age-long question—'After death, what . . . ?' The state of the dead has been the subject of much speculation from the earliest times. Theories concerning it, in endless variation, are found in all religions. Even confining the inquiry to branches of Christianity itself, we are met by considerable divergences among professing Christians. In some cases these divergences may and do constitute serious error. On the other hand, the scriptural teaching is as clear and definite (for all practical purposes) as in any other branch of revelation. The chief requisite in the inquirer is for a careful examination of what the sacred text actually does say.

a. Death and Immortality

The word 'death', as ordinarily used in Scripture, denotes the dissolution of the 'physical' body. This general application is to be distinguished from certain associations which have become attached to it from alien theories, and from two further scriptural usages. These are:

1. *Annihilation.*—There is no example in the whole of the Bible of its certain use to imply complete cessation of being.

2. *Spiritual Death.*—Our Lord and the apostle to the Gentiles clearly teach that unregenerate men are in a state of spiritual death, which may be defined as estrangement and separation from God. This condition exists *now* in this life, while physical well-being is unimpaired. See, *e.g.*, Rom. 8:6; Eph. 2:1; 1 Jn. 5:12.

3. *'The Second Death'*, or *'Eternal Death'*.—This indicates a state where spiritual death (separation from God) is unalterably fixed (Rev. 20:12-15).

It is necessary further to notice that while the power of Satan, sin and death were met and completely defeated at the cross, physical death is still universal. The word used in Scripture (in, *e.g.*, Heb. 9:26) means to 'annul' or bring to no effect. Potentially, sin and death were dealt with completely at the cross. For those who will receive the victory of the cross, physical death is now a gateway into light and life with Christ. God in His purposes for the government of mankind has seen fit to leave physical death as a discipline for the Christian. But it remains unchanged in its terrors for men who reject the cross of Christ, because bodily death as well as spiritual bears the character of divine judgment upon sin (Rom. 5:12. This holds whether Adam was mortal before the Fall or not).

It is clear that Scripture speaks of a continuing personal existence between the disintegration of this earthly body and the 'putting on' of the heavenly body (see section *b*. below, and compare 1 Corinthians 15, which seems to imply some continuum which persists after the dissolution of 'this perishable nature' and waits the assumption of 'the imperishable'). It is customary to describe this as the soul's or spirit's survival of bodily death, and further to talk of this survival as evidence of 'natural immortality' (an expression which on any account is not to be thoughtlessly used). We must remember three points in this connection:

1. God alone possesses inherent and absolute immortality (1 Tim. 6:16).

2. The immortality of life in the resurrection body is clearly something more than this 'natural immortality', for the assumption of this body is termed 'the putting on of immortality' (1 Cor. 15:53, 54). We cannot confine this to the immortality of the body, as if it were merely being put on an equal footing with the (naturally immortal) soul. The whole person will enter upon a new form of existence which can be described as 'immortality'. (We should probably understand 2 Tim. 1:10 in a similar sense. It does not mean that our Lord brought to men a continuation of existence beyond death which had been forfeited as a result of the Fall. On the contrary, He Himself endured to the full the death which resulted from the Fall, and this involved for Him after the point of death the temporary separation of soul from body. The verse either means that Christ has banished the obscurity that surrounds Old Testament eschatology and enabled Christians to contemplate their eternal destiny with complete confidence, or that His resurrection has won for man an eternal life in the resurrection body which is qualitatively quite new, and in comparison with which 'natural immortality' is a very poor second.)

3. Paul also makes clear that being 'naked' or 'unclothed' is an unsatisfactory preliminary to being 'further clothed' with 'our heavenly dwelling' (2 Cor. 5:1-4). This refers to the period of existence between the two forms of bodily life, and reminds us that for the New Testament true human existence is bodily existence, and that the soul's temporary 'un-

clothed' existence must not be thought of as the survival of 'the real man' to the denigration of the body.

b. The Character of the Intermediate Existence

The chief problems which call for attention are whether the soul is conscious or unconscious, whether there is a further development, whether the probation of the soul is terminated by physical death, and what locality is assigned to the departed. For a full discussion the appropriate books must be consulted. The following points should, however, be noted:

1. *Consciousness.*—The chief alternative views are: (i) That the soul is fully conscious. (ii) That the soul continues to exist, but in a state of repose (*cf.* natural sleep). (iii) That the soul dies with the body, and in the same way awaits the resurrection.

Though some passages in the Old Testament might suggest a cessation of consciousness, the New Testament would seem to be clearly in favour of the first view. Our Lord Himself was 'made alive in the spirit' at death (1 Pet. 3:18)—implying consciousness during the period of His 'descent' (see p. 106). Again, although it is in parable, we must not neglect the suggestion of conscious existence in the case of the rich man and Lazarus. Then our Lord from the cross promised to the dying thief, 'Today you will be with me in Paradise.' It is difficult to escape the view that this would bring to the pardoned thief the joy of recognition and a state of felicity. Finally, we may notice that St. Paul was torn between remaining with his converts and departing to be with Christ, which he asserted would be 'far better' (Phil. 1:22–24). He would certainly not describe a state of unconsciousness as superior to that in which he could continue his pastoral care. See context and also other references, such as Revelation 6:9–11.

The arguments brought forward for the view of the 'sleep of the soul' do not seem to be adequate. For instance, that based on the Christian use of the word 'sleep' to describe death does not give sufficient force to the fact that the early Christians saw in it the transformation of the king of terrors into a friend of the battle-weary saint. 'Some have fallen asleep' (1 Cor. 15:6) can as well mean that they have been removed from the sphere of earthly life and activity as that they have been transferred to unconscious existence. There is also an implied comfort to the relatives who survive to know that their loved ones are 'asleep in Jesus'—that is, asleep in that they are no longer troubled by the weariness, anxieties and pains of the earthly pilgrimage. Note also Hebrews 12:23, where the just are described as 'made perfect'. St. Paul speaks of God's bringing with Him those that are asleep, and states that in the meantime such saints are 'at home with the Lord'.

Nevertheless, there remains sufficient uncertainty on this point to allow for a degree of reverent agnosticism, while on the other hand, Scripture leaves us in no doubt at all that it is the assumption of the resurrection body that marks the entrance into the fullness of eternal life.

2. *Development.*—Based on such analogies as that the law of development is universal elsewhere in the individual's and the world's affairs, views have been expressed that the soul does not stand still after death but continues its moral development. While not denying the possibility that, in ways unknown to us, development may take place, yet Scripture is silent as to its nature, and it is unwise for the Christian to speculate on such matters without sure guidance.

3. *Discipline and Probation.*—There are two views which must certainly be held to be erroneous.

(i) *Purgatorial Discipline.*—By a strange exegesis of 1 Corinthians 3:15 some of the Fathers taught that the faithful departed need to complete the process of their sanctification by suffering the refining fires of purgatory. The mediaeval schoolmen carried this teaching further and described four abodes for the departed. The first was for the saints, considered as a special class of pre-eminently holy Christians. The second was for imperfectly sanctified Christians (regarded as the majority of the members of the church). The third was for unbaptized infants, and the fourth for the heathen. The views as to the second abode led on to prayers and masses for the dead and the sale of 'indulgences'. It need hardly be said that there is no scriptural authority for these views and their products.

Quite apart from all other considerations, if purgatory is to be regarded as possessing a relation to justification it directly impairs Scripture's claim for the sole and supreme efficacy of the atonement of Christ. Any eschatological view which reflects upon the complete (and unassisted) efficacy of the sacrifice of Christ is to be rejected without reserve.

(ii) *Further Probation.*—At the opposite extreme from the doctrine of purgatory (which has the effect of adding to the difficulties of the soul in its pursuit of eternal bliss) is the view of a continued probation of the soul in the intermediate state. The latter tends to render the acceptance of Christ here and now less *urgent* and vital to the soul's destiny.

One would have thought that the warnings of Scripture were sufficiently clear and direct to have caused the rejection of this view without extended argument. But differing interpretations of 1 Peter 3:18-20 and 4:6 have caused much discussion among theologians. It is doubtful if they can be made to mean more than that our Lord demonstrated His supremacy in all regions (including that of the kingdom of the dead). We are not told the results of the preaching, and, in any case, 1 Peter 3:18-20 applies to those who died prior to the death of Christ, and may refer to the time of

Noah.[1] There is no similar passage referring to a time subsequent to
Pentecost. On the other hand, there are many stern warnings to those who
neglect or despise the offer of the gospel in Christ (Heb. 2:1–3; *cf.* also Mt.
12:32; the 'great chasm fixed' in the parable of the rich man and Lazarus;
2 Cor. 5:10 and Heb. 9:27).

It cannot be fairly claimed that Scripture gives hope of a future probation. It most clearly and emphatically warns men against neglect and
delay in accepting the present opportunities of salvation.

4. *Locality.*—Briefly the scriptural doctrine is as follows:

(i) In the Old Testament the departed are viewed as possessing a disembodied state in *Sheol*. The latter is regarded as an underworld which
received all the dead. The general descriptions provided in the Old Testament indicate darkness and but faint hopes of future bliss.

(ii) In the Gospels we have a continuation of the same view (the Greek
equivalent being *Hades*). But Luke 23:43 gives our Lord's confirmation of
the division of the departed between *Gehenna* (a place of fire) and *Paradise*
(indicating conscious felicity).

(iii) In the Epistles, beyond a barely possible hint that a difference was
effected in the lot of the faithful departed by the resurrection and ascension
of Christ (see above, and Heb. 11:40; 12:22–24), the chief message is that
the Christian now departs 'to be with Christ', in the conscious enjoyment
of His presence, and that the intermediate state is not to be dreaded but
eagerly anticipated. It should further be observed that New Testament
phraseology does not use 'heaven' for the abode of the righteous, or 'hell'
for that of the wicked, until after its description of the judgment, unless
'the third heaven' of 2 Corinthians 12:2 'is perhaps identical with Paradise'
(C. H. H. Wright).

Scripture perhaps suggests that the rebellious spirits of all ages await
the judgment in Hades (which is described as 'below') and those who die
'in the Lord' await His coming in Paradise, of which we know that it
permits the conscious enjoyment of His presence.

c. The Resurrection

In view of the fact that our Lord Himself referred to the resurrection of
the dead as the oustanding prophecy in His teaching (Jn. 5:28, 29), and St.
Paul reiterates that it is 'a mystery' revealed by the gospel, it must surely be
treated as of primary importance in any consideration of the final phase of
human destiny.

1. In relation to Christ, the resurrection is viewed as being the result
of:

---

[1] See a reliable commentary on these verses, and particularly the relevant section
in Salmond's *The Christian Doctrine of Immortality*.

(i) His atonement. He died and rose 'that he might be Lord both of the dead and the living' (Rom. 14:9).

(ii) His 'power which enables him even to subject all things to himself' (Phil. 3:21; cf. Jn. 5:21, 28, 29).

(iii) The Christian's union with Him (who has self-existence). (Cf. Jn. 5:26; 11:25, 26: 'I am the resurrection and the life.')

2. In relation to the Christian our Lord's resurrection is:

(i) The pledge that he too will rise (1 Cor. 15:20; 2 Cor. 4:14).

(ii) The pattern for his conception of the resurrection body (Phil. 3:21).

The chief problems concern the nature of the Christian's resurrection body. Scripture does not provide us with direct data, and discourages speculation. The student should firmly grasp the fact that Scripture teaches us to view the nature of our own resurrection bodies as identical with that of our Lord's glorified body. He should avoid both a too materialistic view ('it is raised a *spiritual* body', 1 Cor. 15:43, 44)[1] and also over-spiritualizing, such as that the form of the future (ethereal) cloak of the soul bears no relation to the present human body, *etc.*

After comparing Scripture with Scripture, the most we can assert concerning the resurrection body is that:

(i) It will have human likeness, with the possibility that the facial expression may be recognized by those known on earth.

(ii) It will possess new powers unknown to man in his present state.

(iii) It will be 'spiritual', 'imperishable' and 'immortal'.

(iv) It will be 'like' unto our Lord's glorified body.

(v) It will have a definite relation to the present mortal body.

d. Judgment

The resurrection is declared to be the prelude to judgment of all (the redeemed and reprobate alike). They both receive 'the things done in the body'. The appointed Judge is Christ Himself. The reasons for, and the principles of, judgment are clearly delineated in Scripture. The verdict is declared to be absolutely 'righteous'. There is a finality about the statements concerning the execution of justice which is intensely solemn, and yet satisfying to the moral sense. At last wrong shall have received its just recompense.

The lines along which study may most profitably be pursued are:

1. *The Judgment of Christians.*—The question of the guilt of sin does

---

[1] The mediaeval schoolmen went into infinite detail concerning the age and nature of the resurrection body. For example, some held that its appearance was that of the body at the time of death, others that it was like that of our Lord at the age of thirty-three years.

not arise, since it has already been removed by the atoning sacrifice. The judgment is chiefly in the nature of rewards for stewardship. But certain Scriptures, which are filled with warnings to the careless Christian, should be studied. Sin voluntarily permitted to remain in habitual operation in the life of the Christian cannot but cause his serious loss at the judgment-seat. The Christian is never given any encouragement for antinomianism.

2. *The Principles of the Judgment of Non-Christians.*—The following are plain:

(i) The absolute justice of God (Gn. 18:25).

(ii) There will be allowance made for the varying degrees of privilege, both of opportunity and responsibility. Compare our Lord's words regarding Sodom (Mt. 11:24).

(iii) The determining factor in the case of those who have heard the gospel is acceptance or rejection of Christ.

(iv) In the case of the heathen, who have not had the privileges of the gospel, it is suggested that they will be judged on the grounds of the light they had (Rom. 1:19–23; 2:14, 15).

3. *The Results of Judgment.*—The actual words of the final doom are given by the Lord Himself in Matthew 25:41 and 46. There would seem to be no valid reason why the statements should not be taken at their face value. But two erroneous opinions have arisen in the church, which have received extensive acceptance.

(i) The universalists claim that the separation of good and evil will not be everlasting and that finally all men will be reconciled to God.

(ii) The annihilationists teach that the souls who are finally condemned to separation from God will be annihilated and not reserved for eternal punishment. This view speaks of 'conditional immortality'.

For an examination of the various views and their comparison with the orthodox teaching see *The Christian Doctrine of Immortality* (Salmond). Two things are certain. It seems to be abundantly clear that Scripture holds out no hope of a second probation for those who have neglected or deliberately misused their present opportunities. Irretrievable loss awaits the deliberate rejecter of Christ at the throne of judgment.

Scriptures

Human Destiny

1. *The Intermediate State.*—Lk. 16: 19–31; 2 Cor. 5:1–8.

(i) *For the Christian.*—1 Cor. 15:18a; Phil. 1:23; 1 Thes. 4:14, 15; 5:10; Rev. 6:9–11. *Cf.* Jn. 11:26; Heb. 12:23.

(ii) *For the non-Christian.*—Ps. 9:17; Lk. 16:19–31; 1 Pet. 3:18–20.

2. *The Judgment.*

(i) *Those who will be judged.*—Mt. 25:32; Acts 10:42; 17:31; Rom. 2:6, 9, 10; 14:10; 2 Cor. 5:10; Heb. 9:27; Rev. 20:12.

(ii) *The Principles on which Judgment is Meted.*—Gn. 18:25; Mt. 11:20–24; 25:34–46; Lk. 12:47, 48; Jn. 3:18, 19; Acts 10:34, 35; Rom. 2:1–16; 2 Cor. 5:10; 2 Thes. 1:5–10; Heb. 10:28, 29; Rev. 21:8; 22:11, 12.

(iii) *Warnings.*—Mt. 3:7–12; Rom. 2:3, 4; Heb. 2:2, 3; 10:26–31; 12:25; Rev. 20:15.

Questions

1. How do you reconcile Matthew 25:31–46 with the teaching of Scripture elsewhere (*e.g.*, 2 Thes. 1:5–10) that judgment is based on belief or disbelief in Christ?

2. On what biblical grounds have claims been made for (*a*) universalism, and (*b*) 'conditional immortality', and why do you reject these claims?

3. How do you interpret the terms 'paradise' and 'sleep' with reference to the intermediate state of the believer?

BIBLIOGRAPHY

Sir Robert Anderson, *Human Destiny*, Pickering and Inglis, 4th edn., 1895.

G. C. Berkouwer, *The Triumph of Grace in the Theology of Karl Barth*, Paternoster Press, 1956.

E. Brunner, *Eternal Hope*, Lutterworth Press, 1954.

O. Cullmann, *Immortality of the Soul or Resurrection of the Dead?*, Epworth Press, 1958.

H. E. Guillebaud, *The Righteous Judge*, The Phoenix Press, Taunton, advocating conditional immortality.

L. Morris, *The Wages of Sin*, Tyndale Press, 1955.

J. A. Motyer, *After Death*, Hodder and Stoughton, 1965.

S. D. F. Salmond, *The Christian Doctrine of Immortality*, T. and T. Clark, 1907.

H. B. Swete, *The Life of the World to Come*, SPCK, 1917.

3. The Consummation of All Things

It has been well pointed out that there are three 'consummations' evident in the scriptural record of the world's history:

1. The ordering of the world for the creation of the first man.
2. The events leading up to the birth of our Lord.
3. The cessation of the present world system.

Each of the first two consummations ushered in the next phase of God's purpose, and so will the last. At the conclusion of the final judgment God's purpose for the world will be complete. The eternal purpose and saving decrees of the Trinity will have been completely effected, and the church will be in a state of completion and final glorification. There will remain the last of God's purposes to be completed—'Behold, I make all things new.'

Several passages refer plainly to this final consummation of all things (Is. 51:6; 2 Pet. 3:7–13; Rev. 21:1). The references imply not annihilation, but a complete destruction of all links with an old and sinful world and the transformation of the old into a new world, never to know sin and corruption. As with the resurrection of the body, there is both continuity and discontinuity between the old and the new, which is represented both as issuing out of the destruction (Is. 13:9–13; 2 Pet. 3:10–13; *cf.* Heb. 12:25–29), and as consisting in the 'conversion' and liberation of creation (Is. 11:1–9; 35 (*cf.* Lk. 7:22); Rom. 8:21).

No more inspiring study can be undertaken by the student than the tracing of the unfailing fulfilment of God's eternal purposes and covenants with man. Paradise lost in Genesis becomes paradise regained in the Revelation. Between them lies the fascinating story of the promise of, and preparation for, redemption, the work of Christ, and the progress of the redeeming work from Pentecost to the coming of Christ. No higher object of intellectual pursuit is open to man than the study of the being and redeeming work of the Godhead. If this small volume comes to be used by the Holy Spirit to introduce even a few of the author's student friends to a lifelong study of the riches of their inheritance in Christ, it will have served its purpose.

Scriptures

Is. 2:2–4; 65:17–25; 66:22, 23; Acts 3:20, 21; 1 Cor. 15:24–28; Eph. 1:10; Phil. 2:10, 11; Col. 1:20; 2 Pet. 3:10–13 (*cf.* Mt. 19:28); Rev. 20:11; 21; 22.

Questions

1. Will the new creation be entirely new?
2. Is there any connection between the death of Christ and 'the consummation of all things'?

BIBLIOGRAPHY

Richard Baxter, *The Saints' Everlasting Rest*, ed. John T. Wilkinson, Epworth Press, 1961.

K. Heim, *Jesus, The World's Perfecter*, Oliver and Boyd, 1959.

K. Heim, *The World: Its Creation and Consummation*, Oliver and Boyd, 1962.

INDEX